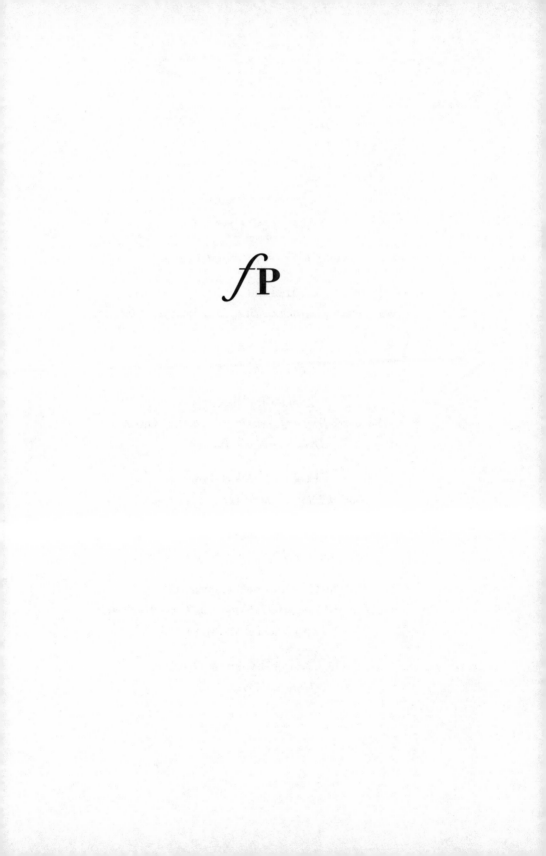

A
MAGNIFICENT
CATASTROPHE

The Tumultuous Election of 1800,
America's First Presidential
Campaign

E D W A R D J. L A R S O N

FREE PRESS
New York   London   Toronto   Sydney

*f*P

FREE PRESS

A Division of Simon & Schuster, Inc.
1230 Avenue of the Americas
New York, NY 10020

FREE PRESS and colophon are trademarks of
Simon & Schuster, Inc.

Designed by Dana Sloan

Manufactured in the United States of America

ISBN-13: 978-0-7432-9316-7
ISBN-10:   0-7432-9316-9

Illustration credits will be found on page 335.

A Book Club Edition

In the spirit of
John Adams and Thomas Jefferson
whose fatherly love and respect for their daughters
ran through and enriched their adult lives,
I dedicate this book to our daughter,
Sarah Marie Larson

"Be assured that to yourself, your sister, and those dear to you, everything in my life is devoted. Ambition has no hold on me but through you."

—THOMAS JEFFERSON TO HIS DAUGHTER, MARTHA
FEBRUARY 5, 1801

"Heaven has blessed you, my daughter, with an understanding and a consideration that is not found everyday among young women. . . . With the most fervent wishes for your happiness, I am your affectionate father."

—JOHN ADAMS TO HIS DAUGHTER, NABBY
AUGUST 13, 1783

"[My] happiness is wrapped up in yours."

—THOMAS JEFFERSON TO HIS DAUGHTER, MARIA
JULY 4, 1800

CONTENTS

PREFACE

$\mathscr{T}$HE RESEARCH that culminated in this book commenced with an invitation to deliver a single lecture on the role of science and religion in the election of 1800. Coming as it did at the sunset of the Enlightenment and the dawn of the Great Revival, the 1800 campaign occurred at the pivot point of massive cultural forces in the history of American science and religion. Those forces necessarily affected the election, and not simply because Thomas Jefferson bore the mantle of Enlightenment science while John Adams invoked Protestant traditionalism as a vital prop for civil society.

Exploring this topic, I found a rich interplay of ideas and actions among protagonists who cared deeply about issues and knew that they were forging the traditions of a great new nation. Jefferson's Republican running mate, Aaron Burr, was the grandson of America's greatest evangelical theologian, Jonathan Edwards, for example, and Adams's Federalist running mate, Charles Cotesworth Pinckney, served for fifteen years as the president of the Bible Society of Charleston. In the end, however, I could not separate the topic of science and religion from other issues driving this critical election that, more than any other, stamped American democracy with its distinctive bipartisan character. Over time, my brief lecture grew into this book dealing with the election as a whole.

As my topic grew, my indebtedness to other scholars grew as well.

For a season, I titled my manuscript "The Founders' Coda" in recognition of the role played by the nation's founders in this election. Here, as participants in an extraordinarily bitter election contest, they transformed the political structure of the American union and set it on its modern course. Their names, first made famous during the Revolutionary Era, sounded again in 1800: Adams, Jefferson, Hamilton, Madison, Jay, Monroe, Gouverneur Morris, George Clinton, John Marshall, Thomas McKean, and even George Washington. For generations, some of the nation's finest historians have examined and reexamined these founders, with an extraordinary flowering of such books published over the past two decades. I have benefited immeasurably from their broad insights in my focused study of the 1800 election. I have also profited from the considerable scholarship on the election itself, including recent books by my friend Susan Dunn, who frequently collaborates with my esteemed former teacher at Williams College, James MacGregor Burns, and by my cross-state colleague within the University of Georgia system, John Ferling. Further, over the years, archivists, librarians and historians have assembled remarkably comprehensive collections of the letters and writings of Washington, Jefferson, Hamilton, Madison, Marshall, and other founders, and of early American newspapers and pamphlets. In exploiting these resources for this book, I have regularized punctuation, capitalization, and spelling. The medieval scholar Bernard of Chartres first spoke of seeing further by standing on the shoulders of giants, and it certainly applies to me in this work.

As a teacher at the University of Georgia and Pepperdine University, I have learned much from my colleagues and students. For this book, I particularly benefited from my collaboration with Georgia's exceptional colonialist, Michael Winship, on a book about the Constitutional Convention, and from research assistance provided by Judkin Browning for my initial lecture on science and religion in the election of 1800. My status as the Russell Professor of American History at the University of Georgia facilitated my investigation of this political topic, and I want especially to thank Charles Campbell, the former

U.S. Senate aide who now chairs the Russell Foundation, for his interest and support. I also had the good fortune of securing research assistance from Michael Coenan, who worked in Athens, Georgia, during 2005–06 as a campaign aide to my former Harvard Law School classmate, Congressman John Barrow. Coenan, now at Yale Law School, immersed himself in the complexities of the 1800 New York election even as he helped his own candidate win reelection. Further, my thanks go to the librarians at Georgia and Pepperdine who assisted in securing source material used in this book and to Philip J. Lampi of the American Antiquarian Society for providing data from the Society's extraordinary First Democracy Project.

Through their assistance, friends and family made this book into a reality. First came my dogged and determined agent, B. G. Dilworth, who pushed and pulled a book proposal out of me. Then came my initial editor at Free Press, Fred Hills, who helped me to reconceive the book's basic structure and saw me through the first draft. Following Fred's retirement, Emily Loose took over my draft chapters and wonderfully transformed them through her editorial suggestions, which were both meticulous in their attention to detail and comprehensive in their conception of the whole. Through it all, my wife, Lucy, and our children, Sarah and Luke, have graciously borne with my preoccupation with this project and encouraged me by their words, actions, and interest. Our dog, Pippin, cheered me on by expectantly lying at my side as I labored on particularly difficult passages—although I suspect his patient expectations revolved more around walks than finished chapters. At every stage, I felt extraordinary support. I hope that the final product is worthy of the assistance that I have received from so many.

—*Edward J. Larson*

MAGNIFICENT
CATASTROPHE

INTRODUCTION

INDEPENDENCE DAY, JULY 4, 1776

*T*HEY COULD write like angels and scheme like demons. Trained as attorneys, they thoroughly mastered that craft only to turn their formidable legal skills toward statecraft. Both men preferred farming to law or politics. But the year was 1776, and their respective colonies—North America's two most populous British domains—had sent them to Philadelphia as delegates to the Second Continental Congress. When all reasonable hope of reconciliation with Britain expired, the Assembly named them to a special, five-member committee charged with drafting a formal Declaration of Independence for the "united colonies." Standing shoulder to shoulder with delegates from the thirteen self-proclaimed sovereign states on that first Fourth of July, John Adams of Massachusetts and Thomas Jefferson of Virginia signed the subtly eloquent document that their committee had crafted. Among the delegates, Adams had argued longest and most effectively for independence. Within the committee, Jefferson had taken the lead in writing the Declaration itself.

John Trumbull's celebratory painting of the signing ceremony puts Adams and Jefferson front and center, with Benjamin Franklin prominently at their side and the other two committee members obscurely in the rear. Lanky and lean with an unruly sandy-red mane, Jefferson at a youthful thirty-three stood head and shoulders above the balding, rotund, but square-shouldered Adams—then a prematurely old forty. "My good man is so very fat," Abigail Adams had written about her husband a decade earlier—and he had only grown stouter with age. Regarding his own portrait, Adams once commented, "He should be painted looking like a short thick archbishop" and, writing from Philadelphia in November 1775, had characterized himself as "a morose philosopher and a surly politician." These comments exposed the inner man. Adams always relished a spirited argument, including with himself, and he inevitably remained his own most astute critic, with his adoring and adored wife a close second. "Vanity," he wrote, "is my cardinal vice."

At over six feet two inches tall, with high cheekbones and deep-set eyes, Jefferson towered over most men of his time even when he slouched—which he often did, especially when seated. Standing, he typically folded his arms tightly across his chest and often had a faraway look. Here, Jefferson's body language betrayed his character as someone who avoided direct confrontation—even with himself. Although Adams's proud combativeness competed with Jefferson's detached coldness in putting off new acquaintances, both men gained the respect of friends and foes alike for their intense self-discipline, studied brilliance, and seriousness of purpose. Along with Franklin and George Washington, they were the central figures in the American Revolutionary leadership.

On that fateful July 4, John Hancock, speaking as president of the Continental Congress and the nearest thing to an elected leader for the aligned but not yet amalgamated states, warned his fellow delegates, "We must be unanimous. There must be no pulling different ways; we must all hang together." Wise and worldly, Franklin reportedly added, "Yes, we must, indeed, all hang together, or most assuredly we shall all hang separately."

As always, Franklin's quip carried more than a kernel of truth. In July 1776, the patriot cause looked bleak. Britain had launched the largest foreign military force in its history against its rebellious American colonies. That force would soon smash the ill-trained and ill-equipped patriot troops in New York and drive them from the field. Philadelphia could have fallen that same year, sending the delegates running for their lives. It did fall a year later. When signing the Declaration of Independence, Benjamin Harrison darkly joked to Elbridge Gerry: "I shall have a great advantage over you, Mr. Gerry, when we are all hung for what we are now doing. From the size and weight of my body I shall die in a few minutes, but from the lightness of your body you will dance in the air an hour or two before you are dead." Harrison, a rotund Virginia planter and direct ancestor of two Presidents, and Gerry, a slender Massachusetts merchant and future Vice President, were family men of substance—not desperate people devoid of hope. The words that Adams spoke and Jefferson wrote in Philadelphia emboldened Americans like Harrison and Gerry to take a historic stand: to stake their lives, their fortunes, and their sacred honor on the cause of freedom. Success or failure turned in large part on how the patriot leaders responded to the challenges they faced in birthing a nation.

For two decades, Adams and Jefferson followed the advice of Hancock and Franklin. They pulled together in war and peace, became friends, and helped to forge a sovereign nation from thirteen dependent colonies. During those fateful years, Adams continued his distinguished service in the Continental Congress; drafted his state's new constitution; joined Franklin as a wartime diplomat in France; and became America's first postwar ambassador to Britain. Although Jefferson left Congress in 1776, he revised Virginia's legal code and served two terms as governor before returning to Congress in 1783 and then joining Franklin and Adams as an American commissioner in Paris.

Jefferson became the country's ambassador to France in 1785, after Franklin retired from that post and Adams moved on to London. Returning home as national heroes following the ratification of a new federal constitution in 1788, Adams was elected America's first Vice President and Jefferson became its first Secretary of State.

The common goals of national independence and sovereignty that united patriot leaders during the Revolutionary Era gave way to differing views on domestic and foreign policy during Washington's second term as President. After 1797, when Adams succeeded Washington as President and Jefferson became leader of the opposition as Vice President, these differences widened into open antagonisms fed by tensions at home and war abroad. The factions led by Adams and Jefferson crystallized into two distinct political parties with competing visions for America's future. They became the public personifications of the warring camps. By 1800, the remnants of their former friendship had ended in a tangle of mutual suspicions and partisan animosities. Adams and many in his Federalist Party feared that Jeffersonian rule would bring political, social, and religious upheaval. Jefferson and his most ardent followers in the Republican Party doubted whether the nation's democratic institutions could survive another four years with Adams at the helm. For both sides, freedom (as they conceived it) hung in the balance. America's two greatest surviving Revolutionary leaders had separated and the country was coming apart. One election took on extraordinary meaning. Partisans worried that it might be the young republic's last.

CHAPTER ONE

FROM FRIENDS TO RIVALS

$\mathcal{A}$LTHOUGH the friendship between Adams and Jefferson took root in Philadelphia during the opening days of the American Revolution, it blossomed in Paris at war's end. Again, the scene included Franklin. For the scene in Philadelphia, John Trumbull created the enduring image of the trio in his monumental painting, *The Declaration of Independence*. They stood together, seemingly larger than life, at the focal point of attention amid a sea of delegates at the Continental Congress, their purposeful eyes gazing forward as if into the future. A war with Britain lay ahead, and the task of building a new nation.

They had changed by the time the war finally ended and they could begin building on the promise of peace. Already the oldest signer of the Declaration in 1776, Franklin was seventy-eight in 1784, stooped with gout and kidney stones, when Jefferson reached Paris to augment the American diplomatic delegation there. Shortly after declaring the nation's independence, Congress had dispatched Franklin to seek French support for the Revolution. Adams joined him in 1778 and, although Franklin had obtained an alliance with France by then, they worked together with a shifting array of American diplomats to secure loans from the Dutch, peace with Britain, and commercial treaties with other nations.

Of middling height and decidedly square shouldered, Adams had added to his girth on a diplomat's diet. Tall for his day, Jefferson had grown into his height by 1784 and typically held himself more upright than before. When the three patriot leaders reunited as diplomats in Paris, the physical contrast between them had become almost comical. Upon making their initial joint appearance at the royal court in Versailles, one bemused observer likened them to a cannonball, a teapot, and a candlestick. America, however, never enjoyed abler representation in a foreign capital.

Franklin arrived in France already a celebrity and enhanced his reputation further while there. Hailed as the Newton of his day for his discoveries in electricity and renowned also as an inventor, writer, practical philosopher, and statesman, Franklin vied only with Voltaire as the public face of the Enlightenment, which then dominated French culture and influenced thought throughout Europe and America. When the two senior savants embraced at a public meeting of the French Academy of Sciences in 1778, it seemed as if all Europe cheered—or so Adams reported with evident envy. "Qu'il etoit charmant," he caustically commented in two languages. "How charming it was!"

The sage of Philadelphia became a fixture in the finest salons of Paris and continued his scientific studies even as he served as America's senior diplomat in Europe. Ladies of the court particularly favored him, and he them, which gave Franklin access to the inner workings of pre-Revolutionary French society. These activities complemented each other by reinforcing Franklin's already legendary stature. Born in poverty on the edge of civilization and content to play the part of an American rustic by wearing a bearskin cap in fashion-conscious Paris, Franklin received honors and tributes from across Europe. A gifted diplomat, he secured what America needed from France to win the Revolution and secure its independence.

While in France, Adams always served in Franklin's shadow. At first, he accepted the shade. "The attention of the court seems most to Franklin, and no wonder. His long and great reputation . . . [is] enough to account for this," Adams wrote during his first year in Paris. Adding to his aggravation, however, was that Europeans seemingly took pains to distinguish him from his better-known cousin, the revolutionary firebrand Samuel Adams. "It was a settled point at Paris and in the English newspapers that I was not the famous Adams," the proud New Englander complained, "and therefore the consequence was settled absolutely and unalterably that I was a man of whom nobody ever heard before, a perfect cipher."

Gradually, Adams turned his rancor on Franklin, which soured their relationship. Except for John Jay (who joined them in negotiating peace with Britain), prior to Jefferson none of the diplomats sent by Congress to work with Franklin and Adams could bridge the growing divide. "The life of Mr. Franklin was a scene of continued dissipation. I could never obtain the favor of his company," Adams observed bitterly. "It was late when he breakfasted, and as soon as breakfast was over, a crowd of carriages came to his . . . lodgings, with all sorts of people: some philosophers, academicians, and economists . . . but by far the greater part were women and children who came to see the great Franklin." Then came formal dinners, parties, and concerts. "I should have been happy to have done all the business, or rather all the drudgery, if I could have been favored with a few moments in a day to receive his advice," Adams complained, "but this condescension was not attainable." Yet, Franklin managed a triumph at every turn despite (or perhaps because of) his socializing, which rankled the Puritan in Adams.

The only respite came in 1779 when, after Franklin secured the alliance with France and became America's sole ambassador to the French court, Adams returned to Massachusetts. He was back in Europe before year's end, however, assigned to work with Franklin and Jay in negotiating peace with Britain.

Despite their animosities, Franklin and Adams labored on with amazing success, each putting his nation's interests above his own. Always blunt and sometimes explosive, Adams was an unnatural diplomat at best. The odd-couple blend of Franklin's tact and Adams's tirades produced results. The alliance with France held, Britain conceded a generous peace, and America gained and maintained its independence from both of those grasping world powers. Between the two men, however, their personal relationship never recovered. Franklin's characterization of Adams stuck to him like tar and stained him forever: "Always an honest man, often a wise one, but sometimes, in some things, absolutely out of his senses."

Both men rejoiced in 1784 when Jefferson arrived in Paris to join them in seeking postwar treaties of commerce and friendship with the various European nations. For Franklin, the attraction was obvious. A scientist and philosopher in his own right, Jefferson shared Franklin's Enlightenment values and religious beliefs. As fellow Deists, they acknowledged a divine Creator but, as Jefferson once wrote, they trusted in "the sufficiency of human reason for the care of human affairs." If they prayed for anything from God, it was for wisdom to seek answers rather than for the answers themselves. Better yet for their relationship, Jefferson accepted Franklin's greatness without a trace of envy. In 1785, when Congress granted Franklin's longstanding request to retire and tapped Jefferson to serve as America's ambassador in Paris, the Virginian stressed that he would merely succeed Franklin: No one could replace him.

Adams seemed as happy as Franklin to receive Jefferson. His "appointment gives me great pleasure," Adams exulted at the time. "He is an old friend . . . in whose abilities and steadiness I always found great cause to confide." Best of all for Adams, Jefferson readily deferred to him and treated him as a senior colleague. "Jefferson is an excellent hand," Adams soon wrote. "He appears to me to be infected with no party passions or natural prejudices or any partialities but for his own country." Adams highly valued these traits. He accepted a political hierarchy founded on talent and believed in disinterested service by the elite. Jefferson seemed to exemplify these characteristics. Adams now spoke of the "utmost harmony" that reigned within the American delegation. "My new partner is an old friend and coadjutor whose character I studied nine or ten years ago, and which I do not perceive to be altered. The same industry, integrity, and talents remain without diminution," Adams observed.

Although Adams may not have noticed it at first, Jefferson had, however, changed. He now carried his height with dignity and hid his insecurities behind an ever more inscrutable facade. Never as self-confident as Adams, Jefferson learned to ignore the type of slights that often enraged Adams. In 1776, frustrations with public life and concerns about his wife's health led Jefferson to resign from Congress and decline appointment as a commissioner to France. He needed time at his beloved Monticello plantation. Once home, Jefferson reclaimed his seat in the Virginia legislature; worked to reform state laws to foster such republican values as voting and property rights, the separation of church and state, and public education; and served two troubled one-year terms as governor during the darkest days of the Revolution. After his wife, Martha, died following a difficult childbirth in 1782, Jefferson agreed once more to represent Virginia in Congress and, two years later, accepted the renewed offer to represent America in Paris. With his wife gone, he needed to leave Monticello as much as he once needed to be there. He grieved for her greatly and kept the vow purportedly made by him to her on her deathbed never to remarry.

During the week that Jefferson arrived, Adams's wife and three younger children joined Adams and their two older children in Paris after five painful years of separation. The Adamses welcomed the lonely Virginian into their happy home. For Jefferson, Abigail Adams became a trusted source of personal and family advice from a woman who was his intellectual equal. She also took Jefferson's two surviving children under her wing at times. He reciprocated in a manner that led John Adams to comment later to Jefferson that, in Paris, young John Quincy "appeared to me to be almost as much your boy as mine." Upon Adams's departure from Paris in 1785 to become the first American ambassador to Britain, Abigail expressed her regret about leaving Jefferson, whom she described as "the only person with whom my companion could associate with perfect freedom and unreserve." To Adams, Jefferson wrote, "The departure of your family has left me in the dumps. My afternoons hang heavy on me."

With both Franklin and Adams gone, however, Jefferson came into his own as the leading American diplomat on the European continent. Immersing himself in French culture as Adams never did, he became attached to the French people and hoped for their freedom from monarchic despotism and Catholic clericalism. "I do love this people with all my heart and think that with a better religion and a better form of government . . . their condition and country would be most enviable," Jefferson wrote to Abigail Adams in 1785. The French royals, personified for some by the debauched queen Marie Antoinette, and many French aristocrats and church leaders lived in splendid isolation from the grinding poverty of the forgotten masses.

For a time, the friendship between Adams and Jefferson survived their separation. In 1787, for example, after Jefferson's closest political ally and confidant in Virginia, James Madison, questioned Adams's character, Jefferson (while conceding Adams's vanity and irritability) replied, "He is so amiable that I pronounce you will love him if ever you become acquainted with him." Two years later, Adams concluded a letter to Jefferson with the words, "I am with an affection that can never die, your friend and servant." At heart, however, it was a friendship between political allies fixed in time and place.

In both Philadelphia and Paris, Adams and Jefferson represented similar or the same interests far from home, and did so with extraordinary passion and ability. This united them. As their political goals for America diverged, however, their ideological zeal drove them apart. These were serious, ambitious men with deep beliefs and grand ideas. Whenever and wherever their paths crossed, Adams and Jefferson were destined to become either fast friends or formidable foes.

During their early lives in the mid-1700s, no one could have guessed that the paths of Adams and Jefferson would ever cross—much less assume overlapping courses during the late 1700s and then collide in 1800. Prior to the coming of the American Revolution, the northern and southern colonies might as well have occupied separate continents. A Virginian and a New Englander—even two such cosmopolitan lawyers as Adams and Jefferson—would have little occasion to meet each other, except perhaps in London on imperial business. Instead they met in Philadelphia at the Second Continental Congress in 1775 with the shared goal of freeing the colonies from Britain's yoke. Their ambitions for themselves and their new nation became the basis for their special friendship.

Ambition marked these men. Both were the first sons in rising families at a time when social custom and inheritance law placed special opportunities and obligations on the eldest male heir. Jefferson's industrious father had greatly expanded the family's land and slave holdings in central Virginia, and passed them to his eldest boy along with a lively intellect, a craving for material possessions, and a fierce streak of independent self-reliance. Adams's father was also driven, but in a pious Puritan sense that pushed him to expand his modest Massachusetts farm, accept positions of trust within his local church and community, and sacrifice to send his firstborn son to Harvard College with a hope that, through formal education, the son could outshine the father in every good and virtuous endeavor. Like his father, Adams tried to live well within his means. Indeed, he enjoyed nothing more than being with his family and smoking a good cigar, both of which he did as often as he could.

Adams and Jefferson drank in their fathers' ambitions and made them their own. "Reputation ought to be the perpetual subject of my thoughts, and the aim of my behavior," Adams chided himself in his diary while still a young lawyer in 1759. He soon wrote to a friend, "I am not ashamed to own that a prospect of an immortality in the memories of all the worthy to [the] end of time would be a high gratification to my wishes." To achieve this goal, he devoted himself to study far beyond the requirements of his profession. Indeed, few colonists of his day could boast of as deep or broad a legal education as Adams's—except perhaps Thomas Jefferson.

At the College of William and Mary, Jefferson chose study over social life in a manner wholly foreign to the convivial spirit of that place as a finishing school for the planter elite. He "could tear himself away from his dearest friends and fly to his studies," one classmate recalled. Others estimated that Jefferson worked fifteen hours a day. He wanted to learn the law, Jefferson admitted, so that he would "be admired." Simply becoming a lawyer and planter was not enough, however, because he continued his bookish studies long after passing the bar and inheriting his father's plantation. Indeed, in 1767, he counseled a young lawyer about the "advantage" of ongoing study, and recommended reading science and theology before breakfast; the law during the forenoon; politics at lunch; history in the afternoon; and literature, criticism, and rhetoric "from dark to bedtime." Jefferson imposed just such a regimen on himself as a young lawyer and continued a disciplined program of self-education throughout his long life. "Determine never to be idle. No person will have occasion to complain of want of time who never loses any. It is wonderful how much may be done if we are always doing," he wrote to his daughter Martha in 1787. "A mind always employed is always happy."

As young lawyers, the greatest challenge faced by Adams and Jefferson lay in gaining sufficient scope for their ambitions. No American colony could provide a suitable stage to display their talents, and the British Empire offered only bit parts to colonial actors. Thinking back in later life about their prospects as ambitious young men, both Adams and Jefferson recalled that initially they could conceive of no higher positions for themselves than appointment to the King's Council (or senate) for their respective colonies. Perhaps that fed their disillusionment with the imperial regime. They wanted so much more than the King would allow his colonists.

Vain to a fault, Adams never hid his ambitions. In 1760, for example, before the first stirrings of the American Revolution, he wrote prophetically to a friend, "When heaven designs an extraordinary character, one that shall distinguish his path thro' the world by any great effects, it never fails to furnish the proper means and opportunities; but the common herd of mankind, who are to be born and eat and sleep and die, and be forgotten, is thrown into the world as it were at random." Adams saw himself in the former class—as did Jefferson—but colonial America could not offer him a "proper means" to glory. Not content with waiting upon heaven to supply the means, Adams examined his options. "How shall I gain reputation?" he wrote in a 1759 diary entry. Shall I patiently build my law practice or "shall I look out for a cause to speak to, and exert all the soul and all the body I own to cut a flash . . . ? In short shall I walk a lingering, heavy pace or shall I take one bold determined leap?" He chose to leap.

In 1765, new stamp taxes on newspapers and other printed matter imposed by Britain solely on American colonists gave Adams his first chance to attach himself to a larger cause. He began testing his revolutionary rhetoric by denouncing the new taxes as "fabricated by the British Parliament for battering down all the rights and liberties in America." This assault appeared in Adams's private diary, however. Although he met frequently with patriot leaders and drafted stern instructions from his town to the colonial legislature condemning "taxation without representation," Adams mostly pulled his punches in public or published his words anonymously, perhaps in part to protect his growing legal practice. When Britain repealed the repressive levy in response to widespread colonial protests, Adams envied the glory heaped upon more-visible patriots, including his fiery cousin Samuel.

By the time of the Townshend Duties crisis in 1768, which erupted after Britain imposed added tariffs on American imports, Adams wrote privately that his legal career "will neither lead me to fame, fortune, [or] power, nor to the service of my friends, clients or country." Determined to make his mark, increasingly he became the public leader of the patriot cause in Massachusetts through his writings, speeches, and government service. He became an early advocate of independence at a time when most Americans still thought that they could work out their differences with Britain amicably. In comparison with his public service, the private practice of law became a "desultory life" for Adams: he called it "dull," "tedious," and "irksome."

Jefferson gradually reached the same conclusion as Adams about the law and his career. He privately dismissed legal literature as "mere jargon" as early as 1763 and abandoned his law practice altogether in

1774, after receiving a sizable inheritance following his father-in-law's death. Almost immediately, Jefferson emerged within the Virginia colonial legislature as a prominent critic of British rule. He had a bearing and intellectual depth that commanded respect—even awe.

Drawing on their years of training and practice, Adams and Jefferson turned from defending private clients to prosecuting the American Revolution. They had found their path to glory and a stage equal to their ambitions and abilities: the United States of America.

Adams went to the First Continental Congress in 1774 as a committed proponent of independence. Jefferson joined him a year later at the Second Continental Congress, which met continously during the American Revolution. They shared a resolve to break with the mother country, making them staunch allies. Their kindred spirits—at once philosophical and practical—also made them friends who could converse and conspire in confidence. In Congress, both men quickly gained the respect and influence that naturally flows to members with firm convictions, superior intelligence, and an ability to persuade others. Although Jefferson spoke little in formal sessions of Congress, Adams recalled that from their first encounters he found the Virginian "so prompt, frank, explicit, and decisive upon committees and in conversation . . . that he soon won my heart"—almost like a younger brother or an adult son.

Together, they pushed and prodded their fellow delegates to accept the inevitability of independence. First, Congress adopted as its own the New England militia besieging the British army in Boston following the battles of Lexington and Concord. Then Adams led the effort to further nationalize these patriot troops by placing George Washington, a Virginian, in overall command. Finally, after the five-member drafting committee delegated the job of crafting the Declaration of Independence to the two men, Adams asked Jefferson to pen the first draft—again hoping to bind the South to the patriot cause.

The Virginian succeeded brilliantly in that task: "We hold these truths to be sacred & undeniable; that all men are created equal and independent, that from that equal creation they derive rights inherent

& unalienable, among which are the preservation of life, & liberty, & the pursuit of happiness; that to secure these ends, governments are instituted among men, deriving their just powers from the consent of the governed; that whenever any form of government shall become destructive of these ends, it is the right of the people to alter or abolish it." Although the committee and Congress made various changes to Jefferson's text, the soaring words and lyrical structure survived. Adams could not have written a first draft more suited to his views. Indeed, the visionary affirmation that "all men are created equal" sounded more like the words of a Massachusetts Puritan than those of a Virginia slaveholder. The expansive "pursuit of happiness" passage, however, was pure Jefferson. The British political philosopher John Locke had spoken of natural rights to life, liberty, and property; but the pursuit of happiness struck Jefferson as so much nobler than simply the acquisition of property, even though Jefferson himself had an insatiable appetite for physical possessions. Indeed, Jefferson's words often soared beyond his actions, leading to enigmatic inconsistencies in his personality that some saw as hypocritical.

Their work together in Philadelphia for a declaration of independence had scarcely ended when Adams and Jefferson parted company. In September 1776, Jefferson left Congress to be with his ailing wife and young children in Virginia. There, he threw himself into efforts to liberalize the state's aristocratic legal code and to end state support for the Anglican Church. He declined the first summons from Congress to serve with Franklin in France, writing to the senior statesman in 1777, "I wish my domestic situation had rendered it possible for me to have joined you in the very honorable charge confided to you." Jefferson fully appreciated the importance of that charge: Securing French support for America's revolution would likely decide the war's outcome. After refusing that call, Adams begged Jefferson to return to Congress. "We want your industry and abilities here extremely," he wrote in May 1777. "Your country is not yet quite secure enough to excuse your retreat to the delights of domestic life." Still, Jefferson remained at home.

Adams ultimately served in France in Jefferson's stead, arriving after Franklin had secured the needed military alliance. Jefferson joined them there in 1784. After Franklin returned home in 1785, for the next three years, Adams served in London and Jefferson in Paris as America's two ranking foreign diplomats. It was a particularly difficult time to serve the country abroad. America had secured its political independence with the signing in 1783 of a peace treaty with Britain. Under the Articles of Confederation, the country remained a loose confederation of states, however, until ratification of the Constitution in 1788. Without an effective national government to represent, Adams and Jefferson could accomplish little. Although they secured a critically needed loan from Dutch bankers, Britain refused to honor its treaty obligation with the United States to evacuate its forts in the Great Lakes region, and France descended toward revolutionary turmoil. After generations of oppression and with the government on the verge of bankruptcy, the people of France arose against their leaders with unexpected violence. Tensions continued between the United States and its former colonial master; America's recent ally, France, could no longer offer any effective assistance. America stood alone in a hostile world and neither Adams nor Jefferson could do much about it as ambassadors.

From their posts in Europe, they watched during 1787–88 as delegates to the Constitutional Convention framed and the states ratified the new national charter. Success remained in doubt until the end. Concerns over representation in Congress divided the small and large states; the issue of slavery already split North from South. The Convention repeatedly bogged down in factional strife and the ratification process became highly contentious in some states.

Concerns about the document reached Americans in Europe and were avidly debated there. Jefferson feared that the Constitution gave too much power to the President, who was chosen by electors; Adams worried that it gave too much power to the Senate, whose members were appointed by the state legislatures. Both thought that it should include a bill of rights. "You are afraid of the one—I, the few," Adams wrote to Jefferson in 1787. "We agree perfectly that the many should have full, fair, and perfect representation. You are apprehensive of monarchy; I, of aristocracy."

Despite their reservations about the compromise document that emerged from the divided Convention, Adams urged that Massachusetts ratify it while Jefferson expressed his qualified support for ratification in Virginia. Having seen what he perceived as the benefits of strong monarchies in Europe, Adams thought that only an effective central government led by a powerful president could forge a stable, secure nation from a multitude of weak, wrangling states. He supported the new Constitution as a means toward that end and thereby gained prominence among those proponents of ratification and a strong national government who called themselves Federalists. Jefferson, in contrast, saw representative democracy and states' rights as the bulwarks of liberty, as against the potential corruption and tyranny of a powerful executive, and he stressed those aspects of the new constitutional union. Although Jefferson did not oppose ratification, he became a leading voice within the faction that included both Anti-Federalists, who had opposed ratification, and more moderate critics of a strong national government. Collectively, its members became known as Republicans or, later, Democrats. These differences in emphasis and constitutional interpretation between Adams and Jefferson sharpened as the government took shape following ratification.

As patriot leaders representing differing factions within the broad constitutional consensus, both men returned to America and took leadership positions in the new government. Serving under President Washington, Adams was elected Vice President and Jefferson was named Secretary of State. Together with others, they endeavored to form a unity government embracing a broad spectrum of federalist-republican opinion. They were convinced that well-meaning leaders could draw together in establishing the union just as they had once united to fight for independence.

Based on their wartime experience of suppressing political differences for the common good, the new government's leaders uniformly condemned factionalism and opposed the formation of political parties. Individuals in Congress and the executive branch should address each issue on its merits, they thought, rather than take partisan positions. For this reason, despite their growing differences, Adams and Jefferson tried to get along. Upon hearing of Adams's election as Vice President, Jefferson warmly congratulated him, "No man on earth pays more cordial homage to your worth nor wishes more fervently your happiness." Adams, in turn, hailed Jefferson's appointment as the first Secretary of State.

The differences dividing Adams and Jefferson reflected a deepening ideological rift that divided mainstream Americans into factions. As the nascent government took shape under the Constitution, the people and their chosen representatives vigorously debated various issues regarding the authority of the national government and the balance of power among its branches and between it and the states. Whether the national government could charter a bank and thus create a national banking system became especially heated, for example. Many doubted if the new national government would long survive. Adams and those calling themselves Federalists saw a strong central government led by a powerful president as vital for a prosperous, secure nation. Extremists in this camp, like Alexander Hamilton, who favored transferring virtually all power to the national government and consolidating it in a strong executive and aristocratic Senate, became known as the ultra or High Federalists. At the Constitutional Convention, Hamilton had unabashedly depicted the monarchical British government as "the best in the world" and famously proposed life tenure for the United States President and senators.

Jefferson and his emerging Republican faction viewed such thinking as inimical to freedom. A devotee of enlightenment science, which emphasized reason and natural law over revelation and authoritarian regimes, Jefferson trusted popular rule and distrusted elite institutions.

Indeed, like French philosopher Jean Jacques Rousseau, Jefferson instinctively revered man in nature. "Those who labor in the earth," such as farmers and frontiersmen, possess "substantial and genuine virtue," he wrote in his 1787 book, *Notes on the State of Virginia*. "The will of the majority, the natural law of every society, is the only sure guardian of the rights of men," Jefferson affirmed three years later. He instinctively favored the people over any institution.

In contrast, Adams and the Federalists tended to distrust the common people and instead to place their faith in the empowerment of what they saw as a natural aristocracy, though one that should be restrained by civil institutions such as those provided by a written constitution with checks and balances. "The voice of the people has been said to be the voice of God, and however generally this maxim has been quoted and believed, it is not true," Hamilton reportedly told the Constitutional Convention regarding a popularly elected legislature. "The people are turbulent and changing; they seldom judge or determine right. Give therefore to the first [or upper house] a distinct, permanent share in the government. They will check the unsteadiness of the second [or lower house]."

Although more moderate in his Federalism than Hamilton, but still unlike the Republican Jefferson, Adams thought that every nation needed a single, strong leader who could rise above and control self-interested factions of all classes and types. Neither an aristocratic Senate nor a democratic House of Representatives would safeguard individual rights, he believed. Indeed, Adams once complained to Jefferson about "the avarice, the unbounded ambition, [and] the unfeeling cruelty of a majority of those (in all nations) who are allowed an aristocratic influence; and . . . the stupidity with which the more numerous multitude not only become their dupes but even love to be taken in by their tricks." Only a disinterested chief executive—the fabled philosopher-king of old—would protect liberty and justice for all. Adams thus combined a Calvinist view of humanity's innate sinfulness with an Old Testament faith that a Moses-like leader could guide even such a fallen people through the wilderness into the promised land of freedom.

Due to these beliefs, Adams supported a strong American presidency. Although Adams always preferred an elected supreme leader to a hereditary one, his thinking leaned too much toward monarchism for Jefferson to stomach, especially when others in positions of power around Adams, most notably Alexander Hamilton, openly praised the "balanced" British constitution with its hereditary House of Lords, representative House of Commons, and still-powerful king. As Washington's Treasury Secretary, Hamilton pushed a centralizing, pro-business program of internal taxes, protective tariffs, a national bank, and close trading ties with Britain. He viewed them as essential for national power, prestige, and prosperity.

Jefferson opposed all these policies as destructive of individual liberty and equality of opportunity. Even more, he feared that they would undermine popular rule by creating an aristocracy of wealth in America, a homegrown elite. He did not want the United States simply to become a better Britain, with its concentrated wealth and power. He dreamed of something new under the sun in America—a land of free, prosperous farmers and workers. His support for their rights was staunch and heartfelt.

The differences between Adams and Jefferson became clear in their responses to Shays's Rebellion, a widely publicized antigovernment protest in Adams's home state of Massachusetts. In 1786, hundreds of western Massachusetts farmers led by Revolutionary War officer Daniel Shays briefly took arms against high taxes and strict foreclosure laws during the economic recession that followed the American Revolution. Massive deflation threatened these protesters with the loss of their property and jobs, while the state government only made matters worse for them by raising taxes to repay bondholders for Revolutionary Era debts.

When news of the uprising reached him in Paris, Jefferson used a metaphor from science to convey his reaction in a letter to Abigail Adams, who was then in London with her husband. "I like a little revolution now and then. It is like a storm in the atmosphere," Jefferson wrote. She was horrified. Speaking for herself and probably her husband, she told Jefferson her views on Shays's Rebellion in no uncertain terms: "Ignorant, restless desperados, without conscience or principles, have led a deluded multitude to follow their standard under pretense of grievances which have no existence but in their imaginations."

Jefferson came to see the episode as significant. From his post in London, John Adams did not sufficiently appreciate the protesters' dire plight, Jefferson later wrote. He feared that Adams took the uprising to mean that even "the absence of want and oppression was not a sufficient guarantee of order" against popular revolts stirred by a demagogue. This disagreement over Shays's Rebellion, however mild it seemed at the time, began to fray the relationship between Jefferson and the Adamses; it was a foretaste of the bitter divisions to come.

The divisions between Adams and Jefferson were exasperated by the more extreme views expressed by some of their partisans, particularly the High Federalists led by Hamilton on what was becoming known as the political right, and the so-called democratic wing of the Republican Party on the left, associated with New York Governor George Clinton and Pennsylvania legislator Albert Gallatin, among others. Proud of his humble origins, Adams always had reservations about Hamilton's elitist agenda. He particularly questioned the wisdom of a national bank and never warmed to Britain. Those reservations were lost on Jefferson, however, who reacted against the whole and all of its parts. Adams supported the basic outlines of the Federalist program, and Jefferson resented it. By 1792, Madison, who always acted on Jefferson's behalf in such matters, was calling for a "Republican" party to oppose Hamilton and the Federalists. For his part, Adams never thought Jefferson did enough to restrain the extreme democrats among his supporters. On both sides, the outlines of party organizations emerged in the rise of partisan newspapers, the coordination of voting by members of Congress, and party endorsements for political candidates.

Washington and Adams were not the primary targets of the Republicans, but they came under fire to the extent that they supported

Hamilton's projects. The Republicans embraced policies that favored popular sovereignty, individual freedoms, low taxes, farms over factories, and a limited national government. During the next three decades, the party's name would evolve from Republican into Democratic, leaving the former label for a later, indirect descendant of the Federalist faction.

Adams's actions as Vice President unwittingly further fed Jefferson's fears that the Federalists would subvert democracy. In 1789, Adams urged Congress to confer a "regal" title on the President, such as "His Most Benign Highness" or (better yet) simply "Majesty," which Jefferson dismissed as "the most superlatively ridiculous thing I ever heard of." Expressing his republican sentiments, Jefferson added, "I hope the terms of Excellency, Honor, Worship, [and] Esquire forever disappear from among us."

Then, in 1790–91, Adams published *Discourses on Davila*, a series of historical essays warning against the dangers of human passion and unchecked democracy. They raised Adams's standing with High Federalists but lowered it among Republicans. In the final essay, he attributed the persistence of monarchism in "almost all the nations on the earth" to the failings of popular rule. "They had tried all possible experiments of elections of governors and senates," Adams wrote, but found "so many rivalries among the principal men, such divisions, confusions, and miseries, that they had almost unanimously been convinced that hereditary succession was attended with fewer evils than frequent elections." Adams's words seemed to support a British-type system in which only the legislative lower house was elected. Certainly Jefferson read them that way. "Mr. Adams had originally been a republican," Jefferson later wrote. "The glare of royalty and nobility, during his mission to England, had made him believe their fascination a necessary ingredient in government."

Jefferson engaged Adams privately about the essays, freely calling him a "heretic" to his face for the antirepublican sentiments expressed in them. A strong presidency, independent of checks imposed by the elected House of Representatives, inevitably threatened democracy,

Jefferson argued, especially if the President took on regal airs. A hereditary monarch was much worse. Adams maintained that the essays simply chronicled the European experience; they did not endorse an American king.

The dispute went public when Thomas Paine's blistering defense of radical democracy in revolutionary France, *The Rights of Man*, appeared in the United States in April 1791. It bore an endorsement from Jefferson expressing his pleasure "that something is at length to be publicly said against the political heresies which have sprung up among us." Politicians read Jefferson's words as a direct assault on Adams's *Davila*, which they were.

A published attack by the Secretary of State on the Vice President threatened to split the administration and clearly irritated Washington. Jefferson apologized for the public affront by saying that he never intended or expected his endorsement to appear in print. Of course "I had in my view *Discourses on Davila*" and Adams's "apostasy to hereditary monarchy and nobility," Jefferson explained in a letter to the President, "but I am sincerely mortified to be thus brought forward on the public stage." To Adams, Jefferson wrote, "That you and I differ in our ideas of the best form of government is well known to both of us; but we have differed as friends should do, respecting the purity of each other's motives and confining our differences of opinion to private conversation."

In his response, Adams formally accepted Jefferson's apology but protested that the damage to his reputation had already been done. "The friendship which has subsisted for fifteen years between us without the slightest interruption, and until this occasion without the slightest suspicion, ever has been and still is very dear to my heart," Adams wrote. In fact, it was all but over. The longtime friends had become political rivals.

During the early 1790s, a raging and widespread war between royalists and republicans in Europe greatly intensified these partisan tensions in

America, which further strained the relationship between Adams and Jefferson. The European war had its roots in the violent fall of the monarchy and rise of republican rule in France, which sent tremors through the royal houses of Europe. France's absolutist ancien régime began to totter in 1788 with the calling of a legislative assembly for the first time in over 150 years. Every French king since Louis XIV had claimed absolute power, but an unprecedented financial crisis, caused in part by helping to fund the American Revolution, forced Louis XVI to convene the old Estates General in order to obtain its consent to raise new taxes. This body consisted of three branches—one each for nobles, clerics, and commoners—with the consent of all three needed to institute any meaningful reforms. The commoners had distinct grievances against the government, however, with the largely disenfranchised masses suffering under heavy taxes and often living in abject poverty following a series of poor harvests.

Soon after it convened, the commoners' Third Estate declared itself the sole legislative authority in France and, absorbing the other two estates, renamed itself the National Assembly. At first, members of the other two estates resisted, but violent protests in support of the commoners and the threat of a nationwide popular insurrection forced the nobles, the clerics, and the King to comply. The army could not control the protesters, and in some places actually sided with the people. A revolution was clearly under way even if the extent of it remained in doubt. The King had lost his claim to absolute power and many sensed that the nobility and established church were vulnerable as well. Ineptly, Louis XVI began playing the various sides against the others in an effort to survive as a limited monarch.

On hand as the American ambassador in Paris, Jefferson welcomed these developments despite the worsening violence. "The revolution of France has gone on with the most unexampled success hitherto," he blithely wrote to Madison in May 1789, after hundreds had died in mass protests and military reactions in Paris and other cities. Countless thousands more were dying from starvation and disease as the economy collapsed under the stress of political disorder and repeated poor harvests. Some of the riots started out as nothing more than mass cries for food from government granaries, then ended in slaughter as troops attacked and protesters reacted. The Queen's alleged response to the masses pleading for bread, "let them eat cake," would seal her fate. She never uttered the famous phrase, but it fit her popular image and rumors that she said it circulated widely at the time.

Jefferson remained in Paris long enough to witness the fall of the royal Bastille prison to the revolutionaries on July 14, 1789. "They took all the arms, discharged the prisoners, and . . . carried the [prison's] governor and lieutenant governor to the Greve (the place of public execution), cut off their heads, and set them through the city in triumph," Jefferson wrote excitedly in his official report. "The decapitation of [Governor] de Launai worked powerfully thro' the night on the whole aristocratical party insomuch that in the morning those of the greatest influence . . . [accepted] the absolute necessity that the king should give up everything."

Impressed by this popular uprising, Jefferson contributed to the fund for the families of those slain storming the Bastille. He naïvely predicted that a constitutional monarchy respecting individual rights would quickly emerge from the ashes of absolutist rule. Jefferson believed that nobles and clerics would readily relinquish power to the people, and he personally urged his friends in the aristocracy to do so.

Viewing events through the lens of the American Revolution, Jefferson saw only better times ahead for France. "We cannot suppose this paroxysm confined to Paris alone," he noted. "The whole country must pass successively thro' it, and happy if they get thro' it as soon and as well as Paris has done." To Madison, Jefferson added, "This scene is too interesting to be left at present." His daughters had grown, however, and he wanted to take them home. Upon arriving with them in America late in 1789, and still planning to return to France without them, he learned that Washington had named him the first Secretary of State. Jefferson never again left the country.

As Secretary of State, Jefferson continued steadfastly to side with the revolutionaries in France even as violence there spiraled out of control. Priests were massacred or driven from the realm for their loyalty to the Roman Catholic Church; nobles fled too, and their property was confiscated; protesters fell by the thousands in military reactions. In 1792, partisans pulled Jefferson's friend, the reform-minded Duc de La Rochefoucauld, from his coach and killed him in full view of his mother and wife. Nevertheless, in 1793, Jefferson wrote of the revolution in France, "The liberty of the whole earth was depending on the issue of the contest, and was ever such a prize won with so little innocent blood? My own affections have been deeply wounded by some of the martyrs to this cause, but rather than it should fail, I would have seen half the earth desolated." He saw the scene much like the English romantic poet William Wordsworth depicted it: "France standing on the top of golden hours / And human nature seeming born again." It was a bloody birth.

In contrast, the events in France horrified Federalists in the United States. Growing ever more radical and powerful, the French National Assembly (reconstituting itself first as the Legislative Assembly and then as the Convention under successive constitutions) took command of the armed forces, nationalized the Church, abolished noble titles and privileges, and made the King virtually its prisoner, holed up and under growing threat first at Versailles and then, by the Assembly's command, at the Tuileries Palace in Paris. Of the Assembly and its impact on France, Hamilton wrote, "It has served as the engine to subvert all her ancient institutions, civil and religious, with all the checks that served to mitigate the rigor of authority." Royalist regimes in Europe led by Prussia and Austria responded to these developments by invading France in 1791 to restore the old order. The invasion served only to radicalize the Assembly still further and precipitate a vicious counterattack. The French people rallied to defend their nation even if they did not otherwise support the revolution.

After riding the whirlwind of revolution for four years, Louis XVI fell from his increasingly titular post as King after fleeing the besieged Tuileries Palace on August 10, 1792, paving the way for the Convention to impose republican rule on France six weeks later. Citizen Louis

Capet, as the revolutionaries delighted in calling the former King, was imprisoned in the Temple fortress by the radical Paris Commune along with his widely despised wife, Marie Antoinette. "I'll tell you what," John Adams reportedly commented, "the French republic will not last three months." Although proved wrong, Adams's prediction surely expressed the hopes of many in his party, some of whom favored revising the Constitution to provide a constitutional monarchy for the United States.

Inspired by republican visions of liberty, equality, and fraternity, the French armies pushed back invading royalist forces and began spreading democracy to neighboring lands at gunpoint. "On this day began a new era in the history of the world," German philosopher Johann Wolfgang von Goethe famously wrote after watching French republican forces rout Prussian imperial troops at Valmy, in France, on September 20, 1792. After he heard of the battle, Jefferson exulted, "Our news from France continues to be good, and promises a continuance; the [extent] of the revolution there is now little doubted of, even by its enemies."

Jefferson had hardly written these words before the Convention tried and guillotined the former King, closed Christian churches, and conscripted the entire population into the war effort. Although the revolutionary government had already nationalized the Catholic Church in France and deported or killed priests who would not swear their allegiance to the new order, radicals in the Convention still feared churches as rallying points for reactionaries. Soon the former Queen followed her husband to the scaffold. A new constitution proposed limiting private property and enshrining the right of revolution. By mid-1793, the Convention's most radical faction, the Jacobins, assumed control. Pressed by opponents from within and without, Jacobins instituted a Reign of Terror to purge France of counterrevolutionaries. Thousands died in public executions, often on mere suspicion of disloyalty, including many of the leading revolutionaries themselves.

The differing views of Federalists and Republicans in America regarding the bloody course of events in France made any attempt at nonpartisan governance by the Washington administration virtually futile. Bitter domestic disputes over national power, informed as they now were by analogies to the affairs in Europe, worsened the situation. By the end of Washington's first term in 1793, the unity government that he had so carefully assembled lay in shambles. Jefferson and Hamilton fought privately for influence within the administration while their respective factions battled openly in Congress and the press. As Vice President, Adams played virtually no part in executive-branch deliberations and was silenced in the Senate, over which he presided, by a new rule limiting debate to senators. Adams grew increasingly distant from both Jefferson and Hamilton, whom he viewed as grasping rivals for power. He had also learned, to his dismay, that Hamilton had secretly discouraged some electors from voting for him in the first presidential election—a slight that Adams neither forgot nor forgave. Jefferson and Hamilton soon resigned from the cabinet but Hamilton, with a stronger stomach for direct confrontation, stayed long enough to fill the still forming executive branch with his followers.

Though a more moderate revolutionary government in France relaxed the Terror in July 1794, as Washington's second term progressed, international tensions continued to dominate partisan debate in the United States. In Europe, France's armies pushed the offense, especially after the rise in the mid-1790s of a young Corsican general, Napoleon Bonaparte. Britain joined the European alliance against France and, with their far-flung empires drawn into the inferno, the whole world seemed at war. "None can deny that the cause of France has been stained by excesses," Hamilton observed at the time. "Yet many find apologies and extenuations with which they satisfy themselves; they still see in the cause of France the cause of liberty. . . . Others on the contrary discern no adequate apology for the horrid and disgusting scenes which have been and continue to be acted." Jefferson fit in the former camp; Hamilton placed himself in the latter one. For many Christians, Jefferson's sympathy for Jacobin assaults on organized religion compounded the suspicions raised by his Deist beliefs. Hamilton and the Federalists repeatedly warned that Republican rule might lead to similar attacks on churches in America. The specter of militant Jacobin anticlericalism turned religion into a heated partisan issue in American politics.

Although many Federalists favored Britain and the royalist alliance while most Republicans supported France and its allies, virtually all Americans hoped that their country could remain neutral in the European conflict and continue trading with both sides. That would prove a great challenge. Europe's leading imperial powers, Britain and France, had fought off and on for over a century, but ideological differences and France's military aggression now increased the bitterness of the battle. Both sides demanded support from other nations and retaliated against those that refused aid. Washington tried to maintain American neutrality but, following Jefferson's resignation as Secretary of State in 1793, his administration increasingly came under the control of Hamilton's pro-British High Federalists. Although suspicious of Britain's designs on the United States, Adams abhorred the revolutionary regime in France and did little to right the balance.

After stepping down as Secretary of State, Jefferson continued working privately with Madison and a growing interstate network of Republicans to oppose the High Federalists' pro-Britain, pro-business policies. Although Jefferson claimed to want out of public life, Adams saw his retirement from the cabinet differently. "Jefferson thinks by this step to get a reputation as an humble, modest, meek man, wholly without ambition or vanity. He may even have deceived himself in this belief," Adams noted at the time. "But if the prospect opens, the world will see and he will feel that he is as ambitious as Oliver Cromwell," who usurped royal authority during the English Civil War. When Madison followed Jefferson into early retirement, Adams added, "It seems the mode of becoming great is to retire [from public scrutiny] . . . upon the same principle that no man is a hero to his wife or valet de chambre." Jefferson and Madison so actively organized and led the Republican reaction to Hamilton's programs that Federalists began calling them the Generalissimo and General of the opposition.

Adding to the tension, British naval vessels began intercepting American ships bound to or from French ports and impressing American sailors for service in the Royal Navy. Washington dispatched Chief Justice John Jay to resolve differences between the United States and Britain. But bargaining from a weak position, Jay's controversial British Treaty did little more than accept British limits on American trade with France in exchange for Britain finally evacuating the last of its pre-Revolutionary War forts on U.S. territory. It even failed to stop the British from intercepting American merchant ships and impressing American sailors. The agreement outraged both Republicans at home and the French government, which retaliated by authorizing the capture of American ships trading with Britain. The fledgling United States had no means to protect its merchant fleet, which was now regular prey to both the British and the French. For the first time, Washington's popularity sagged. Jay reportedly said that he could travel from Boston to Philadelphia solely by the light of his burning effigies.

In 1796, at age sixty-four, Washington announced that he would not accept a third term as President. The posturing for succession quickly evolved into a strange sort of behind-the-scenes competition for office. For the first two elections, no one opposed Washington for the presidency. Now the seat was open. The two emerging partisan factions had not yet evolved into institutionalized parties, and they did not yet have mechanisms for formally nominating presidential candidates. They did, however, have clear leading contenders for that office.

Adams was in from the start. Although he once described the vice presidency as "the most insignificant office that ever the invention of man contrived," he nevertheless saw it as a stepping stone to the presidency. "I am heir apparent, you know, and a succession is soon to take place," he wrote to his wife in January 1796. After eight tedious years as the "Prince of Wales," as he termed the Vice President's position, Adams never would have voluntarily relinquished his claimed right to inherit the throne. Hamilton may have coveted the presidency for himself or preferred a loyal High Federalist for the post over the more moderate Adams, but the Vice President's status made it unlikely that any other Federalist could displace him without fatally dividing the party's electoral vote. Jefferson was the obvious Republican contender. Nobody within his party seriously challenged him.

No candidates openly campaigned for the presidency in 1796 or even publicly declared their interest in holding the job. Washington had acted that way in 1788 and 1792, and his would-be successors were careful to emulate him. Jefferson remained in Monticello; Adams went home to his farm near Boston. Others conspired on their behalf, typically without consulting them.

As it turned out, Adams secured votes from 71 of the 139 electors— or one more vote than he needed for the requisite majority—in what was to be the last old-style presidential election. Jefferson was the runner-up with votes from 68 electors, and, as the Constitution then stipulated, he became the Vice President.

Adams swept the northern states, gaining votes from every elector in New England, New York, and New Jersey. Delaware also went for Adams. Jefferson carried the South and West, except for votes for Adams from one elector in Virginia and another in North Carolina. The two nascent parties had secured regional bases of support, where they dominated state and local politics as well. The middle states of Pennsylvania and Maryland split their votes and emerged as key political battlegrounds of the future. For the only time in American history, partisan opponents served together as President and Vice President.

Immediately after his election in 1796, Adams reached out to the Republicans. He suggested that Madison lead a bipartisan mission to negotiate an end to the trade dispute with France and that, as Vice President, Jefferson serve in the cabinet. Although he accepted the vice presidency, Jefferson declined to work with Adams or support the Federalist agenda. The division between Adams and Jefferson, and their respective factions, had grown too wide to bridge by such means. Jefferson would preside over the Senate as the Constitution prescribed, and use that position to rally the Republican opposition. "My letters inform me that Mr. Adams speaks of me with great friendship, and with satisfaction in the prospect of administering the government in concurrence with me," Jefferson wrote to Madison after the election results became known. "If by that he meant [my participating in] the executive cabinet, both duty and inclination will shut that door.... The Constitution will know me only as a member of a legislative body."

Adams ultimately filled his cabinet with holdovers from the Washington administration. Most of them were High Federalists and more devoted to Hamilton than to their new President. This would cause Adams a great deal of consternation in the coming years.

Adams and Jefferson acted respectfully toward each other during their term together, but always at a distance. Partisan differences had become too fierce for their friendship to survive. As they were walking home together after a preinauguration dinner with Washington, Adams raised the issue of his peace mission to France. He informed Jefferson that Federalist legislators had insisted that only their partisans be sent on the mission. The two old friends soon reached an intersection "where our road separated," Jefferson later recalled, "his being down Market Street, mine off along Fifth [Street], and we took leave; and he never after that said one word to me on the subject, or ever consulted me as to any measures of the government." From that point forward, their paths, and those of their parties, diverged ever more sharply.

The threat from France consumed the Adams administration from the outset and mired it in partisanship throughout. By the time Adams took office in March 1797, French naval vessels and privateers had intercepted hundreds of American merchant ships and France had substantially restricted trade by the United States in retaliation for Jay's Treaty. All this impacted mainly the commercial Northeast, a Federalist bastion, fueling anger at France in that region. Yet, many Americans, especially in the agrarian South, where republicanism held sway, were still most leery of Britain and remained positively disposed toward France and its revolution. Within days after he became President, Adams learned that the revolutionary regime in France had refused to receive the new American ambassador named by Washington, Charles Cotesworth Pinckney, an aristocratic former Revolutionary War general from South Carolina with sympathies toward France's old royalist government and who also was the brother of Federalist leader Thomas Pinckney.

In a bellicose address to Congress two months later, Adams urged Americans to prepare for war even as he reiterated his determination to send a peace mission to France. Reactions to the President's policy followed party lines, with the Republican press becoming especially vitriolic in condemning an alleged rush to war. When Adams pushed ahead with efforts to resolve differences with France, he was, as he had told Jefferson he would be, blocked by leaders of his own party from including Republicans in the peace delegation. Ultimately, Adams chose to send back Charles Cotesworth Pinckney along with Virginia Federalist John Marshall and Massachusetts politician Elbridge Gerry, a political independent and close friend of the President. In March 1798, however, Americans heard that French officials refused to receive the delegation without the United States making an advance payment, which amounted to tribute or a bribe simply to begin negotiations. Americans felt humiliated by the stipulation, which was not how respectful adversaries were presumed to act at the time. The demand was made by three French officials, whom Adams diplomatically identified simply as agents X, Y, and Z, and the incident became known in America as the XYZ Affair. In response, war fever gripped the nation.

Rumors spread of an imminent invasion by France, possibly using freed Blacks from the French West Indies as troops. The threat seemed realistic to some frightened Americans, though not to Adams and never to leading Republicans. By that time, France's revolutionary armies had overrun much of Europe, dislodging long-established political, economic, and religious institutions as they went. America was next, High Federalists ominously warned.

To counter the already crippling impact of French attacks on American shipping, Adams proposed building a navy and raising war taxes. Addressing the purported risk of a Jacobin invasion, in July 1798, Federalists in Congress also passed legislation tripling the size of the regular army from about 4,000 soldiers, who were stationed mainly on the western frontier to deal with threats from Native Americans, to nearly 15,000 soldiers, with the new troops to be stationed in the eastern states. Adams considered this so-called Additional Army unnecessary and Republicans viewed it as potentially dangerous. Deeply suspicious of High Federalist intentions to create a strong central government, Republicans saw a domestic standing army as a clear and present threat to states' rights and individual liberty. Despite his reservations about it, Adams signed the legislation for the Army along with bills for his Navy and the war taxes. These measures steeled the Republicans against him.

In 1798, after debating a declaration of outright war against France, which was backed by High Federalists but vigorously opposed by Republicans, Congress enacted a lesser measure authorizing U.S. warships to engage French vessels in international waters. The resulting naval battles of 1799 and 1800 between American and French ships became known as the Quasi-War. Hamilton pronounced himself "delighted" with Adams's performance in the mounting crisis while Jefferson privately denounced it as "insane." Fearing the worst from France, Americans initially rallied to the President and his party. For the first time in his career, Adams became genuinely popular—and he loved it.

The partisan clashes over the American policy toward France intensified in 1798, when High Federalists in Congress turned to matters of internal security in wartime. The High Federalists claimed that the French government might actually whip up support among its American sympathizers, especially among Republicans and recent immigrants from Europe. Indeed, the French armies had relied on resident aliens and local republicans for help in conquering European territory. France's ambassador, Citizen Genêt, once even appealed for public support in the United States to try to overturn Washington's neutrality proclamation. Some Federalists charged that, in an invasion, France might successfully rally internal opposition to the government, though the Republicans in Congress dismissed this as impossible in America and feared that the Federalists sought simply to clamp down on them. The High Federalists took aim at both foreigners within the country and critics of the government in the ever more partisan and vitriolic press. By this time, a number of openly Republican newspapers had gained popularity, most notably the *Aurora* in Philadelphia, offering some measure of balance against the traditionally pro-Federalist press.

In mid-1798, High Federalists pushed through Congress, and Adams signed, the Naturalization, Alien, and Sedition Acts. These laws raised the bar for citizenship, authorized the deportation of foreigners, and outlawed false and malicious criticism of the government in the press or by individuals, including by opposition politicians. A Federalist judge could readily stretch the interpretation of the Sedition Act to reach virtually any form of negative editorial comment in Republican newspapers, and even many Federalists viewed the measure as a blatant move to suppress the freedom of the press and domestic opposition. These acts "were war measures," Adams later explained, "intended altogether against the advocates of the French and peace with France." Presiding over the Senate when they passed, Jefferson strenuously opposed the acts in both public and private, as extreme encroachments on liberty, as did Republicans generally. At first, however, these measures proved popular with the frightened public and Federalists rode them and America's fears of France to victory in the 1798 congressional midterm elections.

In the last two years of his term, however, Adams's popularity seemingly waned and the Republican opposition gained traction. The naval war with France, which proved exceedingly costly and further disrupted foreign trade, led to a soaring national debt and the collection of ever more taxes, which many Americans resented. Republican attacks on the Adams administration took their toll as the public began to realize that, despite the ongoing naval clashes, France was not going to mount an invasion of America. Before long, the Sedition Act and Additional Army began to seem unnecessary and unwise. Republicans painted them as calculated steps toward imposing an authoritarian regime in the United States, perhaps even to instituting an American monarchy.

Rather than help to defuse partisan differences and unite the country, the proximity of Adams and Jefferson in office as President and Vice President served to personalize every clash and to excite the sense that an epic confrontation between them was imminent in the next presidential contest. The stage was set for the election of 1800: America's first and most transformative presidential campaign.

CHAPTER TWO

CROSSING THE BAR

$\mathcal{H}$E MOUNTED his horse under a lead-gray sky on the morning of Thursday, December 12, 1799, for his daily ride about Mount Vernon, his vast Potomac plantation. Washington may have retired from the presidency nearly three years earlier, but he had not stopped working. He owned thousands of acres in Virginia and over three hundred slaves, many of whom worked as skilled laborers in the plantation's many mills, distilleries, and other craft enterprises. Overseers managed Mount Vernon during his many years of public service commanding patriot forces during the Revolution, presiding over the Constitutional Convention, and leading the nation as its first President. Washington, however, resumed control of his plantation whenever he returned home. He believed that Mount Vernon required his active management to remain profitable and provide a suitable income for himself and his wife, Martha.

Mount Vernon's depleted soils could no longer grow tobacco, which made it a constant challenge to reap a profit from farming. Corn whiskey and wheat flour became the plantation's main cash crops. Washington regularly inspected various parts of his plantation to keep abreast of its operations. Indeed, three months after stepping down as President at age sixty-five, Washington commented about his labors at Mount Vernon, "I have been occupied from the 'rising of the sun to the setting of the same'"—and the work had not diminished with the passing of time. On that gray December day in 1799, he remained outside on plantation business in ever worsening weather for over five hours.

The preceding night, Washington had observed a bright halo around the moon, which he took to forecast an approaching storm. The temperature hovered in the low thirties at dawn and dropped during the day. He donned his greatcoat but not a hat for his ride that morning. Standing nearly six feet three inches tall, with the stature of a stately oak tree, Washington's commanding physical presence contributed to his already legendary charisma. Mounting a large horse simply added to his luster. At a time when people equated equestrian skills with athleticism, Washington was a superb horseman, and it still showed at age sixty-seven.

Although his last surviving brother had died three months earlier and none of his close male relatives had reached age seventy, Washington seemed fit. "I was the *first* and now am the *last* of my father's children by the second marriage who remain," he observed upon learning of his youngest brother's death in September 1799. "When I shall be called upon to follow them is known only to the giver of life." Washington did not expect to hear that call anytime soon. Indeed, he had recently reported on his own "good health" to a Federalist supporter and was planning an ambitious trip to inspect his frontier properties in western Virginia during the upcoming spring. Eighteen months earlier, as fears of a French invasion were sweeping the country, Washington had even accepted formal command of the expanded army—a largely titular post that he filled without leaving home. Now, on his rounds that December day, the General carried a four-year plan for enhancing Mount Vernon's profitability.

After eight years as the nation's President, however, Washington could not refrain from being drawn into national political battles after his retirement. He said that he abhorred partisanship, and he probably believed that all elected officials could rise above factional self-interest and unite on fundamental issues. Yet, he readily took sides in partisan clashes, which usually put him in the company of Federalists. Even as President, Washington increasingly let Hamilton set the tone for the administration—especially after Jefferson left the cabinet in despair over the government's elitist, pro-British tilt. "From the moment . . . of my retiring from the administration, the Federalists got unchecked hold of General Washington," Jefferson later observed. "The opposition too of the Republicans to the British Treaty, and the zealous support of the Federalists in that unpopular but favorite measure of theirs, had made him all their own."

Following Washington's retirement, Jefferson came to eye Mount Vernon as a haven for High Federalist intrigue in Republican Virginia. Washington had grown particularly close to Hamilton during his presidency, treating him almost as the son he'd never had, and that relationship continued after Washington left office. "An Anglican, monarchical, and aristocratical party has sprung up whose avowed object is to draw over us the substance as they have already done the forms of the British government," Jefferson intemperately wrote to a foreign confidant, Philip Mazzei, in 1796. "It would give you a fever were I to name to you the apostates who have gone over to these heresies, men who were Samsons in the field and Solomons in the council, but who have had their heads shorn by the harlot England." Jefferson clearly intended to include Washington among the apostates. After the letter became public a year later, Washington grew to distrust Jefferson in kind.

Washington remained the most popular person in the country as the 1800 election approached. Presumably, he could have regained the presidency if he would accept it. Some High Federalists quietly began pushing for just that. They had become angry with Adams when, earlier in 1799, he had reached out again for peace with France by sending a new team of negotiators to Paris in response to assurances that French officials would receive them honorably. Some leaders within Adams's party began actively conspiring to draft Washington for a third term. Adams, whose popularity appeared to falter as the nation's war fever cooled, could not win reelection, they argued, and his politics were too timid.

The disillusionment with Adams went back further for some High Federalists. Hamilton in particular distrusted Adams as too moderate to lead the nation effectively. He had tried to depress the electoral vote for Adams in 1789, claiming that he did not want anyone to compete with Washington for the presidency. After learning of the effort, Adams suspected that Hamilton may have had more sinister motivations, such as humiliating him in public and perhaps keeping him from becoming Vice President. Later events reinforced Adams's suspicions.

In 1796, Hamilton had made a bolder move against Adams, a harbinger of the intraparty conflict that would break out among Federalists in 1800. He tried to manipulate the Electoral College system to deprive Adams of the presidency and get his own favored Federalist, Thomas Pinckney, elected to the position instead. Hamilton's scheme took advantage of the complex and sometimes seemingly perverse mechanics of the original electoral system.

In their conception of the Electoral College, the Framers foresaw an elite group of well-qualified electors exercising their collective judgment in picking the best-qualified President and Vice President from an open field of leading figures from across the country. Through this process, the Framers hoped to avoid both the formation of national political parties, which were never mentioned in the Constitution, and the development of coordinated partisan voting.

As the Framers designed the system, each elector would cast two equal votes, presumably for their top two choices for President. The most highly favored candidate would become President and the second most highly favored candidate would be placed in line for succession as Vice President. Electors were not permitted to designate on their ballots one vote for President and another for Vice President, however, nor could they vote for two candidates from their own state. The Framers included these peculiar stipulations to prevent state loyalties from overwhelming national interests in choosing the President. They worried that so many electors might favor in-state candidates in balloting that, unless they were forced to vote for someone from outside their own state, no truly national candidate could win the election. But they did not want to bar electors from voting for any in-state candidate. Thus, they gave each elector two votes. Even if each elector cast his "first" vote for his home-state favorite, a national candidate could still emerge out of electors' "second" votes. To further assure that the President would have broad national support, to win the post, a candidate would need to receive votes from a majority of the electors. If none did, the House of Representatives would elect the President by majority vote from among the five candidates with the most electoral votes.

The Framers' vision of how the process would work now seems quaint: independent electors meeting in collegiate settings and using their own judgment in casting their ballots for two individuals whom they deemed best qualified to lead the nation. But the process actually operated much as the Framers intended in 1789 and 1792, when Washington was the clear favorite among all the electors. Aside from Franklin, who died in 1790, Washington was America's only truly national hero: the one indispensable person in forming the new government. No party nominated him for President and he never campaigned for the office. Every elector cast one vote for him on both occasions, and he tried to assemble a nonpartisan administration. In both of those elections, John Adams obtained the second-highest number of electoral votes—despite Hamilton's efforts to suppress votes for him in 1789—giving him the vice presidency.

In 1796, Adams and Jefferson continued the tradition of not campaigning for President, but much else changed. The nation's two ideological factions had been evolving steadily into more organized political parties, and their leaders were working ever more assiduously to induce electors aligned with their party to vote for what amounted to a partisan "ticket" of two candidates designated by the party's caucus in Congress. Presumably, electors would cast their "first" vote for the party's preferred presidential candidate and their "second" vote for its suggested vice presidential pick, even though they could not designate their votes as such. In 1796, the Federalists had agreed on Adams for President and South Carolinian Thomas Pinckney for Vice President.

In their caucus, the Republicans in Congress, while uniformly for Jefferson as President, apparently discussed four candidates for Vice President without settling on one of them for the post.

Hamilton saw an opportunity in the rise of party-ticket voting to unseat Adams. He calculated that if there were two leading contenders for President, each with strong support in one party, as with Adams and Jefferson, then the first votes of electors might be nearly evenly divided between them. There then being 139 electors casting a total of 278 votes, this might leave one candidate with anywhere from 70 to 75 "first" votes versus from 65 to 70 "first" votes for the other, with at least one candidate needing a minimum of 70 votes to gain the required majority.

In this scenario, a vice presidential candidate who had strong party backing for the second votes from Federalists in the North, where that party held sway, and also strong state or regional support in the Republican-dominated South, so that he could also pull second votes there, might actually outpoll both presidential candidates. That was Hamilton's plan for Pinckney, who, as a popular Federalist from South Carolina, had strong support both in his home state and among Federalists generally.

Hamilton expected that Pinckney would get votes from all of South Carolina's electors even if they preferred the Republican Jefferson for President. Some other Southern electors might also favor Pinckney for their second votes. So long as Federalist electors in the North duly gave their second votes to Pinckney, those votes combined with Pinckney's votes from Southern electors should bring the South Carolinian in first, with something over 75 votes.

In the end, the plan backfired. Eighteen pro-Adams Federalist electors in New England, who had discerned Hamilton's scheme, decided not to vote for Pinckney, instead "dropping" their votes from him by casting them for either U.S. Chief Justice Oliver Ellsworth of Connecticut or Governor John Jay of New York, who they knew had no chance of becoming either President or Vice President. In order to drop votes and not inadvertently hurt their favored candidate, electors needed to cast their second votes for someone who had no chance of winning.

Ultimately, Pinckney came in third in the overall voting even though, as expected, South Carolina's eight electors voted for him and Jefferson. Jefferson, Hamilton's old adversary, became Vice President instead of Pinckney, which made Hamilton's frustration with the failure of his scheme even worse.

Now, heading into the 1800 election, Hamilton was still set on displacing Adams. He was one of those urging Washington to run and orchestrating a chorus of like-minded High Federalists.

Unless you consent to stand for the office, Federalist Governor Jonathan Trumbull of Connecticut wrote to Washington in June 1799, "the next election of President, I fear, will have a very ill-fated issue." Adams had barely beaten Jefferson in 1796. Republicans now hated Adams even more than then, and High Federalists distrusted him as a trimmer. Trumbull's letter carried an enclosure suggesting that he wrote on behalf of other High Federalists, including at least one member of Adams's cabinet, Oliver Wolcott. Hamilton naturally concurred.

Washington replied disingenuously that party rather than personality would prevail in the next election and thus he would receive no more electoral votes than Adams. Trumbull rightly responded, "My fears and those of other well-wishers to our country are that neither [Adams] nor any other who could be named will be likely to secure with *certainty* that decided and necessary *totality* of votes which are to be wished unless it be [you]." As an evangelical Christian ruling over a virtual theocracy in Connecticut, Trumbull deeply distrusted Jefferson for his alleged Deism and anticlericalism.

At Hamilton's urging, Federalist senior statesman Gouverneur Morris took up the plea in a December 9 letter to the General. "The leading federal characters (even in Massachusetts) consider Mr. Adams as unfit for the office he now holds," Morris wrote. "You must be convinced (however painful the conviction) that should you decline, then no man will be chosen whom you wish to see in that high office." Morris's letter recited a litany of reasons why Washington, for the sake of his country and his own reputation, must consent to serve. "Ponder this I pray," Morris concluded. Although Adams did not know the extent of the cabal against him, he certainly felt the High Federalists' anger.

Washington never received Morris's letter. On December 12, four days before the letter reached Mount Vernon, he returned from his five-hour ride wet and cold. "About one o'clock it began to snow," the General recorded in his diary for that day, "soon after to hail and then turned to a settled cold rain." Snow hung from his hair when he finally reentered the Mansion House after 3 PM.

The heavy snowfall and his physical condition prevented Washington from riding on Friday, December 13. "He had taken cold (undoubtedly from being so much exposed the day before) and complained of having a sore throat," the General's personal secretary, Tobias Lear, wrote in his journal. "He had a hoarseness which increased in the evening but he made light of it, as he would never take anything to carry off a cold, always observing, 'let it go as it came.'" That afternoon, after it stopped snowing, Washington walked outside to mark some trees for removal. In the evening, he asked Lear to read aloud from the transcript of recent debates in the Virginia legislature. What he heard upset him. Republicans in the legislature had selected James Monroe—a neighbor and close political ally of Jefferson and Madison—as the state's next governor. That choice had stacked the deck for Jefferson in the upcoming contest for Virginia's presidential electors. The General surely went to bed in a sour mood.

For Washington, the upcountry triumvirate of Jefferson, Madison, and Monroe had become the very personification of partisanship; and to him, partisanship represented the gravest threat to freedom. Strong parties might help check and balance the excesses of monarchical power in the Old World, Washington conceded, but would likely subvert the American constitutional union of institutionalized checks and balances. "In this sense," Washington observed in his Farewell Address as President, "it is that your union ought to be considered as a main prop of your liberty." Factionalism, he warned, tends "to put in place of the delegated will of the nation, the will of a party."

Jefferson and the Republicans, in contrast, worried that Federalists had already swept away any meaningful institutional checks contained in the Constitution. "Against us are the executive, and the judiciary, . . . the legislature, all the officers of the government, all who want to be officers, all timid men who preferred the calm of despotism to the boisterous sea of liberty, British merchants and Americans trading on British capitals, [and] speculators and holders in the banks and public funds," Jefferson wrote during the waning days of Washington's second term. The naval war with France, the creation of the Additional Army, and the enactment of the Sedition Act had served only to confirm Republicans' worst fears of the Federalists' supposed authoritarian agenda.

Now, in the run-up to the 1800 election, Republicans mobilized with a new vigor to counter this Federalist hegemony. Their emergence as an ever more organized party deeply distressed Washington, who tended to see Federalists as disinterested patriots and Republicans as little more than domestic Jacobins. Indeed, Washington and other Federalists took to using that French label for their partisan opponents.

Comparing the situation when he left office in 1797 with circumstances in 1799, Washington wrote, "At that time the line between parties was not so clearly drawn, and the views of the opposition [not] so clearly delineated as they are present." By "the opposition," he meant the Republicans, and he went on to lament, "Let that party set up a broomstick and call it a true Son of Liberty, a Democrat, or give it any other epithet that will suit their purpose and it will command their votes in toto!" In a subsequent letter to the same Federalist correspondent, Washington complained that the Republican faction, in its increasingly harsh attacks in the press, is "hanging upon the wheels of government, opposing measures calculated solely for internal defense, and is endeavoring to defeat all the laws which have been passed for this purpose by rendering them obnoxious." To him, the Republicans stood against security, while of course the Republicans saw themselves as standing for liberty.

By selecting Monroe as their state's governor in 1799, Republicans in the Virginia legislature could not have made a more partisan pick—nor one more calculated to enrage Washington and the Federalists. "Virginia's misfortune may be comprised in one short sentence," the *Virginia Federalist* reported: "Monroe is elected."

The bad blood between Washington and Monroe went back to 1794 and the negotiation of Jay's Treaty with Britain. At the time, as a young Republican senator from Virginia, Monroe had led calls to retaliate against Britain for imposing unilateral restrictions on American trade with France. Instead of retaliating, however, Washington had decided to send John Jay to negotiate peace with Britain at almost any price. Then, to keep France from immediately striking back at the United States, Washington asked Monroe to replace America's pro-royalist ambassador in Paris, Gouverneur Morris. Monroe naïvely served Washington's purposes in deflecting French attention from Jay's negotiations with Britain by indiscreetly embracing the republican regime in France. Once the treaty took effect, Washington promptly recalled Monroe from Paris and replaced him with Charles Cotesworth Pinckney, who, like his younger brother Thomas Pinckney, was a wealthy South Carolina lawyer and planter with ties to French royalists.

Feeling that Washington and the Federalists had poorly used him, Monroe returned to the United States intent on setting the record straight. He published an intemperate pamphlet that denounced Jay's Treaty as a calculated surrender to Britain and criticized Washington by name. Washington had retired to Mount Vernon by that time and, unaccustomed to such treatment, he could scarcely restrain himself from lashing back in kind. Now he faced the prospect of this insolent partisan becoming his governor. The entire episode must have come back to the General as he listened to Lear read from the legislative transcript. "He appeared much affected and spoke with some degree of asperity on the subject," Lear reported in his diary. Madison's warm praise of Monroe's character particularly angered Washington. His sworn enemies were at the gate and he was growing old.

Washington awoke in the early hours of Saturday morning struggling for breath. His sore throat had developed into something much worse. It was as if someone were strangling him. Martha wanted to call for help immediately, but the General asked her to wait until dawn. Apparently he feared that she might catch a cold getting out of bed on such a chilly night. By morning, Washington could barely utter a sound and never again spoke above a whisper.

"'Tis very sore," the General said of his throat. Lear sent for Washington's physician, James Craik. Even before Craik arrived, two other doctors were summoned as well. Awaiting their arrival, Washington asked for a bleeding by George Rawlins, the overseer who generally treated Mount Vernon's slaves. In line with standard medical practice of the day, Washington believed that removing some blood might reduce the pressure in his throat. "Don't be afraid," the General counseled his reluctant overseer. "More," he demanded when Rawlins tried to stop. In all, the overseer removed half a pint of blood, but the bleeding did not help.

Dr. Craik repeated the procedure after he arrived and also prescribed a sage-tea-and-vinegar gargle, steam, and a cantharidin blister to draw the swelling to the surface. When none of these reduced the internal inflammation in Washington's neck, Craik bled the patient for a third time and administered two laxatives, which produced a dramatic bowel movement. After the other doctors arrived in the afternoon, they prescribed a fourth bleeding. "The blood came very slow," Lear noted this time. "Was thick."

Washington could barely swallow or breathe. He asked to review his two wills, and had one of them destroyed. "I find I am going," he whispered to Lear. "My breath cannot continue long. I believed from the first attack it would be fatal."

Washington called his illness "an ague"; Craik diagnosed it as "inflammatory quinsy"; the medical team ultimately termed it "cynanche trachealis." During the late eighteenth century, these were just words tied to particular symptoms without any effective treatments linked to them. The youngest doctor in attendance suggested a tracheotomy, which might have helped Washington to breathe, but the other doctors vetoed the procedure as too risky. In all likelihood, Washington had contracted epiglottitis from a bacterial infection in his larynx. If so, then no available medical procedure could have cured him. Indeed, at the time and ever after, critics have charged that the bleedings, blisters, and purges inflicted upon Washington only made matters worse. Clearly, they did not help him. "Let me go off quickly. I cannot last long," he told his doctors at dusk. To Craik, the General added, "Doctor, I die hard, but I am not afraid to go."

The physicians continued to treat Washington with blisters and poultices into the evening but they gave up on his life. "About 10 o'clock he made several attempts to speak to me before he could effect it," Lear noted. "At length, he said 'I am going. Have me decently buried and do not let my body be put in the vault in less than two days after I am dead.'" Once he was certain that Lear understood his request, the General spoke for the last time: "'Tis well." After feeling his own pulse, Washington's hand fell from his wrist and he died. "'Tis well," Martha echoed. "I have no more trials to pass through. I shall soon follow him!" Twenty-nine months later, grieving still and feeling very much alone, she did.

Lear formally notified President Adams of the General's passing. "His last scene corresponded with the whole tenor of this life," Lear wrote. "With perfect resignation and a full possession of his reason he closed his well spent life."

News of the unexpected death shocked Americans and precipitated an outpouring of grief unprecedented in the young nation's history. "Every paper we received from towns which have heard of Washington's death are enveloped in mourning," reported Boston's *Columbian Centinel* on December 28, 1799. "Every city, town, village and hamlet has exhibited spontaneous tokens of poignant sorrow."

President Adams set the tone for many. He grieved openly but in a subtly partisan manner. Responding publicly to a memorial message from Congress describing Washington as the country's father, for example, Adams stressed that, among those still in the national government, only he had served with the General at the First Continental Congress, where the independence movement began. "I feel myself alone, bereaved of my last brother," Adams wrote. By dating the independence movement from the first Congress in 1774, two years before the Declaration of Independence, Adams deftly excluded Jefferson from the band of founding brothers. On the eve of the 1800 presidential campaign, no one in government could have missed Adams's subtext, especially because he sent his response to the Senate, where Jefferson presided.

Adams was now the undisputed head of the Federalist Party, despite the opposition from High Federalists within the party. Washington's death threw off the efforts of Hamilton and his allies who had been trying to persuade Washington to run in Adams's stead. With no Federalist other than Adams enjoying a national reputation, except of course the widely unpopular Hamilton, High Federalists recognized that they now had to support Adams for a second term—at least in public. Privately, however, some continued their scheming to drop him in the end.

Four days after Washington died, his body was entombed in the family's Mount Vernon burial vault. People assembled from miles around to watch as, to the sound of solemn music and muffled drums, a military procession carried the casket from the Mansion House to the vault. A riderless horse with boots reversed in the stirrups followed the bier. After the eulogy, artillery cannons fired a salute. Everyone wore black insignia, with many choosing a darkened badge of the Society of the Cincinnati, an elite organization of former Revolutionary War officers whose badge had come to symbolize the Federalist Party.

As President, Adams ordered that all military stations observe similar "funeral honors" for Washington, which the Army interpreted to mean military processions, gun salutes, solemn music, and spoken eulogies. Hundreds of communities followed suit with funerary processions and eulogies of their own, which enabled countless Americans to mourn Washington's passing in a public way. Perhaps the largest such ceremony occurred on December 26 in Philadelphia, which was still the nation's capital. Congress designated Federalist Representative Henry Lee of Virginia to deliver the eulogy at the event. There he spoke the words that many still use to characterize Washington: "First in war, first in peace, and first in the hearts of his countrymen."

At the time, some Federalists sought to take partisan advantage of the sincere and widespread emotional response to Washington's passing. They planned and led the ceremony in Philadelphia, for example, and Lee's eulogy repeated the Federalist mantra: "Liberty and Order." Republicans, in contrast, stood simply for "liberty" and took the American Revolution's liberty cap, liberty pole, and liberty tree as their symbols. For many conservative Americans, however, the riotous revolutionaries in France had appropriated these symbols and equated them with a reign of terror. Federalists thus stressed the need for "ordered" or "civil" liberty and equated the Republicans' notion of "liberty" with licentiousness and Jacobin mob rule. "Civil liberty," explained Federalist leader John Jay, who then served as New York's governor, "consists not in a right to every man to do just as he pleases, but it consists in an equal right . . . to do . . . whatever the equal and constitutional laws of the country admit to be consistent with the public good." Their firm stand for civil order in turbulent times represented a principal appeal of the Federalists in the 1790s. Stressing this theme in his eulogy, Lee mourned Washington's death coming at a time "when the civilized world shakes to its center [and] when every moment gives birth to strange and momentous changes." He claimed to be hearing Washington plead, from beyond the grave, "Let Liberty and Order be inseparable companions."

Taking up two other Federalist election themes, Lee also claimed to be hearing Washington ask Americans to "reverence religion" and "control party spirit, the bane of free government." Federalists freely denounced Jefferson as a Deist or atheist while calling on America's Protestant majority to support their party's God-fearing candidates. Privately, Washington and Adams inclined toward Deism or Unitarianism, too, but at least they publicly invoked God's blessing on America through displays of civil religion and attended Protestant services. Despite the inroads of Enlightenment thought, particularly among the elites, evangelical Protestantism remained strong in the United States and most Americans valued the role of religion in civil society.

Federalists also equated Republicans with self-interested partisanship and themselves with disinterested public service. A natural aristocracy of virtuous and wise leaders should rule on the call of the people in elections devoid of partisanship, Federalists maintained, and the people should follow. To them, Washington's tenure as President exemplified the ideal: personality over party. In contrast, "the Jacobins appear to be completely organized throughout the United States," one prominent Federalist complained about the Republicans in 1800. "The whole body act with a union to be expected only from men in whom no moral principles exist." For their part, Federalists tended to shun party discipline as inappropriate for public servants, leading one Federalist congressman to observe in 1800, "The Federalists hardly deserve the name of party. Their association is a loose one."

Similar themes to those heard in Philadelphia were sounded in the eulogy for Washington delivered in New York City by the state's incoming Federalist senator, Gouverneur Morris. The 1800 census would show that New York had finally surpassed Philadelphia as the nation's largest city—and both sides viewed New York State's electoral votes as critical to winning the presidency. New York Federalists organized a massive public commemoration of Washington's death for December 31, 1799. Hamilton, who had become like a son to Washington, assumed a central position in the funerary procession, riding after the military contingents and before representatives of various civic associations.

Morris's eulogy cursed the rise of a partisan "faction" in American politics and praised leaders, like Washington, "of decided temper who, devoted to the people, overlooked prudential considerations," as opposed to "cautious men with whom popularity was an object." As Washington's former proroyalist ambassador to Paris, Morris even included a bizarre reference to King Louis XVI as the "protector of the rights of mankind," an apparent slap at Jefferson and the Republicans who defended the revolutionaries who first toppled and then guillotined the French monarch. "Let us raise a standard to which the wise and the honest can repair," Morris proclaimed. Privately, the New Yorker attributed Jefferson's appeal to the people's irresponsible intoxication with popular rule. "When the people have been drunk long enough, they will get sober," he assured a fellow Federalist, "but while the frolic lasts, to reason with them is useless."

Some Republicans resisted efforts to transform memorial ceremonies for Washington into thinly veiled Federalist campaign rallies. "The whole United States mourn for him as a father," observed Benjamin Rush, a renowned physician with Republican ties who attended the ceremony in Philadelphia and afterward critiqued Lee's partisan eulogy as "moderate but deficient in elocution." Philadelphia's leading Republican newspaper, the *Aurora*, reported on various "republican" contingents joining the funerary procession for Washington. "Many will join in ye form that car'd little about him," complained Philadelphia diarist Elizabeth Drinker, a candid and insightful Federalist sympathizer.

Republicans also took part in the ceremony in New York, where all manner of partisan groups accepted the organizers' open invitation for public bodies to join the grand procession honoring the former President. Hamilton must have watched his back as his mounted suite paraded directly in front of partisans from the working-class Tammany Society—the very heart of republicanism in New York City—who held aloft a liberty cap veiled in crape. We mourn Washington too, the Tammanyites seemed to say, and to us, he stood simply for liberty. The contest over the meaning of Washington's life began that last day of 1799—if not before.

*   *   *

One of the points of fiercest contention was the Additional Army. In many major cities, the new troops featured prominently in ceremonies honoring their fallen commander. This seemed appropriate given Washington's military credentials and his role as its head, but it also invited a polarizing partisan response from both Federalists and Republicans. Congress had largely disbanded the nation's military forces following the Revolutionary War, relying instead on state militias for military purposes. When, following the XYZ Affair, Congress prepared the nation for war by creating a navy and greatly expanding the Army, many people had viewed the Additional Army as peculiarly a High Federalist force. Indeed, Adams, believing that the true danger to American interests lay at sea, had not requested any added troops and Republicans had generally opposed the idea. "There is no more prospect of seeing a French army here as there is in heaven," Adams once cautioned his hawkish, High Federalist Secretary of War, Oliver Wolcott.

Privately, Washington agreed with Adams's assessment of the military situation but nevertheless accepted the commission as the Army's leader. He insisted on appointing his own officers corps and, over Adams's strenuous objections, named Hamilton as his Inspector General, the second in command. Two other Federalist politicians with wartime experience, Charles Cotesworth Pinckney and Henry Lee, became major generals, but Hamilton largely organized and led the troops while Washington remained at home.

Republicans had vehemently criticized the domestic military buildup—fearing with some justification that Hamilton might turn the new Army against them. Jefferson in particular worried about a military coup to maintain Federalist hegemony. Even Adams became concerned about Hamilton's intentions when shown private letters from the Inspector General suggesting that he might use the Army to suppress antigovernment "resistance" in Virginia and "take possession" of Florida and Louisiana from France's ally, Spain. "This man is stark mad or I am," Adams later claimed to have said about Hamilton upon reading these and other confidential letters outlining his plans.

As it became increasingly apparent that France would not invade the United States, the Additional Army lost much of its public support. "That army," Adams later commented, "was as unpopular as if it had been a wild beast let loose upon the nation to devour it. In newspapers, in pamphlets, and in common conversation, they [sic] were called cannibals." Cost was one consideration, of course, but the thought of armed young men from various regions encamped in bases scattered across the eastern seaboard worried many Americans who lived quiet lives in insular communities. Feeding those sentiments, Republican newspapers had spread stories of looting and rapes committed by idle soldiers who had no real worry of ever facing French invaders. By 1799, the Army had, on balance, become a decided political liability for Federalists.

Therefore, the prominent role of the Additional Army in so many of the ceremonies marking Washington's death made it a visible symbol of both the partisan gulf separating Federalists and Republicans and the intraparty rift between so-called Adamsites and Hamiltonians. It had always been Hamilton's Army and strictly a High Federalist force, and so it still appeared at the memorial services for Washington. With the need for the Army disputed from the start and negotiations now under way with France, military recruiting, always slow, ground to a halt with the force never reaching even half of its authorized size. A festooned officers' corps comprised largely of aging High Federalist politicians commanded just enough troops to make for impressive dress parades at Washington's many funerary processions.

Though many Republicans participated in the national outpouring of grief, not all of them joined in extravagantly mourning Washington's death. Republican essayist, poet, and newspaper editor Philip Freneau ridiculed the "blasphemous panegyrics" that praised Washington as a god. Emphasizing simple republican virtues, Freneau now wrote of Washington, "He was the upright, Honest Man. This was his glory." For their part, Jefferson and Madison kept a low profile. Even though

Jefferson, as the sitting Vice President, was listed on the official program for Washington's funerary procession in Philadelphia, he did not
attend. Although he surely knew about the ceremony, Jefferson did not
return to Philadelphia for the winter session of Congress until two days
afterward. Indeed, Dumas Malone, Jefferson's most comprehensive
biographer, determined that the man who had once served as Washington's Secretary of State "said nothing in public and appears to have
said nothing in private" about Washington's death. His silence spoke
for him, and his conspicuous absence from the funerary procession
provoked widespread criticism by Federalists, but he probably preferred that to their possible charges of hypocrisy for marching in it,
Dumas observed. Only much later, after the election of 1800, did Jefferson make a private courtesy call on Washington's widow at Mount
Vernon.

Jefferson was not the only prominent Republican leader to miss the
Philadelphia memorial ceremony for Washington. The recently
elected Republican governor of Pennsylvania, Thomas McKean, also
skipped the event. Two weeks later, he pointedly refused to attend a
similar funerary procession for Washington organized by Federalists in
Lancaster, Pennsylvania. Tongues wagged throughout the state as partisans debated the political significance of McKean's actions in light of
the coming presidential election. "Had this party magistrate possessed
one spark of American patriotism," the Federalist *Gazette of the United
States* fumed, other considerations "would not have prevented him
from joining in the general sorrow and affliction of the occasion."

Overwrought partisan opponents could plausibly criticize the
impulsive and temperamental McKean as a "dark and foul-minded
champion of disorganization," as the *Gazette* article did, but hardly for
a lack of patriotism. In the mold of Samuel Adams and Patrick Henry,
McKean was an early and ardent patriot. As a Delaware colonial legislator, he boldly condemned the Stamp Act in 1765 and the Townshend
Duties in 1768. Elected to the First and Second Continental Con-
gresses, McKean joined Adams in advocating American independence
before doing so was either prudent or popular, and he proudly signed

the Declaration of Independence. He later co-authored both the Delaware and Pennsylvania state constitutions and simultaneously served as member of Congress from Delaware and Chief Justice of Pennsylvania. His estate straddled the state line.

Originally a Federalist, McKean so hated Britain from his days as a patriot leader that he gradually broke with Washington over Jay's Treaty and Hamilton's Anglophile policies. Adams's naval war with France clinched McKean's switch to the Republican Party and, with the enthusiasm of a late convert, he had agreed at age sixty-five to stand as its candidate for Pennsylvania governor in October 1799. At the time, partisans on both sides viewed that state's legislative and gubernatorial elections that autumn as virtually the opening round of the 1800 presidential contest.

Already known as the Keystone State for its geographic and political centrality, Pennsylvania certainly appeared key to the election of 1800. The North would go for Adams, most political observers forecast, while Jefferson would carry the South, except perhaps for South Carolina, where there were still Federalist bastions loyal to Thomas and Charles Cotesworth Pinckney. The middle states from New York to Maryland held the balance of power. In 1796, the votes from these states had split between the two leading candidates, with all twenty-two electors from New York, New Jersey, and Delaware voting for Adams, fourteen of Pennsylvania's fifteen electors voting for Jefferson, and Maryland's ten electors casting seven votes for Adams and four for Jefferson. Adams's slender margin of victory had come from the votes of two rogue Southern electors, one from Virginia and one from North Carolina. If either candidate could secure more electoral votes from the middle states this time, he would almost surely win.

Pennsylvania, with its fifteen electoral votes, stood out as the most populous of these middle states. It was also amid a transformation from leaning Federalist to Republican. Looking ahead to the 1800 presidential election in light of the 1799 governor's race, America's flagship

Federalist newspaper, *Gazette of the United States*, predicted, "The effects then of the election of governor will be incalculable."

The governor's role in the presidential election might be substantial because Pennsylvania did not at this time have a set method of picking its electors fixed in law, and the governor could therefore have a significant role in designing that process. Depending how events played out, he might even be the kingmaker.

The Constitution had left each state free to decide how it would select its electors. Most states initially opted to have state legislators appoint electors. As party lines hardened, these legislative choices became ever more partisan. Typically, each party's caucus in the state legislature would put forward a full slate of elector candidates who, if appointed, would support the party ticket. The party with the most legislators would get all the state's electors.

From the outset, a few states allowed voters to choose electors in direct popular elections. Some of these states employed district elections, with voters in each electoral district typically choosing one elector from between two partisan candidates. This approach tended to split a state's electors between the parties, as some districts leaned toward the Federalists and some leaned toward the Republicans. Other states used a general ballot, so that all of the state's electors were chosen by voters from across the state, often from candidates running on two partisan slates. That approach favored all of the state's electors supporting whichever party, and voting for whichever presidential candidate, attracted the most voters statewide.

Further, to identify their candidates for President and Vice President, party members increasingly looked toward the caucus of its representatives in Congress, which was the only venue where politicians from around the nation assembled. Though the Framers had designed the Electoral College to isolate the presidential election process from partisanship, the parties had virtually commandeered the system.

Going into the 1799 Pennsylvania state elections, the Federalists controlled both houses of the Pennsylvania legislature, and though the Republicans hoped to pick up some seats in both, they were not

expected to take control of them. The new legislature would decide
how the state's electors would be chosen in 1800, and lawmakers from
each party would surely try to impose a method that favored their
party. The governor would have veto power over whatever they passed.

Pennsylvania Federalists were especially intent to stack the system
in their party's favor this time because of an ironic turn of events in the
state's last election for presidential electors. Hoping to secure all of
Pennsylvania's electoral votes for Adams in 1796, they had opted for a
statewide general election for electors. The plan backfired, however,
when Jefferson's supporters won a narrow majority in the balloting.
Hence, all but one of Pennsylvania's electors had voted for Jefferson—
the only votes received by the Virginian from any state north of the
Mason-Dixon Line. Those votes, combined with ones from his Southern base, would have given him the presidency except for those two
rogue electoral votes for Adams from Virginia and North Carolina.

To win in 1800, both Federalists and Republicans calculated that
Jefferson would probably need to sweep Pennsylvania's electoral votes
again. His doing so would require the state to reenact its statewide
general-ticket method for selecting electors, and so, of course, Pennsylvania's Federalists now favored either district elections or legislative
appointment for the state's electors. Either system would ensure that
at least some of the electors were Federalists. If McKean were elected
governor as a Republican, however, he could thwart their plans with a
veto.

For their candidate for governor, Federalists countered with
another well-known politician: U.S. Senator James Ross, a leading
High Federalist supporter of the Alien and Sedition Acts who hated
France as much as McKean hated England. The race had become a
clash of titans centered on Philadelphia, the nation's capital. As early as
July 1799, a prominent Pennsylvania Federalist wrote nervously to
Washington, "This state is greatly agitated by the approaching election
of Governor. There is good reason to believe that Mr. Ross will be chosen, but the whole spirit of party will be extended against him."

As the campaign played out, the race turned on national issues, not state ones. McKean supporters tied his opponent to the locally unpopular policies of the Adams administration and the High Federalists in Congress. One Republican broadside denounced Ross as "a British partisan; a monarchist; an advocate of war [with France]; a litigious attorney; . . . [and] a patron of the Alien and Sedition Acts." In contrast, it praised McKean as "a steady patriot of 1776" who supports "peace" and "freedom of press." Another Republican appeal declared, To "the Federalists . . . and their candidate, Mr. Ross, we owe the *Sedition Laws*. . . . To them we are indebted for the *British Treaty*, that parent of our present dispute with France. . . . To them we owe the *Alien Law*, which has set aside trial by jury. . . . Of this party, *James Ross* is the favorite candidate."

In state and congressional elections held in 1797 and 1798, during the rush toward war with France and amid widespread concerns about domestic security, these same issues had tended to cut in favor of the Federalists. On the eve of the 1799 election, however, the Republican *Aurora* proclaimed, "This national infatuation is broken . . . and the free American countenance once more wears the softened lineaments of the independent and benevolent Republican."

Pennsylvania Federalists countered in kind but with less effect. "Mr. McKean is a friend to France," a Federalist pamphlet charged, and "desirous of provoking a war with Great Britain." He favored unlimited Irish immigration, it added, and would countenance domestic discord. Repeating a common Federalist accusation against Republicans, the pamphlet charged, "They have made liberty and equality the pretext, whilst plunder and dominion has been their object." Another Federalist broadside presented the choice as between "happiness and independence" with Ross or "anarchy and insurrection" with McKean. The Federalist *Gazette of the United States* starkly warned that McKean's election would see "the whole state turned into a filthy kennel of Jacobinical depravity."

Religion also played a major role in Pennsylvania's gubernatorial election, but with the traditional roles reversed. In the 1796 presidential election, Federalists had portrayed Adams as a faithful Christian and Jefferson as an infidel bent on driving religion from the public square. In the 1799 Pennsylvania contest, however, Ross was the Deist and Republicans showed that they could give as good as they got. Their campaign literature portrayed McKean as "a devout Christian" and Ross as a heretic. They frequently repeated the charge that Ross publicly denied the Christian doctrine of original sin, and reminded voters that he once sought to delete a provision from the state constitution requiring that officeholders believe in God. Of course, at the national level, Federalists leveled those precise accusations against Jefferson. If the 1799 gubernatorial campaign served as a fair barometer of the nation's political climate, then it forecast heavy weather ahead for the election of 1800.

Federalists despaired when McKean beat Ross by about 5,000 votes out of some 70,000 ballots cast. Not only had the Republicans taken the governorship, they had gained control of the lower house of the legislature, the Assembly, and almost captured the State Senate as well. Nearly 60 percent of Pennsylvania's eligible voters participated in the election—more than twice the percentage participating in the preceding gubernatorial election. The Republicans won on high turnout, with particular strength among Irish and German immigrants. "The Federal Party are so much alarmed at the idea of McKean being chosen governor that they are apprehensive of success . . . next year," the *Aurora* crowed, referring to the 1800 presidential contest. McKean and his Republicans would still have to battle the Federalists controlling the State Senate over the method of selecting electors, but the contest looked tilted in their favor.

Demoralized by their drubbing in the polls, Federalists worried openly about its implications for the upcoming presidential election. "Such a fire has been lighted up in Pennsylvania as will consume the Federal Union," printer John Fenno opined in the *Gazette of the United States*. Characterizing McKean's partisan victory as "an event most disgraceful to our national character," the Federalist Speaker of the U.S. House of Representatives, Thomas Sedgwick, blamed the split between Adams and High Federalists, which he saw as potentially fatal for his fledgling party. "The state of Pennsylvania is a strange medley," Abigail Adams added. Its "late election has withered all the laurels it ever had."

Perhaps the direst predictions came from High Federalist printer William Cobbett, the Anglophile editor of the caustic, opinion-laced *Porcupine's Gazette*, who had suffered in libel actions brought in McKean's court. "The election of my Democratic judge as governor of Pennsylvania, undeniably the most influential state in the union, has, in my opinion, *decided* the fate of what has been called *Federalism*," Cobbett growled. "His success [is] only a sort of onset in the struggle which will terminate in the complete triumph of Democracy." Cobbett viewed Republican "Democracy" as synonymous with "Jacobin" tyranny. Acting on his fears, Cobbett promptly moved his publishing business from Philadelphia to New York, and then to London. He refused to live under Republican rule.

Republicans celebrated across Pennsylvania as word of their victory and its surprising extent spread. For them, it was like Independence Day: bonfires, bands, fireworks, ox roasts, and plenty to drink. Toasts to Jefferson, "the faithful guardian of our rights," inevitably raised the loudest and longest cheers, equaling or exceeding those even for McKean. "May the spirit which dictated the Declaration of Independence preside in the union," one toast to Jefferson proclaimed. It elicited nine cheers compared with only three for a toast to Washington, "the late commander in chief." Republicans in Pennsylvania now sang a new song:

> *Ye true sons of freedom, ye rude swinish throng,*
> *Attend for a while, and I'll give you a song,*
> *It's the triumph of freedom, we now celebrate,*
> *A Republican governor gain'd for the state.*
>
> *Friends of Freedom now since we have gained our cause,*
> *Let's be firm in supporting our country and laws,*
> *But not that curst law of Sedition so ill,*
> *If I do then curse me with an Alien bill.*

Commenting on the results from Monticello, Jefferson wrote to South Carolina Senator Charles Pinckney, the younger Republican cousin of Thomas and Charles Cotesworth Pinckney, "The success of McKean's election is a subject of real congratulation and hope." Of course, Jefferson had carried Pennsylvania in 1796 and still lost. He would need more electoral votes from northern or middle states and solid support from the South to be sure of victory in 1800. The isolated votes in Virginia and North Carolina that had gone to Adams last time must be secured. No one knew this better than the younger Pinckney.

Charles Pinckney lived for politics, and he particularly enjoyed besting his Federalist cousins, who had taken to calling him "Blackguard Charlie" for his allegiance to the Republican cause. As prominent members of South Carolina's inbred aristocracy, the Pinckneys transformed state politics into a family feud. For months, Charles Pinckney had urged Jefferson and Madison to secure the Republican base by pushing Virginia and North Carolina to adopt a statewide method of choosing presidential electors because he was convinced that the majority in both states would be solidly Republican. "The success of the Republican interest depends on this act," Pinckney wrote in a September 1799 letter to Madison. Under a district method of choosing electors, he explained, pockets of Federalism within those two predominantly Republican states could cost Jefferson the presidency in 1800, just as they had in 1796. Using a statewide general ticket would prevent this result. "A single vote may be of great consequence," Pinckney stressed. "This is no time for qualms." The 1798 congressional elections underscored the risk when Federalist candidates won in eight of Virginia's nineteen congressional districts.

Viewing district elections as the most democratic method of choosing presidential electors, Jefferson had favored them as a means to make the inherently elitist electoral-college system somewhat more representative. Without effective state media or communications, local voters might know district candidates, whereas they could not know many of those running statewide. To Jefferson, democracy required informed voters. Practical considerations, however, brought him around to Pinckney's point of view. Any large state using district elections effectively disenfranchised itself in a close presidential contest in which most other states used some form of winner-take-all method of choosing electors—either by a statewide vote or legislative appointment. Splitting a state's electoral votes between opposing candidates effectively negated them.

Once Republicans gained firm control of the Virginia government with Monroe's selection as governor in December 1799, Jefferson endorsed switching to a general ticket for choosing the state's electors. "All agree that an election by districts would be best if it could be general" throughout the nation, he wrote to Monroe, "but while ten states choose either by their legislatures or by a general ticket, it is folly and worse than folly for the other six not to" use some winner-take-all approach. Madison, then serving in the state legislature, recognized that his party had enough power to push through the change. "The present assembly is rather stronger on the Republican side than the last one," he wrote to Jefferson on January 12, 1800. "It is proposed to introduce tomorrow a bill for a general ticket in choosing the next electors." In January, majority Republican lawmakers dutifully enacted Madison's bill calling for a statewide election for electors, but only after a bitter partisan debate and by an unexpectedly narrow margin. The new election law all but assured that Jefferson would sweep Virginia's twenty-one electoral votes this time, the most of any state.

Between Virginia's general-ticket law and McKean's triumph in Pennsylvania, the pieces seemed to be falling in place for a Republican victory in 1800. The election remained nearly a year away, however, and essential uncertainty over the outcome remained. Even with all their electoral votes, Virginia and Pennsylvania could not quite guarantee the margin of victory for Jefferson. He had received virtually all their votes four years earlier and still lost. True, if he carried all their votes this time and every other vote he had won in 1796, he would win by one vote—but he could not necessarily count on doing so well everywhere. Other than Pennsylvania, the middle states—New Jersey, Maryland, and Delaware—remained predominately Federalist. Pockets of Federalism in the Carolinas also threatened to undermine Jefferson's Southern base and subtract votes from his 1796 total. In addition, in Virginia and Pennsylvania, Federalists immediately began working to salvage some electoral votes.

In Virginia, Federalists tried to shame Republicans into restoring district elections, and, with legislative elections scheduled for April, well before the balloting for electors in November, they even dreamed of gaining control of the legislature and then restoring district elections themselves. A statewide general ticket will effectively "exclude *one third* at least of the citizens of Virginia from a vote for the president of United States," one partisan complained—the one-third in Federalist-leaning districts. A widely reprinted Federalist broadside denounced the general-ticket law as violating "the ancient usages of elections and [voters'] established rights" of choosing from among candidates in local races rather than between party ballots in statewide ones. Underscoring this point, critics of the law noted that Virginia had never conducted a statewide election for any office: Should partisan considerations trump democratic traditions?

Republicans responded with a pamphlet, *A Vindication of the General Ticket Law*, which defended the principle of winner-take-all balloting as "best calculated to preserve to every state in the union the full extent of that power which the Constitution intended to confer." As the most populous state, Virginia should have the most electoral power, the Republicans argued, and only a winner-take-all approach would secure it.

Of course, the same electoral calculus applied in other states and to both parties. As the contests over voting methods heated up in Pennsylvania and Virginia, partisan lawmakers in other states took heed. Fearing that Republican electors might win in one or two of their state's electoral districts, Federalists in control of the Massachusetts government soon responded effectively in kind to Virginia Republicans by switching from district elections to legislative appointment for presidential electors. Explaining his desire to "guard against *one* anti-federal vote from Massachusetts," a Bay State lawmaker warned that "one vote may turn the election." Cautious Federalists in neighboring New Hampshire also opted for legislative appointment. Ultimately only three states—Kentucky, Maryland, and North Carolina—stuck with district elections for choosing presidential electors in 1800, four fewer than in 1796. Two others—Rhode Island and Virginia—used a statewide general ticket for electors, which would likely result in one party carrying all the electoral votes because voters would presumably vote along party lines in such a contest. The rest used some form of legislative appointment.

In Pennsylvania, despite McKean's victory and their strong showing in legislative races, Republicans could not yet count on sweeping the state's electoral votes in 1800. They had taken control of the lower house of the state legislature along with the governorship in 1799, but Federalists had clung to power in the upper house. Both houses and the governor would have to agree on the method of choosing electors, and Federalists in the upper house firmly opposed any approach that might favor Jefferson. They would demand either district elections or legislative appointment, which would surely secure some Federalist electors, over the statewide ballot favored by McKean and the Republicans. As long as they controlled the State Senate, even by a narrow margin, they would have the power to hold out for their preference, or force a stalemate. If lawmakers failed to resolve the issue of how the state chose its electors, Pennsylvania might have to abstain altogether from voting in the presidential election.

Federalists went into the 1800 election never having lost the presidency and firmly in control of both houses of Congress due to their strong showing in the 1798 midterm elections. With their leaders split over Adams's peace initiative with France and critical state elections going against them in Pennsylvania and Virginia, however, their prospects for 1800 had dimmed even while Washington lived. As the only person whom all Federalists admired, Washington had held the party together and given it meaning. A few years earlier, Jefferson had predicted that the nation's "republican spirit" would revive once Federalists could no longer rally around Washington. For beleaguered Federalists, their leader's passing came at a critical time. "The death of the General!" one prominent Federalist had exclaimed late in 1799. "God help us!" His words spoke for an entire party.

Throughout the 1790s, Republicans were defined largely by their opposition to Hamilton and the High Federalist agenda. People called them "the antis." With Washington gone and their unity shattered by Adams's overture to France, Federalists were fast becoming "the antis"—defined mainly by their opposition to Jefferson and the Republican Party. The initiative heading into the 1800 election had passed from the Federalists to the Republicans by the end of January, but the outcome was far from certain and partisanship now reigned supreme.

CHAPTER THREE

"ELECTIONEERING HAS ALREADY BEGUN"

*J*HE NEWS resounded like rolling thunder as it spread across America. "The French Republic is overthrown," the Federalist *Gazette of the United States* reported on February 7, 1800. The name Napoleon Bonaparte hung in the air everywhere. The republic's greatest general had staged a coup and taken effective control of France. Americans sensed that this new earthquake in European politics would shake their country too, but no one yet knew exactly how. Federalists and Republicans alike struggled to retain their balance in the wake of the shocking news.

If they agreed on nothing else, Federalists and Republicans agreed that events in the Old World still influenced those in the new one. The cataclysmic European conflicts gave energy and meaning to the American partisan disputes. Indeed, they had largely given them birth. Bonaparte's coup d'état cast all in doubt. Although it occurred in November 1799, word of the event did not begin reaching American ports until January 1800, with complete reports arriving only in February.

For over a decade, political developments in France had dominated the news in America. "That revolution which has been the admiration, the wonder, and the terror of the civilized world had, from its commencement, been viewed in America with the deepest interest," observed John Marshall, whose principled stand against negotiating with France during the XYZ Affair effectively launched his legendary career in American public service. Second only to Britain, France had influenced the course of American political, social, and cultural development for two centuries. Always the other world power with designs on eastern North America, France had alternately threatened and enticed Americans since colonial times. After trying to conquer Britain's New World colonies in the 1760s, France helped them to gain their independence in the 1770s. So many Americans still admired Louis XVI for his role in their struggle for independence that his portrait continued to hang in a position of honor at the U.S. House of Representatives in 1800—more than seven years after his own people had overthrown and beheaded him.

The fascination of Americans with the French Revolution crossed party lines and stemmed in part from the sense that the American Revolution had played an important role in transporting visions of liberty and democracy onto the world stage. At the dawn of the French Revolution, for example, Washington wrote optimistically to Jefferson in France, "The rights of mankind, the privileges of the people, and the true principles of liberty seem to have been more thoroughly discussed and better understood throughout Europe since the American Revolution." Jefferson concurred. He wrote back to Washington, "The [French] nation has been awakened by our revolution." This bond between the two nations had survived into the 1790s despite growing doubts among High Federalists. Even when France's short-lived constitutional monarchy fell to republican rule in 1793, Washington (in words probably written by Jefferson as his Secretary of State) reassured French officials that "the union of principles and pursuits between our two countries [is] a link which binds still closer their interests and affections." Capturing the spirit of the day, John Marshall wrote, "There seems to be something infectious in the example of a powerful and enlightened nation verging toward democracy."

Virtually all Americans had initially welcomed the French Revolution as heralding a new birth of freedom in Europe. The absolute authority of the King in prerevolutionary France and the oppressive power of its nobles and clerics found little support among Americans, who claimed a heritage of representative government, personal liberty, and economic opportunity from their days as British colonists. Their revolution defended and expanded these rights, Americans believed, without directly challenging the established social and religious order. As the French Revolution pushed far beyond its American predecessor, however, in repudiating political, economic, and religious traditions and opening new horizons for radical social change, many Americans, led by the High Federalists, began having second thoughts. Now the French had fallen under military rule, a fate anathema to the basic principles of the United States and the American Revolution.

Federalists took one lesson from the French experience: Unfettered democracy under the influence of a leveling faction produces anarchy, atheism, and then tyranny. "I much fear that this country is doomed to great convulsions, changes, and calamities," Maryland Senator Charles Carroll of Carrollton, an extreme High Federalist, wrote to Hamilton in 1800. "The turbulent and disorganizing spirit of Jacobinism, under the worn out disguise of equal liberty, and rights and division of property held out as a lure to the indolent and needy, but not really intended to be executed, will introduce anarchy which will terminate here, as in France, in a military despotism." In his arch-Federalist newspaper, William Cobbett tried to awaken his readers to the Republican threat at home by raising the guillotine. "The friends of order and humanity [are] dilatory, like the persons of the same description in France," he warned. "They seemed to be waiting till the sons of equality came to cut their throats."

Alarmists in America saw parallels where none existed. They now equated a series of easily suppressed tax revolts over the past two decades—Shays's Rebellion against Massachusetts tax and foreclosure laws in 1786, the Whiskey Rebellion against national excise taxes in 1794, and Fries's Rebellion against national war taxes in 1799—with the massive popular uprisings that plunged revolutionary France into chaos, even though the scale and causes of them differed greatly. "If our people cannot be brought to bear necessary taxes," Fisher Ames sternly advised Treasury Secretary Oliver Wolcott in January 1800, "I am afraid they are unfit for an independent government."

During the 1800 presidential campaign, Ames became the brooding conscience of Federalism by incessantly invoking in published essays and private letters the specter of France to rally opposition to Jefferson's election. Regardless of his personal prudence, Jefferson "must act as his party will have him," warned Ames, a recently retired member of Congress who would later be offered the presidency of Harvard College. "Behold France—what is theory here, is fact there," he asserted. "The men, the means, the end of such a government as Jefferson must . . . prefer will soon ensure war with Great Britain, . . . alliance with France, plunder, and anarchy." In a widely circulated essay, Ames added that if in the presidential election the American Jacobins "should prevail, the people would be crushed, as in France, under tyranny more vindictive, unfeeling, and rapacious, than that of Tiberius, Nero, or Caligula."

In countless Federalist editorials, Bonaparte came to personify the likely consequence of excessive republicanism. Endlessly compared to Caesar and Cromwell, he became the tyrannical usurper of legitimate authority—put forward as a warning for true patriots. "Behold France, that open hell, still ringing with agonies and blasphemies, still smoking with sufferings and crimes, in which we see their state of torment, and perhaps our future state," Ames wrote. "Friends of virtue, if you will not attend the election, and lend to liberty the help of your votes, within two years you will have to defend her cause with your swords." To Federalists, Jefferson now became "the great arch priest of Jacobinism and infidelity."

No less stark in their rhetoric, Republicans drew a very different moral from Bonaparte's military coup: A standing army threatens popular democracy. At first, America could only guess what Bonaparte intended to do with his political power. "Whatever his views may be," Jefferson wrote to Samuel Adams early in 1800, "he has at least transferred the destinies of the republic from the civil to the military arm. Some will use this as a lesson against the practicability of republican government. I read it as a lesson against the danger of standing armies." Madison made similar comments to Jefferson at the time. "Whether the lesson [from Napoleon's coup] will have the proper effect here in turning public attention to the danger of military usurpations," he wrote, "is more than I can say. A stronger one was perhaps never given, nor to a country more in a situation to profit by it."

Republican printers picked up this theme and published it throughout the land. "Nothing more solemnly points out the danger to free governments from a standing army than the recent events of France," the *Aurora* noted. Every reader knew which standing army these Republicans feared: the Additional Army now led by Alexander Hamilton. In private letters and conversations, Republicans began referring to Hamilton as "our Bonaparte." "The enemies of our Constitution are preparing a fearful operation," Jefferson warned a fellow Virginian in February 1800. "Our Bonaparte, surrounded by his comrades in arms, may step in to give us political salvation in his way." Indeed, in February 1799, Hamilton had privately proposed just such a military maneuver against radical Republicans in Virginia. Perhaps getting wind of this threat, Adams worried aloud in March 1799 to his political confidant, Elbridge Gerry, that some extreme Federalists "were endeavoring to get an army on foot to give Hamilton the command of it and then proclaim a regal government."

For over a decade, Jefferson and the Republicans had stressed the fundamental similarities linking the French and American experiments with democracy and expressed their hopes that both experiments would ultimately turn out all right. Indeed, they regularly complained that royalists in England and Federalists in America exaggerated the excesses of republican France. For some Republicans, seeing their cause as an integral part of an international movement magnified its significance and their own importance.

Upon learning that Bonaparte had imposed military rule in France, however, they began pointing to differences between the two cases and arguing that, contrary to Federalist warnings, greater democracy in America need not lead to a Napoleonic outcome. "The people of [France], having never been in the habit of self-government, are not yet in the habit of acknowledging that fundamental law of nature by which alone self-government can be exercised in a society," Jefferson wrote upon hearing of Bonaparte's coup. "I mean the *lex majoris partis* [or law of the majority]." In contrast, he implied, Americans took that principle to heart. "It is very material," Jefferson added, for American citizens "to be made sensible that their own character and situation are materially different from the French; and that whatever may be the fate of republicanism there, we are able to preserve it inviolate here." Jefferson especially worried that if Bonaparte declared himself leader for life and brought peace to his troubled land, then Americans might become more receptive to High Federalist notions of a lifetime president or American monarch. "The late defection of France has left America the only theater on which true liberty can have a fair trial," Madison lamented to Jefferson.

The tightly knit network of Republican papers reported the news from France in Jeffersonian terms. In their striving for liberty and democracy, a long essay in the *Aurora* explained, the French "had to struggle not only against all the evils of the most enormous and corrupt [religious] hierarchy that ever existed, against the most numerous and useless body of privileged idlers that ever aggrieved a nation, but against the wide spread influence of a wicked, debauched, and unprincipled court." The legacy of religious, aristocratic, and monarchic domination made stable republican rule much more difficult to sustain in France than in the historically self-governing American states, the essayist suggested. "Our vessel is moored at such a distance," Jefferson wrote of the French, "that should theirs blow up, ours is still safe, if we will but think so."

Republican newspapers widely reprinted rumors that British agents had aided Bonaparte in his coup and suggested that they might support an American military usurper as well. The Republicans had Hamilton and his Additional Army squarely in their sights in doing so. Adams

later viewed such newspaper attacks on the Army—"a thousand anecdotes," he called them, "propagated and believed,"—as central to the
Republican campaign against him.

Federalists had the legal means to fight back against such Republican
attacks, and they readily used them now. Back in 1798, during the
height of political and military tensions with France following the XYZ
Affair, Federalists in Congress had pushed through the Sedition Act
with the purpose of silencing critics of the government in the name of
national security. The law made it a crime, punishable by fine and
imprisonment, "to write, print, utter or publish . . . any false, scandalous and malicious writing or writings against the government, . . . the Congress, . . . or the President of the United States, with
intent to defame." Jefferson had denounced the measure as "palpably
in the teeth of the Constitution" and even Hamilton viewed it as
imprudent, but, with strong support from High Federalists in Congress, it passed on what amounted to a party-line vote, and Adams had
signed it into law.

Outraged by the Act and companion measures raising the bar for
citizenship and authorizing the deportation of aliens, Republican-
dominated state legislatures in Kentucky and Virginia passed resolutions secretly drafted by Jefferson and Madison challenging the
constitutionality of the Alien and Sedition Acts. The Kentucky resolution went so far as to declare the acts "altogether void and of no force."
Privately, Jefferson characterized this entire period of High Federalist
lawmaking as a "reign of witches."

Undeterred by the outcry that had followed enactment of the Sedition Act, Federalist prosecutors made partisan use of it from the start,
and now brought ever more prosecutions during the run-up to the
presidential election. Even before its passage, Federalists had freely
admitted that the Sedition Act targeted the Republican press. After all,
they passed the law as a wartime security measure, and many of them
viewed Republican printers as potentially dangerous (and possibly

treasonous) Francophiles. At the time, most American newspapers were openly partisan, with some going so far as to include party labels in their mastheads. Many received financial support and editorial copy from party sources. As a rule, newspapers did not then practice balanced reporting. Diversity came through the variety of publications within a community (many of them low-budget, four-page weeklies) rather than from various voices collected within any one source. Readers expected to receive slanted reports with little distinction between news articles and editorial commentary. The best way to silence a partisan viewpoint was to shut down its newspapers. Aside from pamphlets, no other means of mass communication then existed.

Although a majority of newspapers wore a Federalist face, Republican outlets more than made up for their lesser numbers by their intense partisanship. Through Philadelphia's *Aurora*, Boston's *Independent Chronicle*, and New York's *Argus* (all of which supplied original copy for other newspapers), the Republican voice was heard across the land. Each of these three papers had become the subject of multiple prosecutions under the Sedition Act or related laws. In all, federal attorneys brought at least seventeen indictments against Republican newspapers between 1798 and 1800, with most of these cases intended to shut down presses during the run-up to critical elections. Some succeeded in that objective, but new Republican papers quickly replaced shuttered ones. "The most vigorous and undisguised efforts are making to crush the republican presses, and stifle enquiry as it may respect the ensuing election," one Republican senator privately advised Madison in April 1800.

With Adams's full knowledge, Secretary of State Timothy Pickering coordinated the legal assault. According to Pickering, the Sedition Act could not possibly violate the Constitution because it punished only "pests of society and disturbers of order." Partisan attacks on the Additional Army particularly incensed Pickering, a Hamilton loyalist.

Simply referring to the federal troops as a "standing army" could serve as grounds for an indictment. To the Revolutionary War generation in the United States, including both Federalists and Republicans, the term carried a sinister meaning. Under popular rule, Americans then commonly believed that citizen soldiers would turn out in sufficient numbers to defend their country in times of foreign invasion or domestic insurrection, and then return home after the danger passed. State militias acted in this manner and provided the bulk of American forces at the time. The citizen-soldier ideal was personified by George Washington. In contrast, Americans saw foreign tyrants using professional "standing armies" to usurp or maintain power against the popular will. In this respect, among the despotic "abuses and usurpations" of power listed to justify the American Revolution, the Declaration of Independence specifically charged George III with having "kept among us in times of peace standing armies." Even if not used to subdue popular rule, Americans at the time tended to view soldiers in a peacetime standing army as armed and potentially dangerous idle young men living well at taxpayer expense.

This is why in 1798, when Federalists in Congress authorized a full-time force to counter any potential invasion by France, they pointedly called it an "Additional Army"—as in one temporarily added to deal with a particular danger—rather than a permanent or standing army. Always fearful that Hamilton might use the force against them, or even to usurp power for himself, Republicans naturally denounced it as a "standing army." The term stung. If believed, it could cost votes for Adams and other Federalists. Responding to criticisms of the Army, in May 1800, Adams ordered it disbanded, which caused him grief from both High Federalists, who still strongly supported it, and suspicious Republicans, who questioned his motives. By this time many saw Adams's decision as purely motivated by politics, including some disgruntled members of his own party. By "a disbanding of the army," the uncompromising High Federalist printer William Cobbett observed disapprovingly, "Adams was now laying in a provision of popularity against the ensuing election for President." It was too late for him to win over many Republican voters, however.

*   *   *

Adams moved to disband the Army shortly after two high-profile trials focused national attention on Republican denunciations of it as a "standing army." These prosecutions, both heard in April before prominent High Federalist justices of the United States Supreme Court sitting as trial judges for criminal prosecutions, involved printers charged with violating the Sedition Act. Their indictments covered more than simply their depictions of the federal military as a "standing army," but that became a key issue in both cases and the only grounds for conviction in one. Occurring as they did during the election season, and clearly timed to shut down Republican presses before the election, these cases became an integral part of the presidential campaign. For Federalists, they showed the government's patriotic commitment to maintaining domestic security and civil order. For Republicans, they demonstrated Adams's despotic disregard of individual liberty.

The first trial involved Charles Holt, a fiery iconoclast who, in 1797, opened the first Republican newspaper in the rock-ribbed Federalist state of Connecticut. He called it *The Bee* because of its sting. Federal prosecutors indicted Holt for publishing a reader's letter suggesting that, although Americans would readily give their lives to defend their country, no worthy recruits would "devote their valor to promote the views of ambition or to oppose their country and prosperity with a standing army." In his charge to the jury, Justice Bushrod Washington (the former President's nephew) declared the "publication to be libelous beyond even the possibility of a doubt" and virtually instructed the jurors to convict Holt, which they did. His three-month incarceration shut down *The Bee* for a significant segment of the election season.

Less than a week after Holt's conviction in Connecticut, the Northumberland, Pennsylvania newspaper printer Thomas Cooper, a radical English émigré with legal training and a bitter, biting wit, went on trial in Philadelphia before Justice Samuel Chase. Although Cooper had attracted the administration's attention with a 1799 article that Adams denounced as a "libel against the whole government and, as such, ought to be prosecuted," the 1800 indictment involved a political handbill.

Among other partisan accusations, it charged Adams with seeking to maintain a standing army. Abigail Adams had already pronounced her judgment in a letter to her sister stating that Cooper, "in his former mad democratic style, abused the President, and I presume subjected himself to the penalty of the Sedition Act."

Conducted in Philadelphia, the nation's capital, Cooper's trial became a sensational political event. Pickering attended it daily along with two other members of the cabinet and several leading members of Congress. "A more oppressive and disgusting proceeding I never saw," Republican Senator Stevens Thomson Mason complained in a letter to Madison. "Chase in his charge to the jury (in a speech of an hour) showed all the zeal of a well fee'd lawyer and the rancor of a vindictive and implacable enemy." In that charge, Chase articulated the Federalist argument for prosecuting sedition, and made it stick against Cooper. "If a man attempts to destroy the confidence of the people in their officers, their supreme magistrate, and their legislature, he effectually saps the foundation of the government," Chase told jurors. "A republican government can only be destroyed in two ways: the introduction of luxury or the licentiousness of the press." Upon Cooper's conviction, the court sentenced him to six months in the local prison, which the *Aurora* dubbed "Chase's repository of Republicans."

Both convictions backfired on Federalists by transforming small-town printers into nationally known martyrs to the cause of a free press. Republican newspapers depicted the trials as politically motivated election-year witch hunts. Far from silencing Holt and Cooper, both men denounced their convictions in articles from jail and emerged from incarceration more defiant than ever. Holt resumed publishing *The Bee* in time for the election, swinging at every Federalist in sight. "Punishment only hardens printers and pleases the fellows," he wrote, "for they come out of jail holding their heads higher than if they had never been persecuted." Cooper emerged from jail in Pennsylvania hailed by Republicans in public celebrations as "the conspicuous victim of the sedition law . . . and the able advocate of universal liberty."

Federalists hoped that criminal convictions would discredit antigovernment printers—and perhaps they did, in some eyes—but they also galvanized the opposition and turned the Sedition Act into a major issue in the presidential campaign. Vermont voters had already rendered their verdict on the Act in the fall of 1798 by reelecting to Congress a Republican politician and printer, Matthew Lyon, convicted of violating it. Carried back into office on a wave of sympathy aroused in part by graphic depictions of his confinement in a common cell with hardened criminals, Lyon won by a two-to-one margin over the Federalist printer who helped to put him in jail.

When Federalists in Congress passed the Alien and Sedition Acts within weeks of authorizing a larger army during the summer of 1798, Jefferson had begun dreading their next move. "I consider these laws as merely an experiment on the American mind to see how far it will bear an avowed violation of the Constitution," he wrote. "If this goes down, we shall immediately see attempted another act of Congress declaring that the President shall continue in office during life, reserving to another occasion the transfer of the succession to his heirs and the establishment of the senate for life."

Although the course of events Jefferson feared never materialized, an effort seen by some as being in the same spirit was made later. In February 1800, following his defeat in Pennsylvania's bitter gubernatorial contest, James Ross introduced a bill in the U.S. Senate that could have all but given control over choosing the next President to the Federalist-dominated Congress. As originally drafted, the Ross Bill would have created a thirteen-member "Grand Committee" to rule on the qualifications of presidential electors. Each house of Congress would appoint six of its members to the committee, and the Chief Justice would chair it. As amended in the Senate, the thirteenth member became a senator chosen by the House of Representatives rather than the Chief Justice. "The report of the majority of the said committee shall be final and conclusive determination of the admissibility or inadmissibility of the votes given by the electors for President and Vice President," the legislation stated. That provision would have authorized a partisan committee, meeting in secret, to nullify any number of electoral votes and thereby to swing the election as it chose.

Publicly, the bill's sponsors claimed that it would simply provide a procedure for weeding out invalid electoral votes, such as those cast either by electors never "properly appointed" or for an ineligible presidential candidate. Privately, they acknowledged that it targeted a particular threat posed by Pennsylvania.

In fact, Ross may not have intended anything more with his bill than to guard against electoral-vote shenanigans by Pennsylvania Governor Thomas McKean, whom he had good reason to distrust. Following McKean's election, Federalists in control of the Pennsylvania Senate refused to accept Republican proposals to reenact the law providing for the election of presidential electors by a statewide general ticket, which both sides thought would once again award the state's electoral votes to Jefferson. They wanted electors chosen by districts, which would surely secure at least some votes for Adams. By February, it became apparent that a stalemate might ensue.

Federalists worried what McKean might do if no election law passed in Pennsylvania. "There being no law in the state," U.S. House Speaker Theodore Sedgwick noted in a letter to another High Federalist, "the governor had declared, and the Jacobins propagated the report, that he would call on the people, by proclamation, to choose electors and that he would return their votes." In short, Federalists feared that McKean might order an extralegal statewide election by executive fiat. Treasury Secretary Oliver Wolcott warned darkly, "If this course should be pursued, and the choice of a president should depend on the votes of Pennsylvania, a civil war will not be improbable." Ross wanted a mechanism in place to exclude any such tainted electoral votes from counting.

If this represented the full extent of Ross's intent, however, then his bill overreached its objectives. In fact, since Federalists controlled both houses of Congress, under Ross's proposal, a committee of their choosing would effectively decide which electors could vote from every state.

In their growing (and also understandable) paranoia, Republicans read this sweeping purpose into the overbroad bill. Some intemperate Federalists fed Republican fears. "This bill was a sweeper," the incendiary Federalist printer William Cobbett wrote. "It would . . . have, in reality, placed the election of the President in the hands of the Senate alone. That it would be much better for the country were the election in the hands of the Senate is certain; but it would have been fairer to pass a law directly to that effect." The debate over this so-called Ross Bill showed the level of distrust that had descended on national politics by early 1800.

During the Senate's contentious debate over the bill, Charles Pinckney of South Carolina took the lead in outlining Republican concerns. "In every state where the election is strongly contested, there will of course be a minority," he explained. If that losing side was Federalist, then its members could "easily discover the means of raising objections to the validity of the return of electors, insist that they themselves are elected, proceed to the length of meeting and voting, and transmit to Congress a [second] return." The Federalist-dominated Grand Committee would then decide which return counted. This led Pinckney to ask rhetorically, "Knowing the situation of the Union, how differently some states think from others, [and] how divided Congress have been for some years on certain great and trying subjects," who can doubt the potential for partisan abuses in vote counting that could "throw almost every state into [violent] scenes which can never arise but from this bill?" Both sides could threaten civil war over this issue. Such objections did not deter the Senate from passing the bill over unified Republican opposition, however, and sending it to the House of Representatives, where moderate Federalists held the balance of power between High Federalists and Republicans.

The Senate debated the Ross Bill in closed sessions with the text of the legislation kept secret until the *Aurora* published a pirated copy of it in late February 1800. Then the public storm burst. Republicans charged that the bill would violate states' rights and undermine popular rule. Virginia Senator Stevens Thomson Mason spoke of its "obnoxious principles." Republican organizer John Beckley called it "a deadly blow . . . aimed at us." Madison declared that it violated the Constitution by giving Congress too much control over choosing the President. Protests flowed from Republican presses. "The bill brought into the Senate by Mr. Ross," one editorial charged, "was as daring an attempt on the Constitution of the United States as that of Bonaparte on that of France."

The *Aurora* led the Republican outcry with almost daily reports critical of the Senate and its "alarming attempt upon the freedom of this state." One of its articles compared Ross's Grand Committee to the aristocratic "Venetian Council" that had long held the power to choose leaders in the Italian republic of Venice. Another asked, "If there was nothing dangerous or hostile to the liberties of the people in this Bill, why has its publication given those who support it so much and such extraordinary alarm?"

Senate Federalists struck back at the *Aurora*'s pugnacious editor, William Duane, by taking the unprecedented step of forming a Committee of Privilege to investigate his publication of the pirated bill. Born in colonial America to Irish parents, reared in Ireland, and deported from British India for publishing an antigovernment newspaper in Calcutta, Duane had irritated Federalists ever since he had taken over the *Aurora* in 1798, following the death of its crusading founding editor, Benjamin Franklin Bache, a grandson of Benjamin Franklin. "Is there any thing evil in the regions of actuality or possibility that the *Aurora* has not suggested of me?" Adams complained to Pickering in 1799. "The matchless effrontery of this Duane merits the execution of the alien law. I am very willing to try its strength upon him." Twice indicted for sedition but never under the Alien Act, the wily Duane managed to escape conviction and keep publishing his paper. Now the Senate sought to punish him directly.

Inevitably, the *Aurora*'s secondhand reports of closed Senate proceedings on the Ross Bill contained inaccuracies, some of them potentially inflammatory. The Committee of Privilege investigated these false statements as well as Duane's publication of the bill itself. "The right of self-preservation is vested in the Senate," High Federalist Senator Uriah Tracy argued in support of pursuing Duane. "If it is admitted that we have the right of protecting ourselves within these walls from attacks made in our presence, it follows of course that we are not to be slandered and questioned elsewhere." In mid-March, the Senate (in a series of bitterly contested, highly partisan votes) accepted the committee's finding that, by his publications about the Ross Bill, Duane had breached Senate privileges. It ordered him to appear before the Senate for sentencing.

Instead of presenting himself, Duane went into hiding until Congress adjourned. The Senate responded by ordering Duane's arrest for contempt, but could only plead for assistance in catching him. No one helped. Duane continued feeding copy to the *Aurora* on a daily basis, including scathing attacks on the Ross Bill and the proceedings against him. One Republican senator described the scene to Madison: "Although you and *all* persons in the U.S. (including, no doubt, army and navy) are called on to assist in apprehending him, he is not yet taken."

Taunting his hapless and ham-fisted Senate persecutors, a notice in the *Aurora* stated that written messages delivered to Duane at the newspaper's office would "be sure to reach him in less than 48 hours." In so far as public opinion mattered, Marshall thought that the Senate misplayed its hand badly. "Questions of privilege are delicate in their nature," he commented on the case, "and such as are most apt to interest the public mind against those who exercise the power of punishing for its breach."

Even as Republicans publicly bewailed Senate action on the Ross Bill, Jefferson (who watched over the entire affair as Vice President) privately took comfort in the measure's uncertain prospects in the House of Representatives. Under the Constitution, the House alone chooses the President in case of a tie or the failure of anyone to receive votes from a majority of electors. Given this institutional consideration, Jefferson doubted that House members would go along with a bill giving power over the electoral process to senators. He foresaw a deadlock between the Senate and House on the issue, as did Senator Stevens Thomson Mason of Virginia. Writing to Madison in March, Mason predicted "that the House of Representatives will hardly be induced to accede to an arrangement which will place the Senate on an equal footing with themselves."

In the House, John Marshall led the effort by moderate Federalists to rewrite the Ross Bill. He did not believe that Congress should delegate power to rule on the qualification of electors to a committee. First, Marshall raised constitutional concerns. "On this question," wrote House Speaker Theodore Sedgwick, a High Federalist proponent of the bill, "I had a long conversation with [Marshall], and he finally confessed himself (for there is not a more candid man on earth) to be convinced. . . . He then resorted to another ground of opposition. . . . Although the power was not indelegable, yet he thought, in its nature, it was too delicate to be delegated."

Marshall agreed with Sedgwick and other High Federalists that Congress should have some means to exclude ineligible electoral votes, but he felt the Ross Bill went too far. The first-term congressman from Virginia stood his ground on principle against the House Speaker, who privately complained that Marshall read the Constitution narrowly like a criminal statute rather than broadly to serve partisan purposes. He offered alternative legislation, which passed the House, to create a special joint committee to advise Congress on the admissibility of disputed electoral ballots, but the Senate wanted more. "Let me do what I will," Marshall wrote to his brother about the dispute that swirled around him. "I am sure the [Republicans] will abuse me and therefore I need only try to satisfy myself." Ultimately, Federalists in the House and Senate failed to reach a compromise on the legislation and it died.

*   *   *

The session of Congress that began in December 1799 by marking Washington's death and ended in May 1800 remained mired in partisan discord throughout and accomplished little in the end. Abigail Adams saw it coming. "Next week Congress meet," she wrote at the outset. "Electioneering has already begun. There will be more things aimed at than will be carried by either Jacobins or Federalists—but the Jacobins are always more subtle and industrious than their opponents." The High Federalist Speaker of the House advised his partisans in December 1799, "In all our measures, we must never lose sight of the next election of President." Members of Congress on both sides followed this approach, prompting Fisher Ames to comment midway through the session, "Our parties in Congress seem to regard that approaching election as the only object of attention."

When the session ended, Jefferson expressed relief that it had not gone too badly for his party. "Congress will rise today," he wrote to Madison. "On the whole, the Federalists have not been able to carry a single strong measure in the lower house the whole session. When they met, it was believed they had a majority of twenty; but . . . public opinion sets so strongly against the federal proceedings that this melted off their majority and dismayed the heroes of the party. The Senate alone remained undismayed to the last. Firm to their purpose, regardless of public opinion, and more disposed to coerce than to court it, not a man of their majority gave way in the least."

At the time, of course, voters elected members to the House while state legislatures appointed senators. Frustrated by his failure to push through High Federalist measures, House Speaker Sedgwick also attributed what he called "a real feebleness of character in the House" to the influence of public opinion on moderate members, particularly John Marshall. "He is disposed on all popular subjects to feel the public pulse," Sedgwick wrote. "Doubts suggested by him create in more feeble minds those which are irremovable." At the time, politicians had to trust their instincts regarding public opinion. No one conducted polls.

Jefferson could not count Federalist defeats as Republican victories, however. Failure of the Ross Bill did not assure him of Pennsylvania's crucial electoral votes. A partisan stalemate over adopting a method to choose electors in that state remained possible. In the face of continued intransigence by Federalists in the State Senate, McKean disavowed earlier suggestions that he might order a statewide election by executive fiat. With or without Ross's Grand Committee, he concluded that Federalists in Congress would find some way to disallow the votes. McKean decided to wait until the October Pennsylvania legislative elections. If the Republicans took control of the State Senate from the Federalists, then he would call an eleventh-hour special session of the legislature to appoint electors. If the Republicans failed to gain the majority, then Pennsylvania might not vote. Nothing in the national Constitution actually required states to cast electoral votes, and no state could do so without enacting a method for choosing electors.

With nine months to go before the Electoral College met on December 3, Jefferson viewed the political landscape much as other seasoned observers did. "This seems to be the prospect. Keep out Pennsylvania, Jersey, and New York, and the rest of the states are about equally divided," he wrote to Madison on March 8, 1800. States favorable to the Federalists, which included the five New England states, Delaware, and Maryland, would have 52 electors; the pro-Republican southern and western states of Virginia, the Carolinas, Georgia, Kentucky, and Tennessee would have exactly the same number of electors. In 1796, all but three of the former group had voted for Adams while all but two of the latter had voted for Jefferson. These five rogue electors had been selected in district elections, with the three for Jefferson in Maryland and one each for Adams in Virginia and North Carolina. Most observers, including Jefferson, expected similar returns from these states in 1800. They constituted each candidate's base. "Then the event depends on the three Middle States before mentioned," Jefferson concluded in his letter: "If Pennsylvania votes, then either Jersey or New York giving a Republican vote decides the election. If Pennsylvania does not vote, then New York determines the election." Jefferson naturally assumed that Pennsylvania, with McKean as governor and the Republicans firmly in control of at least one house of the state legislature, would vote for him, if it voted.

Under this electoral calculus, Jefferson needed to carry either New York (with twelve electors) or New Jersey (with seven) even if he received votes from all fifteen Pennsylvania electors. He needed at least New York if Pennsylvania did not vote. In both New York and New Jersey, state legislators selected the electors and had chosen all Federalists in 1796. The Federalists still controlled the legislatures of both states going into 1800, but elections that year would decide which party held the most seats in each when it came time to choose electors in the fall. In each state, whichever party held the most seats in its legislature would get all of its electors. New Jersey was virtually a lost cause for the Republicans, but New York had a mixed political tradition. Although Federalist icon John Jay had served as New York's governor since 1795 and Hamilton lived in New York City, Republican stalwart George Clinton served nine terms as governor prior to Jay and had carried New York's electoral votes for Vice President against Adams in 1792. During the 1790s, one of New York's U.S. Senate seats had passed back and forth between Hamilton's Federalist father-in-law, Philip Schuyler, and Republican Aaron Burr as the state legislature twice changed hands between the parties. In 1800, the Republicans could at least hope to retake the New York legislature, but Hamilton and his followers would oppose them.

All political eyes now turned toward New York, which held its state elections in April. The legislature chosen in that election would name New York's electors. Considering everything that needed to fall into place for him to gain votes from a majority of the electors, and despite the advances made by Republicans in Pennsylvania and Virginia, Jefferson concluded, "Upon the whole, I consider it as rather more doubtful than the last election." Without New York, he would again likely fall just shy of a majority. Although he did not express his views so clearly in a letter, Adams apparently viewed the prospects in much the same way as Jefferson did and looked to New York with equal anticipation.

CHAPTER FOUR

BURR *V.* HAMILTON

*I*F THE ROAD to the presidency in 1800 lay through New York, then Jefferson would have to ride to victory on Aaron Burr's Republican campaign machinery. At the time, few politicians fully trusted Burr and many actively disliked him—but no one doubted his influence over local politics in New York City, which then dominated that of its state. In April 1800, New York voters would elect the legislature empowered to select the state's twelve presidential electors, with New York City's large delegation in the lower house holding the balance of power. In 1796, Federalists controlling the state legislature had selected electors loyal to Adams and Thomas Pinckney. If Jefferson could capture those votes this time, he would likely win the election. Only Burr could deliver them by orchestrating a Republican takeover of the state legislature, but he would have to beat Alexander Hamilton to do so.

New York boasted a gallery full of High Federalist luminaries. During the spring of 1800, Alexander Hamilton commanded the nation's Army from his headquarters in New York City, Gouverneur Morris took office as the state's new senator, and John Jay served as governor in Albany. Federalists controlled both houses of the state legislature going into the April legislative elections and rejected a Republican proposal to choose presidential electors by district elections, which surely would have split the state's electoral vote in 1800. By retaining legislative appointment for presidential electors, New York Federalists hoped to deliver all of them for their party's candidates just as they had in every previous presidential contest. Burr had other ideas, which required a Republican victory in the April elections. With a singleness of purpose that awed friend and foe alike, he set about to make it happen. Hamilton, already Burr's rival, stood determined to stop him and maintain Federalist rule in New York. The contest became a historic clash within the larger presidential campaign.

The 1800 census reported that New York City had finally surpassed Philadelphia as the nation's largest city and principal port. Yet, this increasingly cosmopolitan city—founded by the Dutch in 1626, conquered by the British in 1664, and bloated by German and Irish immigrants during the late 1700s—could not comfortably contain two men with such enormous egos and soaring ambitions as Burr and Hamilton. Short in stature but strikingly handsome and able to charm, they were destined to come into conflict repeatedly and have their relationship end in a deadly duel. The election of 1800 neither began nor finished their rivalry for power and influence; rather, it intensified it greatly.

The parallels and perpendicularities between the two men were almost eerie. Born during the mid-1750s within a year of each other, Burr and Hamilton came from dramatically different backgrounds. Son of Aaron Burr Sr., a noted theologian and Princeton College president, and Esther Edwards, the scholarly daughter of the legendary evangelical minister Jonathan Edwards, Burr boasted a matchless American pedigree dating back to the earliest Puritan settlers of New England. "I have never known, in any country, the prejudice in favor of birth, parentage, and descent more conspicuous than that in the instance of Colonel Burr," John Adams once observed. In contrast, Adams slurred Hamilton as "a bastard brat of a Scotch peddler" for his out-of-wedlock birth to a drifting trader and married Frenchwoman on the British West Indies island of Nevis. Adams made the comment about Hamilton in 1806, long after their bitter personal and policy disputes, which Adams never forgot or forgave, became public.

Both Burr and Hamilton lost their parents at an early age and became wards of maternal relatives. Burr gained easy entry into

Princeton while Hamilton overcame all odds by securing a place at King's College (later Columbia) in New York. Burr considered following his father and grandfather into the ministry but soon rejected the idea and never again showed marked interest in religion. Like Hamilton, Burr enjoyed a self-gratifying life punctuated with extramarital affairs. The Revolutionary War interrupted their academic studies, with both men joining the patriot army, serving on Washington's personal staff, and rising to the rank of colonel. Whereas Washington grew to rely heavily on Hamilton and trust him implicitly, the General quickly lost faith in Burr and had him transferred to combat positions, where he served with distinction. Years later, Washington insisted that Hamilton become his second-in-command for the Additional Army over President Adams's objection, but refused Adams's recommendation that Burr become a brigadier general in the same force. "Colonel Burr is a brave and able officer," Washington conceded at the time, "but the question is, whether he has not equal talents at intrigue." The comment infuriated Adams, who, when later recalling it, denounced Washington's pick, Alexander Hamilton, as "the most restless, impatient, artful, indefatigable and unprincipled intriguer in the United States, if not the world." Burr and Hamilton inevitably excited passions.

After the Revolutionary War, both men gained eminence as two of the brightest lawyers in the booming city of New York. As attorneys, Burr and Hamilton occasionally collaborated on cases—including as co-counsel for the defense in a sensational murder trial during the weeks leading up to the election of April 1800. They married well and joined the city's social elite, although Burr's extravagant expenses often exceeded his sizable income. Each of them compounded his personal influence by attracting and sustaining a trusted circle of loyal lieutenants. Hamilton tended to draw in men of independent means and social standing, some much older than himself. Burr, in contrast, attracted a small corps of rising young New Yorkers, known as Burrites, who devoted themselves to his causes. "It was ever one of his characteristics to secure inviolable the attachment of his friends," one of them later wrote. "It was here that Colonel Burr was all powerful, for he possessed in a preeminent degree the art of fascinating the youthful."

Politics consumed both men by the late 1780s, but they chose different sides. Hamilton and his father-in-law, Philip Schuyler, became leading Federalists; Burr gravitated toward the circle of the state's seven-term Anti-Federalist (and later Republican) governor, George Clinton, first when serving in the state legislature and then as Clinton's attorney general. Within state politics, their relative prominence rose and fell as power passed back and forth between the two parties during the 1790s, even as Hamilton gained national influence as Washington's principal adviser and Treasury Secretary. When Clinton's faction took over the state legislature in 1791, for example, legislators chose Burr to replace Schuyler in the United States Senate, but Schuyler reclaimed the seat from Burr six years later after Federalists took back the legislature. In an effort to reach beyond their Southern base, Republicans looked to New York—a critical battleground state in the North—for their vice presidential candidates. The first nod went to Clinton, in 1792, and then again to him in 1804 and 1808. In 1796, however, many national Republicans favored Burr, but he secured only thirty electoral votes when some Southern Republican electors gave their second votes to Samuel Adams or Clinton. The experience both fed Burr's national ambitions and drove him to insist on strict party loyalty should he again stand for the vice presidency.

In contrast to Hamilton, who remained a principled High Federalist and accumulated political power through ideological purity, Burr saw his path to glory through pragmatic politics. He took ideologically inconsistent stands on various issues and even courted Federalist support for a possible run against Clinton as governor in 1792—a move that Hamilton blocked within his party. Still smarting from his father-in-law's defeat for the Senate at Burr's hands a year earlier, Hamilton warned a Federalist confidant at the time, "As a public man [Burr] is one of the worst sorts—a friend to nothing but as suits his interest and ambition. Determined to climb to the highest honors of state and as much higher as circumstances may permit—he cares nothing about the means of effecting his purpose." Drawing on a historical analogy that his own opponents leveled against him, Hamilton concluded, "If we have an embryo-Caesar in the United States, 'tis Burr."

Losing his U.S. Senate seat in 1797 did not deter Burr. Again elected to the state legislature a year later, he supported legislation benefiting his investments, including a bill chartering the Manhattan Company, a banking institution disguised as a water company that offered borrowers a Republican alternative to the Bank of New York and the local branch of the Bank of the United States, both of which Federalists controlled. Defeated for reelection in 1799 amid accusations of self-dealing, Burr determined to build a Republican political machine that would stabilize his political fortunes. He set his sights on the April 1800 legislative election with the goal of securing the state for Jefferson and the vice presidency for himself. Hamilton stood in the way. In his brooding historical novel about Burr, Gore Vidal has his antihero say at this point in the narrative, "I suspect that when Hamilton looks at me he sees, in some magical way, himself reflected." It would have been a mirror image with many parts reversed.

Partisans on both sides and in all parts of the country watched the New York City election closely. Analyzing the overall contest for President in a March letter to Madison, Jefferson stressed the significance of that one local election for the ultimate outcome. "If the *city* election of New York is in favor of the Republican ticket, the issue will be Republican; if the Federal ticket for the city of New York prevails, the probability will be in favor of a Federal issue," he wrote. "The election of New York being in April, it becomes an early and interesting object."

Federalists attached similar importance to the event. "We are full of anxiety here about the election of our members to the legislature," Hamilton's close friend and political ally Robert Troup observed in March. "We must bring into action all our energies; if we do not . . . Jefferson will be in." As the election neared, Maryland's Charles

Carroll of Carrollton wrote nervously to Hamilton, "It is asserted with confidence by the anti-federal party here that all your electors will vote for Mr. Jefferson as president; if such an event shall really happen, it is probable he will be chosen; of such a choice the consequences to this country may be dreadful."

The precarious balance of both national and New York State politics made the city election pivotal. Assuming, as most then did, that Adams would carry the Northeast and Jefferson would sweep the South and West, New York's twelve electoral votes might well decide the difference. Certainly they were critical for Adams's victory in 1796, and could be again in 1800.

Federalists held an eight- or nine-seat majority in the New York Senate prior to the April election, but only a slight edge in the lower house (or State Assembly). Members of both houses voted as a single body for presidential electors, with each senator and assemblyman having an equal vote. New York City, then a densely packed urban center confined to the southern end of Manhattan Island, chose its thirteen members of the State Assembly in a single citywide election, with voters from all seven of the city's wards able to vote for each of the seats. If either party swept the city's thirteen Assembly contests—which the Federalists had done by a wide margin in the previous election—then that party would likely hold a majority of seats in the next state legislature and gain all of New York's electoral votes.

Burr explained this to Jefferson in a private meeting on January 18, 1800, and Jefferson passed the explanation on to Virginia Governor James Monroe. "In the new election which is to come along in April, three or four in the Senate will be changed in our favor," he wrote based on Burr's analysis. "In the [Assembly], the county elections will still be better than last, but still all will depend on the city election."

Going into the city election, party leaders on both sides expected to win. Following his meeting with Burr, Jefferson confidently predicted, "At present there would be no doubt of our carrying our ticket there." On the eve of the election, High Federalist Christopher Gore, a future Massachusetts governor and United States senator, wrote from New

York City to the American ambassador in London, "Your fellow citizens here are busy electioneering. The parties are desirous of securing their favorites, and each is sanguine. Hamilton is sure of success and I understand the other side is equally so." By their nature, both Burr and Hamilton exuded confidence, but only one of them could win this contest.

Despite its early date, the New York City election became the clearest test of popular opinion on the 1800 presidential race ever conducted in a competitive setting. The local press focused squarely on national issues, not state ones. The looming showdown between Jefferson and Adams subverted the local race to national ends and relegated the Assembly candidates to the role of willing surrogates for the presidential aspirants.

Observing in late April that "the election of a president on either side depends upon the city of New York," the Federalist *Commercial Advertiser* urged "every friend to the Constitution and peace of his country to make the most vigorous exertions in favor of the Federal interest." Those became the Federalist campaign themes: preserve the current constitutional order and domestic security by voting for the entire party ticket. The local press rarely mentioned any of the state issues that normally dominate legislative campaigns. "Citizens choose your sides," another New York Federalist newspaper proclaimed. "You who are for French notions of government; for the tempestuous sea of anarchy and misrule; for arming the poor against the rich; for fraternizing with the foes of God and man; go to the left and support the leaders, or the dupes, of the anti-federal junto. But you that are sober, industrious, thriving, and happy, give your votes for those men who mean to *preserve the union* of the states, the purity and vigor of our excellent Constitution, the sacred majesty of the laws, and the holy ordinances of religion." Christianity means nothing to Jefferson and his friends, many articles charged: "The devil is in their hearts," one declared.

In a flood of editorials, articles, and letters published in local Federalist newspapers during the weeks leading up to the April election, writers argued that Jefferson, Burr, and Clinton had opposed ratifying the Constitution and still hoped to abolish it—and with it, domestic peace and prosperity—for their own personal gain. "Great God, is it possible?" one Federalist asked, even "the apostate Madison," who coauthored the Constitution, is "now leagued with them." Clinton served as an easy target because, as governor, he led the opposition to ratifying the federal Constitution in New York. Jefferson and Burr initially had qualms about the amount of power concentrated in the national government under the Constitution, but they did not oppose its ratification.

Federalists warned that with Jefferson at the helm, the United States would become like revolutionary France, where Jacobins overthrew the civil order and Christian religion. "Merchants, your ships will be condemned to *rot* in your harbors for the *navy* which is their protection Jefferson will *destroy*," a typical Federalist editorial charged. "The temples of the most high will be profaned by the impious orgies of the Goddess of Reason, personated as in France by some common prostitute." After relating a long parade of horribles, another editorial implored voters, "It is for you to decide whether these gloomy presages shall be realized, or whether we shall continue to flourish in our present splendor." In a single sentence that summarized the entire campaign, one editorial declared, "Those of you who wish to preserve your liberty, religion, and the Constitution of the United States will support the Federal ticket with a long pull, a strong pull, and ALL pull together." Vote for the entire Federalist slate, it urged New Yorkers.

Federalist publications, while explicit in their attacks on Jefferson, spoke in generalities about their own candidates and policies. Beyond their names and party affiliations, little appeared in the press about the thirteen candidates whom Hamilton rounded up to run on the Federalist ticket for the Assembly. Only two incumbents chose to stand for reelection, and the others had virtually no political experience. Most were tradesmen. John Adams later dismissed them as "men of little weight, obscure in name, poor in purse, mean in talents, and meritorious only in [that] they were confidential friends of the great and good Hamilton." Abigail Adams called them "men of no note, men wholly unfit for the purpose." Republicans openly speculated that Hamilton picked them solely because of their personal loyalty to him.

In 1796, even though Hamilton had tried to swing the final electoral-vote tally to Thomas Pinckney over Adams, he had worked vigorously to deliver New York for the Federalist ticket. The relationship between Adams and Hamilton, never good, had soured still further since 1796, and this may have influenced Hamilton's choice of legislative candidates. Adams's impulsive temperament, independent streak, and distrust of Hamilton had fueled the tensions between these two proud men, but his decision to send peace negotiators to France in 1798 and hostility toward the Additional Army had turned Hamilton into an implacable foe.

By the time of the New York elections, Hamilton told friends that he could no longer support the President's reelection. Adams knew of these comments and thereafter viewed Hamilton's actions with utmost suspicion. Indeed, Hamilton at this time was actively, if still secretly, conspiring with other High Federalists to replace Adams as the party's presidential candidate with some politically viable member of their own faction, most likely Thomas Pinckney's brother, Charles Cotesworth Pinckney. Having New York's twelve electors in his pocket could give to Hamilton as much influence over the Federalists' choice for President as those same electors would give to Burr over the Republicans' choice for Vice President. "Hamilton, who ruled Washington," Adams bitterly observed at the time, "would still rule if he could."

Not feeling the sting of Adams's temper and naturally favoring peace over war, the public tended to side with the President over Hamilton and the High Federalists, which incensed them all the more. To keep out the Republicans, Hamilton would not yet risk an open break with Adams even as he schemed to unseat him. To achieve his objectives, Hamilton instead apparently decided to promote individuals loyal to him for the New York legislature rather than secure the strongest Federalist candidates, some of whom might favor Adams. With the New York legislature under his sway, Hamilton could then secure the selection of High Federalist electors more loyal to him than to Adams. At least Adams believed this was the motive for Hamilton's choice of lackluster legislative candidates. If true, it was a high-stakes gambit. Some historians have suggested that Hamilton simply wanted to reach out to common voters with a commoner's ticket—but that hardly fit his elitist style. He typically sought to stand tall rather than stoop low. Perhaps defensive about the Federalist slate, Hamilton's friend Robert Troup observed at the time, "It is next to an impossibility to get men of weight and influence to serve" in the lowly legislature. Regardless of the reason for their choice, according to reports that later reached Adams, when Burr read the list of Federalist candidates, he said of Hamilton, "Now I have him all hollow."

Even more striking, the Federalist press rarely mentioned Adams even when it denounced Jefferson by name. "If the Federal ticket for the state legislature is carried, a Federal president will be chosen," one typical appeal noted. "If the Jacobin ticket succeeds, Mr. Jefferson will be president." These few words spoke volumes. If Hamilton held New York for the Federalists, then its electors would do his bidding—and it was clear enough to many that he had little interest in Adams's reelection. Both Hamilton and Burr played a multidimensional game of politics, but they still needed the right cards to win.

New York's Republican press responded to its Federalist counterpart by stressing the commitment of its party to constitutional liberty. Pushing national issues to the fore, it denounced Federalists for the Alien and Sedition Acts, "the standing army and useless navy," high war taxes, the soaring national debt, creeping monarchism, and a ruinous allegiance to pro-British policies and British-style aristocracy. "Peace or war, happiness or misery, opulence or ruin! These depend on the results of the approaching election. If the friends of liberty are zealous, the system of EQUAL RIGHTS will yet flourish," one Republican writer exclaimed. "The political happiness of America hangs suspended upon the fruit of your activity upon the present occasion," another added. "Rise then with Republican firmness, with energy and patriotic activity, in defense of those invaluable rights for which during the Revolution you fought and bled."

On the eve of the election, New York's leading Republican newspaper warned its readers that Federalists would charge "that whoever disapproves of the administration of our government is an enemy to the Constitution." Stand firm, it urged readers, for "if you waver, if you hesitate, if you neglect in this respect your duty, you will wreck upon the shoals of aristocratic design the vessel of state which includes in it the liberties and happiness of the people."

Republicans sensed that the public mood in New York was shifting in their favor. Two years earlier, at the height of the XYZ Affair and rumors of a French invasion, Americans had sought security even at the expense of civil liberties—and Federalists in New York and elsewhere had done well. As fears of war passed and the cost of preparedness became apparent, the pendulum of popular opinion had begun swinging back toward the Republicans, as reflected in the Pennsylvania legislative elections six months earlier.

"A little patience," Jefferson predicted in 1798, "and we shall see . . . the people, recovering their true sight, restore their government to its true principles. It is true that in the meantime we are suffering deeply in spirit and incurring the horrors of war and long oppression of enormous public debt." In March 1800, he advised Madison, "The Republican spirit beginning to predominate in Pennsylvania, Jersey, and New York . . . there is the strongest expectation that the Republican ticket will prevail in the city election of New York." On the second day of voting in that much-anticipated election, Jefferson anxiously wrote to Congressman Edward Livingston, one in an extended family of moderate New York Republicans that included his brother Robert, the state's long-serving chancellor, and his cousin Brockholst, an eminent lawyer and future U.S. Supreme Court Justice. "By this time I presume the result of your laborers is known to you," Jefferson observed. "Whatever it may be, and my experience of the art, industry, and resources of the other party has not permitted me to be prematurely confident, yet I'm entirely confident that ultimately the great body of the people are passing over from them. . . . The madness and extravagance of their career is what ensures it."

Jefferson had good reason to worry about the art, industry, and resources that Hamilton poured into the New York City election, but neither of them could have anticipated Burr's extraordinary effort on behalf of the Republican ticket. Ever since, political historians have marveled at his innovative techniques in urban electioneering.

Burr laid the foundation for victory in 1799 when, as a state legislator, he had secured the charter for the Manhattan Company, which broke the Federalist banking monopoly in New York City. By the spring of 1800, artisans and owners of small businesses could openly support Republican candidates without fear of losing access to credit. Indeed, bank records suggest that the Manhattan Company significantly stepped up operations to coincide with the election. "The [Federalist] bank influence is now *totally* destroyed," Burr protégé Matthew Davis boasted in a preelection letter to Republican congressional leader Albert Gallatin, "the Manhattan Company will, in all probability, operate much in our favor." Other partisans made similar comments at the time, and some later historians have seen the bank's role in the city election as decisive. One stanza of a Federalist poem deriding the rise of republicanism in New York aptly noted:

> *Here, when all other measures fail,*
> *To turn the newly balanc'd scale,*
> *Manhattan's Bank pours in its stream,*
> *The Fed'ral party kick the beam . . .*
> *A Bank, upon occasion's spur,*
> *To discount notes for Colonel Burr.*

At the very least, as this poem suggests, the Manhattan Company balanced the scales between Republicans and Federalists in New York City.

Building on this foundation, Burr recruited a stellar slate of candidates for the State Assembly to stand against Hamilton's lackluster list. As Davis explained to Gallatin, "Mr. Burr is arranging matters in such a way as to bring into operation all of the Republican interests." This meant uniting the Clinton, Livingston, and Burr factions of the local party in a common effort. Clinton had stepped down in 1795 after six terms as governor, yet Burr persuaded him to permit his name to head the list of Republican candidates for the State Assembly. Brockholst Livingston represented his clan on the ticket. Washington's first Postmaster General, Samuel Osgood, who once led a company of minutemen at the Battles of Lexington and Concord, lent his name. Perhaps most remarkable of all, at Burr's urging, General Horatio Gates, whose fabled victory at the Battle of Saratoga turned the tide in the American Revolution, emerged from retirement at age seventy-four to stand for election to the Assembly.

Few of these candidates actually campaigned for office, and some of them had no intention of actively serving in the Assembly. Indeed, according to Davis (who participated in the meetings at which Burr pleaded with Clinton to join the ticket), the proud former governor reserved "to himself the right of stating in conversation that his name was used without his authority." As for Gates, Burr later felt it necessary to remind the infirm general when to vote for presidential electors—presumably he did not otherwise attend legislative sessions in Albany. Yet, the united ticket of Republican luminaries served its purpose. "I believe we shall offer to our fellow citizens," Davis wrote to Gallatin, "the most formidable list ever offered them by any party in point of morality, private and public virtue, local and general influence, etc. . . . If we carry this election, it may be ascribed principally to Col. Burr's management and perseverance. Hamilton fears his influence."

While the Republican press hailed the party ticket as the finest assemblage of senior statesmen ever put forth for such lowly offices, the city's two leading Federalist newspapers could only fume. "They have got names to which respectability *has been* attached," the *Commercial Advertiser* noted, but "the citizens of New York will see through it." None of these candidates cared about the state's business, it charged, they cared only about electing a President. "Citizen Clinton does not go to the Assembly for the purpose of mending roads, nor Citizen Burr for that of digging wells," the *Daily Advertiser* commented. Charging that "their sole object in standing candidates is to secure the election of Mr. Jefferson," the *Commercial Advertiser* dismissed Gates as "tottering over the grave with a mind utterly impaired" and characterized Clinton as "smiling at the thought of having done his best to destroy that Constitution which he voted against adopting." An election-day squib in the *Daily Advertiser* reminded voters of Gates's infamous defeat at the Battle of Camden: "If the General *runs* as well at the election, he cannot fail of success." Such jabs had little impact on voters. Commenting on Gates's election, one observer later wrote of "the veterans of the Revolution abandoning their party to vote for their old comrade and leader."

Once he secured strong candidates through personal negotiations, Burr staged a formal nominating process to engage the party. First, the Republican county committee met to nominate Burr's hand-picked slate; then, a party caucus open to all interested voters accepted the nominations. Long after those events, one participant remembered Burr's instructions for the party meeting: "As soon as the room begins to fill up, I will nominate Daniel Smith as chairman, and put the question quickly. Daniel being in the chair, you must each nominate one member. . . . We must then have some inspiring speeches, close the meeting, and retire."

Republican Party subcommittees met in each ward and worked tirelessly for the entire ticket. Burr had loyal lieutenants spread throughout the city, and his palatial home served as the campaign headquarters, with refreshments served at all hours and mattresses in the rooms for exhausted workers. "Our organization was completed by dividing the city into small districts," the observer recalled, "with a committee appointed to each, whose duty it was to canvass the district and ascertain the political opinion of each voter by going from house to house." These lists guided later efforts to get voters to the polls for the election.

If not correct in every detail, this account fits the surviving record of those near-spontaneous events. The parts of America's first urban party machine fell into place that spring by trial and error.

Federalists also held caucuses and campaign rallies, but they did not generate as much enthusiasm as did the Republican meetings. "Never have I observed such a unity of sentiments, so much zeal, and as general a determination to be active," Matthew Davis wrote to Gallatin following the Republican county meeting. In contrast, he reported that dissension marked the Federalists' nominating conclave. "So much for the friends of good order and regular government," Davis added dryly.

Feverish partisan activity continued throughout the campaign. Each side organized groups of merchants and artisans on behalf of its ticket. Burr apparently put in place a highly organized fund-raising scheme that taxed Republicans according to their ability and willingness to contribute. Abigail Adams claimed that the Republicans spent $50,000 on the campaign, which (if true) was an unprecedented amount for the time—the equivalent of about $750,000 today. At the outset of the campaign, Burr reportedly "pledged himself to come forward and address the people in firm and manly language on the importance of the election and the momentous crisis at which we have arrived." He fulfilled this pledge by vigorously portraying Federalist warmongering and abuses of civil liberties as a crisis of American democracy. "Many people wonder that the ex-senator and would-be vice president can stoop so low as to visit every low tavern that may happen to be crowded with his dear fellow citizens," the *Daily Advertiser* commented accusingly, "but the prize of *success* to *him* is well worth all the dirty work." Hamilton campaigned as well: "Every day he is seen in the street hurrying this way and darting that," glad-handing individuals and speaking to small groups, a critic observed.

When the polls finally opened on April 29 for three days of balloting, normal business came to a halt across the city and electioneering took over. "Both parties were very warmly engaged," Elizabeth DeHart Bleecker noted in her diary, "and it is very doubtful which ticket will be successful."

Events hampered the Federalist effort. On the first day of voting, word reached the city that the British frigate *Cleopatra*, then moored in New York harbor, had recently captured two American merchant vessels and sent them as prizes to Canada. This affront reminded voters of the inadequacies of Jay's Treaty and hurt the Federalists, who were associated with pro-British policies. "Can it be possible that the Federal Party in this country are so blinded by prejudice and actuated by party spirit that they cannot see the danger of close connection with that people," a hastily prepared partisan handbill describing the incident said of Federalists' ties to the British. "Let us go forward to our polls, give our suffrage to the men who have once released us from the tyrannical yoke of Britain, and who now come forward once more to secure to you that liberty they have so hardly earned." Running a slate of candidates headed by several aging Revolutionary War heroes, the Republicans had invoked the Spirit of '76 against the "British party" in American politics. A prominent High Federalist soon wrote to the U.S. ambassador in London about the timing of "the unconciliating conduct of Capt. Bellows of the *Cleopatra*" and its probable influence on the New York election.

Following common election practices of the era, party leaders (but not candidates) positioned themselves at polling places to encourage their voters and intimidate all others. Hamilton and Burr threw themselves into this practice. "They repeatedly addressed the people and did all that men could do," one Burrite observed. "They frequently met at the same polls and argued in the presence of large assemblages the debatable questions." Some accounts had Hamilton going from poll to poll on a white horse—jeered in some wards, cheered in others—and Federalist officers from the national Army stationed at some polls in full regalia. "I have been night and day employed in the business of the election," Hamilton's friend Troup reported after the final day of voting. "Never have I witnessed such exertions on either side before. I have not eaten dinner for three days." Burr matched Hamilton stride for stride (though not on horseback). Indeed, he stood for (and won) election from a neighboring county so that he could more freely campaign in the city. Defying convention, Brockholst Livingston addressed voters at the polls even though he was a candidate.

Republican efforts focused on New York's sprawling Sixth and Seventh Wards, located on the city's expanding northern fringe. Crammed with foreign immigrants and home to many native-born African-Americans and impoverished European Americans, each of these wards contained over twice as many voters as any of the three wards at Manhattan's southern tip, where most of the city's wealthiest citizens lived. These northern wards promised the most votes for Republicans. The densely populated Sixth Ward contained the least desirable housing in the city, while the geographically larger Seventh Ward included a mix of neighborhoods.

Various reports suggest the extent of Republican efforts in these two critical wards. The party dispatched German-speaking poll workers to the heavily German Seventh Ward, for example, and in both wards it organized transportation for poor voters, many of whom lived far from their ward's central polling place. One account spoke of "carriages, chairs and wagons" appearing on the streets for Republican voters. "This morning, Mr. Robert Livingston drove an old Negro to the poll at the Seventh Ward, a distance of five miles in his own elegant chair," the Federalist *Commercial Advertiser* reported snidely, yet the man "voted for the Federal ticket to the utter amazement and confusion of his dear friend Bobby." An April 30 article in the same newspaper noted, "The purse-proud landlord of the Seventh Ward, Henry Rogers, stood at the poll yesterday in obedience to the orders of Burr to solicit, and to overawe, and to brow beat the voters." Burr stationed himself in the Sixth Ward on April 30, and then moved on to the Seventh Ward for May 1. "This day has he remained at the poll of the Seventh Ward, *TEN HOURS*, without interruption," his exhausted follower Matthew Davis wrote at day's end. "Pardon the hasty scrawl: I have not eaten for fifteen hours."

*   *   *

Then it ended. By 12:00 on the night of May 1, the outcome was clear. "Republicanism Triumphant," Davis emblazoned across the top of a midnight letter to Albert Gallatin at the national Congress in Philadelphia. With virtually identical numbers for all their Assembly candidates, Republicans had won by an average of some 450 votes—or about 8 percent of the total. The Sixth Ward, the city's poorest, accounted for the entire margin of victory. Without its votes, every Republican candidate would have lost. The huge Seventh Ward voted Republican too, but more narrowly than the Sixth. As in Pennsylvania earlier, the allegiance of new immigrants to the Republican cause tipped the scale. In this sense, the Naturalization and Alien Acts had hurt the Federalists. Federalist candidates meanwhile swept the three southernmost wards— home to the city's wealthiest residents—by nearly a two-to-one margin. Vote totals from the middle two wards split about evenly. Despite a deeply divided electorate, city-wide voting gave all thirteen Assembly seats to Republicans.

When word of the outcome reached Philadelphia by post, the U.S. Senate adjourned for the day. "The New York election has engrossed the whole attention of us, meaning by 'us' Congress and the whole city," Gallatin wrote from Philadelphia. "Exultation on our side is high; the other party are in low spirits." The political ground had shifted seismically under the nation's politicians. Congressman Edward Livingston actually spoke of "an earthquake." New York's twelve electoral votes, which had gone to Adams in 1796, would move to Jefferson's column for 1800. Federalists and Republicans alike struggled to digest the news and determine what it meant for themselves and their party. Passing the glad tidings on to Madison, Virginia Congressman John Dawson exclaimed, "Dear Sir! The republic is safe. Our ticket has succeeded in the city of New York."

First came the crowing and finger-pointing. "To Colonel Burr we are indebted to everything," Davis proclaimed in his midnight letter to Gallatin. In a longer letter four days later, he reiterated, "The management and industry of Colonel Burr has [sic] effected all that the friends of civil liberty could possibly desire." Gallatin's father-in-law, retired senior Navy officer James Nicholson of New York, agreed about Burr's contribution. "His generalship, perseverance, industry, and execution exceed all description," Nicholson wrote playfully. "I [recommend] him as a general far superior to your Hambletons, as much so as a man is to a boy." For his part, in a letter to Jefferson, Burr wrote, "The victory is complete and the manner is highly honorable. On the part of the Republicans there has been no indecency, no unfairness, no personal abuse. On the other side, the influence and authority of office have [been] openly perverted." He surely knew that the Virginian would want to see their victory in such terms. To a local Federalist, Burr reportedly boasted, "We have beat you by superior management."

Federalists took their defeat particularly hard because they had not anticipated it. Only a year earlier, their Assembly candidates had averaged 60 percent of the vote in the city. Although they received nearly as many votes in 1800 as in 1799, their percentage of the total dropped to about 46. Just as in Pennsylvania, Republicans had won on high turnout in areas of their strength, especially in the Sixth and Seventh Wards, where the number of voters jumped by 40 percent.

The reversal shocked Federalists. "But yesterday they were arrogant and certain of our defeat," Edward Livingston wrote about the reaction of Federalists in Congress to news of the election, "today there is a most auspicious gloom on the countenances of every Tory." From New York, John Jay's twenty-four-year-old son, Peter, wrote to his father, "The event of the election here is as unexpected as it is mortifying." He gave due credit for the outcome to Burr, who he said "contrived everything and put everything in motion," but also blamed his own party for inadequate preparation. "The Federalists were as usual supine till the eve of the election," young Jay wrote, "then they did their duty—I doubt whether more activity and exertion were ever employed on a similar cause"—but it came too late. Postelection analysis in the Federalist *Commercial Advertiser* expressed a similar view. "They do not confine themselves to three days exertion," it said of the Republicans, "they devote weeks, months, even the year itself to secure their purposes." Abigail Adams put it bluntly soon after hearing the news. "These people at the head of whom was Burr laid their plan with much more skill than their opponents," she wrote.

As Burr claimed and his opponents conceded, the Republicans won in part through superior organization. They presented a united front for Jefferson and against Adams. Theirs was no longer the party of disorder—it was the Federalist Party that had begun to splinter. Hamilton and the New York Federalists, by contrast, while vigorous in their efforts, had not rallied behind Adams. Abigail Adams observed that "the defection of New York . . . was produced by the intrigue of two men": Burr, who "seized the lucky moment of mounting into power upon the shoulders of Jefferson," and Hamilton, who "sowed the seeds of discontent and division amongst the Federalists." In blaming Hamilton, she reflected the views of her husband. "Hamilton has been opposing me in New York," the President angrily complained to his High Federalist Secretary of War on May 5. "He has caused the loss of the election." As Adams saw it, by contriving to put forward Assembly candidates loyal to himself, Hamilton had alienated Adams's supporters in New York and depressed the party's vote.

Some Republicans saw the result as a vindication of their principled stand against Federalist restrictions on civil liberties. "To reign by fear and not by affection was ever bad policy," a writer for the *American Citizen* commented following the election. "I am confident that the people of America are too fond of freedom to surrender it passively; and that whenever any body of men disclose views inimical to their interests, they will hurl them into insignificance." In a letter to Jefferson, Chancellor Livingston interpreted the election as "a lesson to the future place" of any party guilty of violating individual rights. "Thank God," he wrote, "the people are roused from their lethargy."

Hamilton could scarcely believe the election results. For two days after the polls closed in New York City, he nurtured the hope that returns from across the state would preserve a Federalist majority in the legislature. Other ardent Federalists held similar hopes. By May 4, however, Hamilton conceded that the Republicans had won. Some reports described him as "a figure of rage and despair"—but these inevitably came from Republicans, who wished it so. Hamilton never totally despaired about anything. He instinctively devised solutions for his problems, and he certainly viewed the prospect of Jefferson's elevation to the presidency as one of the most serious problems that he or the country had ever faced. Ever since they had served together in Washington's cabinet, Hamilton had viewed Jefferson as a dreamy idealist who could neither effectively lead a government nor restrain the radically egalitarian and potentially violent elements within the Republican Party. Further, Hamilton despaired of Jefferson's ideals. Hamilton wanted a strong central government to foster commercial development; Jefferson idealized individual freedom, states' rights, and the family farm. Hamilton also feared that Jefferson's ardent anticlericalism, if made national policy, could destabilize the social order by dissolving the glue of civil religion that helped to hold the country together.

During the first week of May, Hamilton gathered with other New York Federalists to discuss their options. According to an account of their meeting leaked to the Republican press, someone there proposed asking Governor Jay to call a special session of the lame-duck legislature and have it "invest him with the power of choosing the electors." At least with respect to the choice of New York's presidential electors, this would effectively undo the election results. When someone else objected that this "might lead to civil war," a third person in the room "observed that a civil war would be preferable to having Jefferson for president."

A day's ride away in Philadelphia, the *Aurora* published a story about the proposal on May 7, describing it as "a new and extraordinary instance of the confirmed depravity of a faction." A Federalist paper in New York promptly dismissed the story as an "infamous lie," but in fact its substance was true. Some local Federalists met in New York City with Hamilton and some congressional Federalists met in Philadelphia with Hamilton's father-in-law, Senator Schuyler, to discuss ways to salvage at least a portion of New York's electoral votes.

Whatever the initial proposal, it changed by the time it reached the governor. On May 7, Hamilton and Schuyler sent separate letters to Jay requesting that he recall the state legislature for the purpose of authorizing district elections for choosing New York's presidential electors—the very procedure that Federalist legislators had rejected when the Republicans had proposed it prior to the state legislative elections. "This measure will not fail to be approved by all in the Federal Party," Hamilton assured Jay. With district elections inevitably splitting the state's electoral votes, Schuyler expressed confidence "that Mr. Jefferson's election will be defeated."

In his letter, Schuyler stressed that he wrote on behalf of "our federal friends in Congress," including John Marshall (whom he mentioned by name). "I am aware that there are weighty objections to the measure but . . . in times like this in which we live, it will not do to be overscrupulous," Hamilton argued. "The scruples of delicacy and propriety, as relative to a common course of things, ought . . . not to hinder the taking of a *legal* and *constitutional* step, to prevent an *atheist* in religion and *fanatic* in politics from getting possession of the helm of the State." Hamilton may have thought that these charges against Jefferson would resonate with Jay—a devout Christian and former Chief Justice of the U.S. Supreme Court.

Both Hamilton and Schuyler expressed their grave, and undoubtedly sincere, concern for the nation's survival under Republican rule. Schuyler denounced Jefferson as "pervaded with the mad French philosophy." Hamilton described the Republican Party as "a composition indeed of very incongruous materials but all tending to mischief— some of them to the overthrow of the Government by depriving it of its due energies, others of them to a revolution after the manner of Bonaparte." Defending the Constitution and preserving the "social order" justified extreme means, Hamilton maintained. "It is impossible to appreciate all the painful results that may ensue from Mr. Jefferson's conduct should he be president," Schuyler added. "It seems to me that these considerations will justify the measure of calling the Legislature." Expressing a view shared by virtually all Hamilton biographers, Ron Chernow concluded that "Hamilton's appeal may count as the most high-handed and undemocratic act of his career." It sought to overturn the expressed will of the people through a second election conducted under different rules after his opponents had fairly won the first one.

Despite his High Federalist leanings and strong party loyalty, Governor Jay did not even dignify these letters with written replies. Even though one of them came from the commander of the Army and the other from a United States senator, Jay simply filed the letters for posterity, which has judged them harshly. He jotted his own opinion on Hamilton's letter: "Proposing a measure for party purposes, which I think it would not become me to adopt." From a soft-spoken gentleman like Jay who had served under Washington and imbibed late-eighteenth-century notions of public service and personal honor, "for party purposes" constituted a biting indictment. The New York election stood.

Even as New Yorkers voted in their late April elections, news spread regarding the results of Virginia's state legislative contests, held on April 23. To assure that Jefferson would this time sweep the state's twenty-one electoral votes, allowing for no rogue Federalist electors, the old, Republican-dominated legislature had changed the law to have voters choose electors by a statewide vote in 1800. Federalists tried to make the new law into an issue during the April legislative campaigns. They wanted to restore the old method of choosing electors by district elections. A new legislature could revise the law in time for the fall election.

Although most voters probably did not either fully understand or greatly care how they chose electors, rumors persisted in the nation's capital that Virginia Federalists had found a winning issue. Federalist House Speaker Theodore Sedgwick reported hearing it from "several of our friends," yet confessed he had not the "faintest hope" of his party's candidates prevailing in the state on that or any other issue. "Pray how is the general ticket relished in Virginia?" Republican Congressman John Dawson worriedly asked Madison three months before the election. Federalists "report that it is universally abhorred," Dawson noted. Madison thought otherwise: "I have no reason to believe this to be the fact," he replied. Nevertheless, in March, Virginia Republicans published a twenty-three-page pamphlet justifying the law as a fully constitutional means to maximize the state's influence in the upcoming presidential contest. "That the election of Mr. Jefferson was an effect expected or rather hoped for by the friends of the measure is readily admitted," the pamphlet stated.

This straightforward explanation apparently satisfied voters. Three days before the election, Madison reported to Jefferson about the state legislative campaign, "I find that considerable exertion is used to raise prejudices against the measures of the last session of [the] Assembly, especially the novel mode of appointing electors. I am not possessed however of any evidence of their success that deserves attention." By April 26, as returns trickled in from across the state, Monroe assured Jefferson, "The elections so far as we have intelligence are almost universally in favor of the Republican cause." The next day, Madison wrote from Virginia regarding the Federalists, "The patrons of usurpation and aristocracy will have little encouragement from this quarter." Republican candidates won virtually everywhere in the state and reportedly did so by large margins.

The election results from New York and Virginia, coming as they did six months after McKean's victory in Pennsylvania, panicked Federalists and elated Republicans. All three elections turned on national issues and directly impacted the electoral vote. In six months, the situation had reversed from the Republicans having to sweep virtually every remaining winnable electoral vote to the Federalists bearing that burden. To compensate for the loss of New York's electors, Federalists would need to hold New Jersey, win more electoral votes in Maryland and North Carolina than they won in 1796, and carry South Carolina. If Pennsylvania voted, they would also need at least some of its votes.

Because of the heightened importance of the Carolinas, Pinckney might now have the best chance of any Federalist to cobble together the votes needed for victory.

As early as March, Jefferson commented about the mood at the nation's capital, "The Feds begin to be very seriously alarmed about their election next fall. Their speeches in private as well as their public and private demeanor to me indicate it strongly." The shift became apparent to everyone by May. Commenting in early May on the latest Republican victory, the *Aurora* gloated, "The results of the New York election must speak to the Federal administration in a very emphatical manner, how general and decisive the public opinion is against their measures."

Abigail Adams could count the votes accumulating against her husband as well as anyone. She saw only darkness ahead. The Republicans had added twelve electors to their already formidable fifty-odd elector base, with only seventy needed to win. "New York, by an effort to bring into their assembly anti-Federal men, will make also an anti-Federal ticket for president . . . at the sacrifice of all that good men hold dear and sacred," she wrote to her sister on May 5. "Much animosity is springing up between South and North and East. A whole year we shall hear nothing else but abuse and scandal, enough to ruin and corrupt the minds and morals of the best people in the world. Out of all this will arise something which (though we may be no more) our children may live to rue." John Adams and other Federalists knew that they must act quickly and decisively to right the situation. In order to do so, they needed to present a united front against the Republicans, but the growing rift between Adams and the High Federalists would prove a great challenge for the party that had ruled America since the Constitution was ratified.

CHAPTER FIVE

CAUCUSES AND CALUMNY

*H*AVING ORCHESTRATED the Republican victory in the New York City election, Aaron Burr promptly set out to claim his reward—designation as the party's choice for Vice President. Burr's chief lieutenant, Matthew Davis, served as his agent. No candidate for national office in America had ever been so brash. Washington had appeared positively reticent about putting himself forward for President. Adams and Jefferson had worn a similar face when seeking national office, as had Clinton in 1792 and Thomas Pinckney in 1796.

The product of urban politics and a full generation younger than Washington, Adams, and Jefferson, Burr could not keep himself out of sight or above the fray. He yearned for high office and never hid his ambitions, which made some politicians distrust him.

Already in 1792, during his first year as a senator from New York and only age thirty-six, or one year older than the minimum age to serve as President, Burr had pushed himself forward as a candidate for Vice President. That year the Republicans had launched an effort to oust Adams from the post. In the election—America's second for President—everyone assumed that all electors would cast one vote for Washington's reelection, which they did. The contest for Vice President remained in doubt, though, and some Republican leaders had sought to push Adams aside by encouraging Republican electors to cast their second votes for an agreed alternative, which ended up being eight-term New York Governor George Clinton. Jefferson, then serving as Washington's Secretary of State, would have been their logical choice, but he was effectively excluded from consideration because he came from Virginia, the same state as Washington, and the Constitution bars electors from voting for two people from their own state. At the time, no Republican could hope to win without electoral votes from Virginia. Republicans needed a candidate from another state. Burr had sought the nod by seeking the cooperation of party leaders in New York and Pennsylvania.

Following a flurry of letters among leading Republicans, the choice had gone to Clinton over Burr due to the long-serving governor's greater stature and more reliable Anti-Federalist credentials. In comparing these two options for the vice presidency, Virginia Senator James Monroe had written to Madison, "Some person of more advanced life and longer standing in public trust [than Burr] should be selected for it, and particularly one who in consequence of such service had given unequivocal proofs of what his principles really were." Having voted for the Declaration of Independence as a member of the Continental Congress but against the Constitution as speaker of New York's ratifying convention, Clinton had a long history of patriotic service as a principled Anti-Federalist. The pragmatic Burr, in contrast, had flirted with both factions during his brief political career. Madison concurred with Monroe in favoring Clinton over Burr, and their opinion prevailed.

Clinton ultimately received the united electoral votes of four states—New York, Virginia, North Carolina, and Georgia—placing him a strong third behind Washington and Adams. This contest between Adams and Clinton had etched the first outlines of coordinated partisan balloting for national office. Considering Washington's popularity and Adams's stature, the Republican candidate had done surprisingly well, and the choice of Clinton over Burr probably contributed to this outcome. Burr, however, would not be deterred.

In 1796, still in his first term as a U.S. senator, Burr had tried again for the vice presidency. The Federalists had quickly settled on South

Carolina's Thomas Pinckney as their candidate for Vice President, without ever formally meeting to discuss the matter. Republicans not only considered a wider field but employed a novel process for doing so. Their congressional members met together in secret to discuss their options—the first time that a party's representatives and senators had ever caucused to discuss candidates.

Although a necessary evil to establish and maintain party unity in an age before primary elections and nominating conventions, closed caucuses carried an odor of conspiratorial factionalism from the Revolutionary Era, when both patriots and loyalists met in private to plot the other's destruction. Factional scheming would give way to open political discourse in the sunshine of American democracy, the patriotic vision proclaimed. Caucusing was reviving with the rise of partisan politics, but it remained unpopular with the public.

In their 1796 secret caucus, Republican lawmakers discussed at least four candidates for the vice presidency: Burr, Senator Pierce Butler of South Carolina, Senator John Langdon of New Hampshire, and Chancellor Robert Livingston of New York. Although members attending the caucus apparently never voted on these individuals and did not, as a group, endorse any one of them, Burr seems to have been the favorite, enjoying particularly strong support in the middle states, especially Pennsylvania, where partisan leader John Beckley affirmed that "the whole body of Republicans are decidedly in favor of Burr." Republicans, however, made little attempt actually to coordinate their voting for Vice President.

In the ensuing Electoral College balloting, Burr had proved most popular with Republican electors in the middle and western states. In Jefferson's strongholds in the South, however, most Republican electors had cast their second votes for more senior and reliable Anti-Federalists, particularly Clinton and Samuel Adams of Massachusetts—two popular, older leaders who had initially opposed ratification of the Constitution and apparently were overlooked at the congressional party caucus.

The vote totals in 1796, with Adams and Jefferson coming in first and second while their parties' other candidates trailed far behind, demonstrated that disciplined party voting did not yet dominate the Electoral College. Many electors still voted their consciences or sectional loyalties. Finishing a poor fourth behind Adams, Jefferson, and Pinckney, Burr professed to feel betrayed by Southern Republicans—particularly Jefferson's Virginia electors, who gave fifteen votes to Samuel Adams, three to Clinton, and only one to Burr.

Following his Herculean efforts on Jefferson's behalf in the 1800 New York City election, in the 1800 presidential election Burr demanded more loyalty from Republican electors than he had received in the past. Party discipline, not ideological purity or sectional loyalties, should prevail in the casting of electoral votes, he argued.

Hitching himself to Jefferson and the rise of partisan voting, Burr set his sights on being chosen as the sole Republican vice presidential candidate this time. As in 1796, Republican members of the U.S. House of Representatives and Senate again planned to caucus secretly to make their vice presidential nomination. The brilliant Swiss émigré Albert Gallatin served as the Republican leader in Congress. On May 11, at the boardinghouse in Philadelphia where many Republican lawmakers lodged during congressional sessions, he convened the caucus. Its timing would enable Burr to capitalize on his recent efforts for the Republican ticket in New York if he struck fast. Matthew Davis had already laid the groundwork for Burr to do so, undoubtedly with his mentor's full knowledge and encouragement.

During the campaign in New York, Davis had sent Gallatin regular reports highlighting Burr's efforts on behalf of the party. The colonel "has effected all" and "principally" caused the victory, the letters gushed in words that as likely came from Burr as from his adoring protégé. After the party ticket prevailed in New York City, Davis sent a final letter to Gallatin expressly raising the issue that had been the topic of open speculation in the city throughout the campaign. "It is generally expected that the vice president will be selected from the state of

New York," Davis wrote on May 5. "Three characters only can be con-templated, viz., George Clinton, Chancellor Livingston, and Colonel Burr." Dismissing the first as too old and the second as too timid, Davis concluded, "Colonel Burr is therefore the most eligible character, and on him the eyes of our friends in this state are fixed as if by sympathy for that office."

In his mind, Gallatin had already narrowed the choice to two of these three New Yorkers. On May 6, even before receiving Davis's final letter, Gallatin wrote from Philadelphia to his wife, then visiting her family in New York City. "Who is to be our vice president, Clinton or Burr?" he asked. "This is a serious question which I am delegated to make, and to which I must have an answer by Friday next." That was the appointed day for the secret Republican caucus.

To discover which person New York Republicans favored as Vice President, Gallatin asked his wife's illustrious father, retired Navy cap-tain James Nicholson, to survey local sentiment. Nicholson instead went straight to Clinton and Burr. Here the record becomes fuzzy. Nicholson and Clinton later wrote that, in line with conventional prac-tice, Clinton played the reluctant candidate, much as he had when Burr asked him to stand for the State Assembly two months earlier.

Nicholson pressed him about the vice presidency, Clinton wrote in an 1803 letter. "After much conversation on this subject, I finally agreed that in answering Mr. Gallatin's letter he might mention that I was adverse to engage in public life, yet rather than that any danger should occur in the election of president . . . I would so far consent as that my name might be used without any contradiction on my part," he recalled. Burr also initially expressed his willingness to stand as Jeffer-son's running mate, Clinton and Nicholson reported, but then became enraged when Nicholson told him that Clinton's name would also go forward to Philadelphia. "He would have nothing more to do with the business," Burr reportedly told Nicholson, and would instead run for governor. To placate Burr, Nicholson (with Clinton's consent) altered his response to Gallatin.

Nicholson's letter to Gallatin did not mention any of the alleged behind-the-scenes posturing by Clinton and Burr. It simply endorsed Burr as the choice "of all the Republicans in this quarter that I have conversed with." According to the letter, Clinton "declined" to run due to "his age . . . and attachment to retired life" and endorsed Burr as "the most suitable person" for the vice presidency. The wily Burr then played the reluctant candidate whose conditional no actually meant yes. "He seemed to think that no arrangement could be made which would be observed to the southward," Nicholson wrote of Burr's reluctance, "alluding, as I understand, to the last election, in which he was certainly ill used by Virginia and North Carolina. I believe he may be induced to stand if assurances can be given that the Southern States will act fairly." Without a solemn pledge of solid support by Republican electors in all states, Burr was well aware that he could gain the caucus nomination and still come in third or fourth in an election that Jefferson won. "Burr says he has no confidence in the Virginians," Gallatin's wife added in a separate letter. "They once deceived him, and they are not to be trusted."

By encouraging party-line voting by electors pledged to partisan unity, Burr's expressed goal was to garner one vote from every Republican elector, which could result in his getting as many votes as Jefferson. Indeed, any astute politician could readily recognize that completely straight party-line voting would lead to a tie vote between the party's two candidates. Such an outcome could be catastrophic. The Constitution stipulated that in the event of a tie between two candidates, each with votes from a majority of the electors, the House of Representatives would pick between them by majority vote. In the House balloting, each state would have one vote. At the time, due to an even partisan split in some state congressional delegations, neither party controlled a majority of them. The Federalists could thus use their power in Congress to block Jefferson's election.

During the campaign, Republican leaders never seemed to doubt that some Republican electors would, in the end, drop their votes for Burr, either on their own initiative or at the direction of a party leader. After all, it was clear that no Republican elector actually favored Burr over Jefferson for President, but the Constitution prohibited them from officially designating one vote for President and another vote for Vice President. Eliminating one or more votes for Burr was the only way Jefferson could win the election without a troublesome House vote.

Forty-three Republican members of Congress reportedly attended the secret caucus, which formally tapped Jefferson as the party's nominee for President and Burr as its choice for Vice President. At the time, presumably to maintain the appearance of an open party, participants did not publicly acknowledge that the meeting had occurred.

Ironically, after Federalists held a closed, but not secret, caucus to choose their candidates for national office within days of the secret Republican one, the Republican *Aurora* gleefully condemned it as a "fractious meeting . . . unknown to the constitution or law." Other Republican newspapers also questioned the authority of a "self-appointed" caucus to "dictate" nominations without ever suggesting that Republican lawmakers held a similar gathering. Indeed, in an autobiographical writing published four decades later and after a stellar career of public service that transcended partisanship, Gallatin still defensively maintained that Republican caucuses were infrequent, informal, and nonbinding during his tenure in Congress.

No record exists of what transpired within the Republican caucus on May 11—only Gallatin's private report of the results. "We had last night a very large meeting of Republicans in which it was unanimously agreed to support Burr for Vice President," he wrote privately to his wife in New York on May 12. Jefferson denied playing any direct role in the choice. "It is our mutual duty to leave those arrangements to others and to acquiesce in their assignment," Jefferson wrote to a Southern supporter about himself and Burr. "He has certainly greatly merited [the support] of his country, and the Republicans in particular, to whose efforts his have given a chance of success."

Perhaps because of their secret nature, caucuses could not in themselves enforce party discipline. Burr wanted more than a mere expression of support: Only pledges of personal honor would bind participants to their caucus commitments. He sought them following the caucus.

Republicans soon spoke openly of their mutual commitment to vote equally for Jefferson and Burr. When rumors spread that, to prevent a tie, some Southern electors would not vote for Burr so that Jefferson would be certain to prevail over Burr in the final tally, Burrite David Gelston wrote accusingly to Madison on Burr's behalf, "*Can we, may we*, rely on the integrity of the southern states?" Madison responded by openly urging Governor Monroe to make sure that all Virginia's electors duly voted for Jefferson and Burr. "It would be superfluous to suggest to you the mischief resulting from the least grounds of reproach, and particularly to Virginia, on this head," he wrote to the governor. Madison, Monroe, and Jefferson each assumed that others would, nonetheless, make sure that at least one Republican elector in some state would not vote for Burr. None of them wanted to be personally responsible for the breach of trust, however.

Burr now had the nomination and a pledge of support covering all Republican electors. He responded by campaigning conscientiously for the party ticket and never, as far as the record shows, overtly breaking his implicit commitment to support Jefferson. If he did watch out for himself along the way, it was nothing more than he expected from others.

The Federalist caucus, though on its surface less contentious, involved more convoluted subcurrents than the Republican one. For Jefferson's running mate, Republicans had chosen someone already known for his independent ambition and lack of long-term party loyalty yet able to deliver key electoral votes. Jefferson would later call Burr a "crooked gun or other perverted machine whose aim or stroke you could never be sure of," while Monroe and other leading Republicans had long viewed him as unreliable. Some observers predicted that Republicans would soon regret choosing Burr. In contrast, for their second candidate, Federalists tapped a reliable subordinate and party loyalist, Charles Cotesworth Pinckney, the elder brother of their 1796 vice presidential candidate, Thomas Pinckney.

Although seemingly obvious on its face to the public, the choice of Pinckney for the national ticket, in fact, threatened to split Federalists along a critical fault line. Party insiders knew that Pinckney's loyalties ran toward Hamilton rather than Adams, and that Hamilton had backed Pinckney's brother over Adams in 1796. Indeed, after the caucus in 1800, senior Federalist leader Fisher Ames privately commented on the "singular and mysterious" state of his party's politics: "The plot for an old Spanish play is not more complicated with underplot." The choice may have been perverse in some respects, but there was good strategy behind it, especially for High Federalists.

Like the Republicans, the Federalists caucused in the wake of the New York City election, which cast a pall over their gathering. To retain the presidency without New York's electoral votes, Federalists needed to peel some votes away from Jefferson in the South. With its established aristocracy, the Pinckney family's power base, and its relative independence from national partisan politics, South Carolina offered the best prospects for them. This is why they turned once again to one of the wealthy and influential Pinckney brothers—who were South Carolina's leading Federalists—to run with Adams. Born into power and privilege in Charleston, both brothers studied law in England, received military training in France, and inherited vast lowcountry plantations with hundreds of slaves. In the afterglow of negotiating a popular 1795 treaty with Spain that peacefully resolved the nation's southwestern border with Louisiana and opened New Orleans to American commercial traffic, Thomas Pinckney had been the Federalists' logical choice in 1796 for trying to break the Republicans' grip on the South. Every South Carolina elector voted for him and Jefferson; none voted for Adams.

By 1800, Thomas's older brother, Charles Cotesworth, had emerged as the strongest candidate to run with Adams on the party ticket. One of three commissioners named to negotiate outstanding differences with France in 1797, the older Pinckney famously defended America's honor by refusing to pay the bribe allegedly sought by French officials in the XYZ Affair. "No, no, not one sixpence," he purportedly replied, or, "Millions for defense, but not one cent for tribute." Both versions circulated widely in the United States, and made him a national hero—at least until taxpayers began paying those millions. After the ensuing breakdown of negotiations led to fears of war with France, Pinckney agreed to serve under Washington and Hamilton as commander of Southern forces in the Additional Army even though, as a general during the Revolutionary War, he had outranked Hamilton. With his brother Thomas then serving in the U.S. House of Representatives and his cousin Charles in the U.S. Senate, Charles Cotesworth joined Adams on the party's agreed upon, though unofficial, national ticket.

In a controversial twist, rather than endorse Adams as President and Pinckney as Vice President, the thirty-or-so Federalist members of Congress attending the caucus agreed simply to endorse both men and urge all Federalist electors to vote for them equally. Presumably party moderates and High Federalists were able to reach consensus at the caucus only on these terms. The agreement left Hamilton free to hope that this time a plot like the one he had hatched in 1796 would succeed and his candidate would outpoll Adams. To work, the effort would require strict party-line voting by Federalist electors in the North while at the same time a repeat of favorite-son balloting by South Carolina's electors. If all Federalist electors duly voted for both candidates—with no one dropping votes from Pinckney, as some had done with his brother in 1796—and if South Carolina's electors again voted for a candidate from their state's most powerful family, then Charles Cotesworth Pinckney would almost surely win the presidency.

Hamilton had suggested this approach in a May 4 letter to Federalist House Speaker Theodore Sedgwick, a caucus leader. Reminding the Speaker of the 1796 effort to bring Thomas Pinckney in ahead of Adams, Hamilton declared that, following the loss in New York, such an effort was now the party's best option for retaining the presidency. "To support *Adams* and *Pinckney* equally is the only thing that can possibly save us from the fangs of *Jefferson*," he wrote.

The scheme might succeed in 1800 where it had failed in 1796,

Hamilton reasoned, because Adams had lost so much High Federalist support by then due to the resumption of peace negotiations with France. Although moderates within the party welcomed the peace mission, High Federalists hated it. Enough electors from New England might now knowingly go along with his scheme for it to work, in contrast to those who had scuttled it last time. "It is therefore essential that the Federalists should not separate without coming to a distinct and solemn concert to pursue this course *bona fide,*" he wrote to Sedgwick.

The strategy behind the caucus agreement was clear to all astute political observers. Jefferson immediately dubbed it a "hocus-pocus maneuver," presumably referring to the substitution of the popular candidate, Adams, by the High Federalists' choice, Pinckney. Adams guessed Hamilton's game as soon as he heard what the caucus had done, and he was livid. Following the caucus, Fisher Ames neatly summed up the political situation when he wrote: "It is understood by most persons that Pinckney's chance is worse than Jefferson's and better than Adams's."

Sedgwick described the caucus in words that echoed Hamilton's instructions for it. "We have had a meeting of the whole Federal Party on the subject of the ensuing election and have agreed that we will support, *bona fide,* Mr. Adams and General Pinckney," he wrote. "If this agreement be faithfully executed we shall succeed, but otherwise we cannot escape the fangs of Jefferson." As a leading member of Congress from Massachusetts who had long supported Adams, Sedgwick had felt personally betrayed when the President reopened peace negotiations with France in 1799. "Had the foulest heart and the basest mind in the world been permitted to select the most embarrassing and ruinous measure," Sedgwick commented at the time, "perhaps it would have been precisely the one which has been adopted." In his report of the Federalist caucus, Sedgwick pointedly added, "It is true that the late conduct of the President has endeared him to the great body of the Federalists, but it is equally true that it has created an entire separation between him and those whom he theretofore deemed his best friends." Sedgwick counted himself among the friends estranged by the President's conduct toward France. He was ready to reciprocate in kind.

Following the caucus, U.S. Senator Samuel Dexter of Massachusetts, a moderate, complained about the party's treatment of its President. Passing Dexter's objections on to Hamilton, Sedgwick wrote, "He says that however those who have had the opportunity of personal observation may esteem the character of Mr. Adams, as he is viewed by the great majority of Federalists, he is the most popular man in the U.S." The public would blame Hamilton and the High Federalists if the agreement led to Pinckney becoming President over Adams, Dexter reportedly warned, and "this will crumble the Federal Party to atoms."

Revealing the full depth of his hatred for Adams, Hamilton responded angrily to the comments by Dexter. "He is, I am persuaded, much mistaken as to the opinion entertained of Mr. Adams by the Federal Party," Hamilton replied to Sedgwick. "For my individual part, my mind is made up. I will never more be responsible for [Adams] by my direct support—even though the consequence should be the election of *Jefferson*. If we must have an *enemy* at the head of the government, let it be one whom we can oppose and for whom we are not responsible."

Hamilton promised to honor the caucus agreement as long as it appeared to hold "in the East," but if it faltered there, he would support only Pinckney. In short, if it seemed that New England electors were breaking ranks to drop votes from Pinckney, as they had done to his brother in 1796, then Hamilton would urge other electors to drop votes from Adams. "'Tis a notable expedient for keeping the Federal Party together to have at the head of it a man who hates and is despised by those men of it who in time past have been its most efficient supporters," Hamilton noted bitterly. A flurry of letters ensued from Massachusetts Federalists committing their state legislature to appoint electors who, in the words of one, "would vote unanimously for Adams and Pinckney."

Republicans could scarcely contain their glee over the still private but no longer secret split within Federalist ranks. The caucus decision to support Adams and Pinckney equally was public knowledge, and the split that underlay it was obvious enough to astute observers. Republicans speculated openly about the ulterior motives behind the caucus decision and used it to undermine support for the Federalist ticket among those loyal to the President. The Republicans, Fisher Ames warned fellow Federalists, "would join in the cry to make any [Federalist] opposed to the President unpopular" simply as a means to divide the opposition and discredit High Federalists. Of course, the Republicans did not like Adams, but they could join with moderate Federalists in denouncing High Federalists for opposing him as a means to further split the opposition. Feeding the division within the Federalists, the *Aurora*'s editor circulated and later published an old letter by Adams questioning the patriotism of the Pinckney brothers and suggesting "much British influence" in Thomas Pinckney's 1792 appointment by Washington as the American ambassador in London. Every move served to deepen the wedge between Adams and the High Federalists and expose their differences. Soon their private dispute erupted in public.

John Adams had a temper that could explode into uncontrollable outbursts of verbal abuse. With time and reflection, he typically brought his emotions under control and responded rationally to situations, but for the moment he could appear, as Benjamin Franklin had famously observed, "absolutely out of his senses." In May, Hamilton's private campaign to topple Adams touched off an outburst that opened the rift within the Federalist Party for all to see and reverberated throughout the presidential campaign.

In all likelihood, Adams's outburst was prompted by the one-two punch of news about the New York elections and the ensuing Federalist caucus. With the former, Adams learned that Jefferson had gained the advantage in the contest for the presidency; with the latter, he realized that his own party had virtually abandoned him for Pinckney.

Adams blamed Hamilton for his plight. Not only did Adams suspect that Hamilton had conspired to undermine his presidency from the outset (due at least in part to jealousy), but he also believed that Hamilton had lost the New York election by picking weak candidates loyal to himself and then masterminding the caucus vote for Pinckney. "Hamilton had opposed my election as Vice President in 1788 and my election at every subsequent period as Vice President and President," Adams later wrote, and "divided the Federalists of New York . . . [by] selecting a list of representatives for the city in their state legislature who [would] concur with his plan in the choice of electors of president" to "bring in General Pinckney." Claiming that informers had told him about Hamilton's plots in advance, Adams attributed the Republican victory in New York to the reluctance of his friends to support Hamilton's candidates. Adams may have exaggerated Hamilton's direct role in his worsening prospects, but he reacted as if he believed it.

Immediately after the New York elections and Federalist caucus, Adams moved against the Hamiltonians within his administration. He had retained three of them in his cabinet from the Washington administration: James McHenry, Timothy Pickering, and Oliver Wolcott. In Adams's eyes, only Wolcott performed his job well. All three men actively conspired with Hamilton while serving in Adams's cabinet and shamelessly sought to undermine Adams's peace initiative with France. McHenry was inept as well as disloyal. Republicans especially despised Pickering for his vigorous enforcement of the Sedition Act against their partisan newspapers. "Mr. Pickering would have made a good collector of the customs but he was not so well qualified for a Secretary of State," Adams noted about his stern, proud foreign minister. "He is a man in a mask, sometimes of silk, sometimes of iron, and sometimes of brass. And he can change them very suddenly and with some dexterity." Adams later joked, "Pickering could never be happy in heaven because he must there find and acknowledge a superior." Four months earlier, Wolcott confided to a friend that Adams "considers Col. Pickering, Mr. McHenry, and myself as enemies; his resentments against General Hamilton are excessive; he declares his belief at the existence of a British faction in the United States."

Ostensibly to discuss a minor administrative matter, Adams invited McHenry for a private meeting on May 5 that turned into a verbal assault. All the President's pent-up fury fell on this meek man, who wrote poetry and spoke with an Irish lilt. The President "became indecorous, and at times, outrageous," McHenry wrote to his nephew about the encounter. "I had done nothing right." Adams listed McHenry's supposed transgressions, major and minor, from aiding Hamilton's power grab in the Army and subverting Adams's peace mission to buying shoddy clothes for the troops and refusing a military commission for the lone North Carolina elector who voted for Adams in 1796. McHenry denied none of the major charges against him. Indeed, in the letter to his nephew, who served as an American diplomat in Europe, McHenry defended his efforts to subvert the peace mission on classic High Federalist grounds: "The kind of war we waged with France gave us little to fear from her, effectively shut out French principles, [and] was calculated to . . . preserve the friendship of England."

Following his meeting with the President, McHenry set down his recollection of the exchange and sent it to both Adams and Hamilton. Adams reportedly declared, "Hamilton is an intriguer—the greatest intriguer in the world—a man devoid of every moral principle—a bastard and as much a foreigner as Gallatin. Mr. Jefferson is an infinitely better man; a wiser one, I am sure, and, if President, will act wisely." The President then turned on McHenry: "You are subservient to Hamilton, who ruled Washington. . . . Washington saddled me with three Secretaries who would control me, but I shall take care of that." Wolcott could stay, the President suggested, but the other two must go. McHenry submitted his resignation the next day.

In the letter to his nephew, McHenry described Adams's degree of agitation on this and other occasions vividly. "At times he would speak in such a manner of certain men and things as to persuade one that he was actually insane," McHenry wrote. When Hamilton learned what happened, he exclaimed in a letter to McHenry, "Oh mad! Mad! Mad!"

Next came Pickering. On May 10, in a terse letter that gave no substantive reasons, Adams asked for the Secretary of State's resignation.

Pickering replied in his customary peevish fashion that, due to the importance of his work and the financial needs of his family, "I do not feel it to be my duty to resign." In what Adams later called "one of the most deliberate, virtuous, and disinterested actions of my life," he instantly fired Pickering.

As soon as he heard about the sackings, Hamilton sent the outgoing Secretary of State an urgent letter asking him to purloin from department files "all such documents as will enable you to *explain* both *Jefferson* and Adams. You are aware of a very curious journal of the latter when he was in Europe, a tissue of weakness and vanity." Rumors suggested that Adams had bared his soul a bit too candidly in his official reports from Europe during his diplomatic missions there. Hamilton wanted material to use against Adams in the worst way—even if it meant stealing it—and justified the request by adding that "real integrity" required exposing charlatans. Pickering received Hamilton's letter too late to act upon it. "I intended to have done precisely what you suggest respecting Mr. Adams['s] journal," he wrote back to Hamilton, but he never had a chance. The President discharged Pickering without notice, and the Secretary left office on the same day. Hamilton would have to look elsewhere for damaging material on Adams.

Adams's dismissal of McHenry and Pickering represented more than simply retribution against personal foes; it fit into a larger shift by the President toward the political center. Having secured his Federalist base the best that he could by obtaining at least a co-nomination for the presidency at the party's congressional caucus, Adams apparently felt free to moderate his policies in advance of the election. The party was committed to support him at least equally with Pinckney, and so the High Federalists could not now dump him. He was free to reach out in directions that might appeal to voters in Pennsylvania, Maryland, North Carolina, and other places where popularity might still translate into electoral votes. Firing McHenry and Pickering was only the beginning.

Before the end of May, Adams took a series of further steps that appealed to moderates. First, he named Massachusetts Senator Samuel Dexter to replace McHenry as Secretary of War and Virginia Representative John Marshall to replace Pickering as Secretary of State. During the preceding legislative session, Dexter and Marshall had shown a measure of independence from High Federalists in Congress. Then, on May 14, Adams signed into law a bill authorizing him to discharge the Additional Army. "This bill amounted to a disbanding of the army," the angry High Federalist printer William Cobbett complained, "because it was well known that Adams, who was now laying in a provision of popularity against the ensuing election for President, would issue orders for disbanding the moment the Congress adjourned." Adams did so the next day by directing McHenry, who remained in office until the end of May, to transmit an order disbanding the Army "to Major Generals Hamilton and Pinckney." Finally, on May 21, Adams issued a bold pardon of a man who had led a popular uprising against federal war taxes; a man whom High Federalists wanted to hang as a grim lesson to all.

John Fries was a former Revolutionary War officer. In 1799, he had led up to four hundred east-central Pennsylvania farmers and townspeople in armed but largely nonviolent resistance to the collection of federal property taxes imposed in 1798 to pay for military preparedness against France. These taxes represented the least popular part of the Federalist war effort. Even though no one was physically injured by the tax resisters, High Federalists cast them as Jacobin revolutionaries who imperiled public order and national security. Proclaiming that the actions of the tax resisters "amount to treason," Adams had ordered a force ultimately composed of nearly 3,000 federal and state troops to subdue them.

Fries's so-called rebellion died down long before the troops arrived. Federal marshals riding with that army nevertheless arrested over ninety persons involved in it. Following a series of highly politicized trials, Supreme Court Justice Samuel Chase—already hated by Republicans for his treatment of Sedition Act violators—sentenced Fries and two of his closest confederates to hang for treason. Thirty-two others received jail sentences. All of them acknowledged their guilt, promised to obey the law, and petitioned for executive clemency.

Upon receipt of the prisoners' petitions in mid-May, Adams asked his cabinet for advice. In a joint response, the cabinet declared the sentences both "just" and calculated to inspire "the well disposed with confidence in the government and the malevolent and fractious with terror." Every cabinet member affirmed that at least Fries should hang; Wolcott added that all three convicted traitors should die. He stressed, "The cause of humanity will be most effectually promoted by impressing an opinion that those who are brought to trial, and convicted of treason, will not be pardoned." While still Secretary of State, Pickering had written to the President about Fries's conviction, "I feel a calm and solid satisfaction that an opportunity is now presented in executing the justice of the law to crush that spirit which, if not overthrown and destroyed, may proceed in its career and overturn the government."

Now, on May 21, having come to view the underlying criminal activity as a "riot" rather than an insurrection, Adams rejected his cabinet's advice and issued a blanket pardon. Fries and his followers went home. The presidential pardon incensed High Federalists but proved popular in Pennsylvania, where Adams still hoped to win electoral votes. Everywhere, it reinforced the generally favorable view of Adams as a political independent. He would take a middle course in the campaign between Jefferson and the High Federalists.

So public was the break between Adams and the High Federalists that the *Aurora* ran an article asserting that there were now three parties represented in the U.S. Senate—Republicans, Adamites, and Pickeronians—with each having about equal numbers in that body. "The latter party consists of those who have leagued with *Hamilton* and are easily designated by their English connections," the newspaper noted. They were the High Federalists: the elite of the "aristocratic" party, according to the *Aurora*. They had no true national candidates. Indeed,

Adams and Jefferson were the only two American politicians with national followings.

Many High Federalists now recognized the virtues of manipulating the Electoral College so as to slip Pinckney in ahead of Adams without giving a majority to Jefferson. For some High Federalists, however, the overarching aim became to purge their party of Adams, even if it meant losing the presidency. "The miserable policy of regarding *men* not *measures* will defeat the hopes of the most enlightened and truly patriotic citizens," Pickering complained regarding Adams's continued popularity among middle-of-the-road Americans and many rank-and-file Federalists.

Once Congress adjourned in mid-May and its members returned home, letters became virtually the only means of private communication among party leaders. Trying to coordinate the electoral vote and debating whether to honor the caucus agreement or reject Adams for Pinckney became the object of countless letters among High Federalists. Many read like Shakespearean soliloquies: Whether 'tis nobler to support Adams and retain the presidency or defy him openly and risk Republican rule became the overriding question for High Federalists.

By the end of May, Pickering and Wolcott joined Hamilton in privately urging Federalist electors to break with Adams regardless of the consequences. "The cause of Federalism (which we consider to be the cause of our country) will be as little or as less in jeopardy under Mr. Jefferson than under Mr. Adams," Pickering observed. From within Adams's own cabinet, Wolcott wrote, "It is with grief and humiliation, but at the same time with perfect confidence, that I declare that no administration of the government by President Adams can be successful." He added, "I am no advocate for rash measures, and know that public opinion cannot be suddenly changed, but it is clear to my mind that we can never find ourselves in the straight road of Federalism while Mr. Adams is President." For these men who had worked under Adams, principle prevailed over the presidency. Wolcott now characterized Adams's reelection, not Jefferson's election, as "the greatest possible curse: A presidential administration which no party can trust."

Most High Federalists, however, still disagreed with the extreme measure of publicly repudiating the President. "An open attack, if made soon on [Adams], would, I fear, divide our force and perhaps give some [electoral] votes to Jefferson," Fisher Ames wrote in June. "Instead of analyzing the measures of the man who has thus brought the cause into jeopardy," he admonished Wolcott about his attacks on Adams, "you must sound the tocsin against Jefferson." Believing that a "Jacobin President" represented a greater threat to ordered liberty than another term for Adams, Ames warned, "A thousand ways of attacking property are plausible, popular, and fatal."

Writing on behalf of High Federalists in the Northeast, New Jersey Senator Richard Stockton also cautioned Wolcott that, although they shared his utter alienation from Adams, "nothing further was practicable than the plan proposed in Philadelphia of running two candidates." He added, "None of us think that affairs are so desperate as to believe that Mr. Adams, with all his weaknesses . . . can be a worse man than Jefferson." In a like manner, South Carolina Congressman Robert G. Harper wrote to Hamilton that, while Southern Federalists favored Pinckney over Adams, "they are however convinced that no direct attack can safely be made to drop or supercede Mr. Adams. It would create uncertainty, division, and defeat."

Pinckney also urged his Southern supporters not to break publicly with the President. "If any alteration should take place in the agreement entered into in Philadelphia," he wrote in mid-June, "it should originate in the Eastern states; otherwise we shall be inevitably divided, and the Anti-Federalists obtain the success which I am sure they will not if the Federalists are united, active, and energetic." The call to repudiate Adams should come first from Federalists in New England, Pinckney reasoned, because if it came from Federalists in any other region, New Englanders would likely rally around their native son. Although highly critical of the President in private, Pinckney still viewed the caucus agreement as the best means for the Federalists to retain the presidency.

In his doleful letters lamenting Adams's conduct and his own mis-
treatment, McHenry captured the High Federalists' angst. "Have our
party shown that they possess the necessary skill and courage to
deserve to be continued to govern?" he wrote to Wolcott about the
continuing party support for Adams. "They did not (with few exceptions), knowing the disease, the man, and his nature, meet it, when it
first appeared, like wise and resolute politicians. . . . Nay, . . . they write
private letters. To whom? To each other. But they do nothing to give a
proper direction to the public mind." Someone should speak out
against Adams, McHenry believed, but he left the task to others.

Plotting against the President themselves, High Federalists now
could see only the worst in his every move. In 1800, for example, Jefferson had remained in the nation's capital later than his customary
return to Monticello in April. This unexplained act coupled with
Adams's firing of McHenry and Pickering in early May touched off
rumors within Federalist circles that Adams and Jefferson had entered
into a secret pact to run on a united ticket. "I have good reason for
believing that Pinckney and McHenry have been sacrificed as peace
offerings," House Speaker Theodore Sedgwick wrote to Hamilton in
mid-May, suggesting that the dismissals of these two partisan cabinet
officers sealed a deal between the President and the Vice President. Jefferson had remained in the nation's capital until Adams consummated
the bargain by his actions, the speculation ran. One version of the
rumor had the men agreeing to exchange their current positions, with
Adams becoming Jefferson's Vice President. Another version had
Adams serving a second term as President and then supporting Jefferson for the post. Adams hotly denied the rumors, and his wife found
them disgusting. The fact that some High Federalists believed them
showed the level of distrust that divided the party. Even Pinckney conceded in June that, if true, a deal by Adams "to form a party with Jefferson" would justify Federalists in abandoning the caucus agreement
to support Adams.

The cumulative effect of the New York election and all the ensuing
intraparty intrigue fundamentally destabilized the Federalist Party.

"All our friends here are in sad anarchy," Gouverneur Morris observed from New York in early June.

Even as the Federalists went to battle among themselves, the Republicans took every opportunity to assail them, and they had substantial material to use against them. High or low, Federalists had held power for twelve years and could not escape blame for unpopular taxes, excessive spending, and perceived abuses of power tending toward authoritarianism or, as their critics like to call it, monarchism. The Republicans continuously hammered them on these issues, but never more abusively than in the campaign tract *The Prospect before Us*, by scandalmonger James Thomson Callender. In late May, with Adams's full support, the government tried to silence Callender by invoking the Sedition Act one last time. To many, however, the high-handed use of a wartime measure to suppress political criticism during the campaign served only to reenforce the Republican case against continued Federalist rule.

After moving to the United States in 1793 to escape an indictment for sedition in Britain, Callender made a career of exposing the public and private misdeeds of Federalists. His sensational *History of the United States for 1796* accused Hamilton of speculating in government securities, while he was Treasury Secretary, to pay off the husband of his mistress, Maria Reynolds. In a stunningly selfish and self-destructive defense of his public honor, Hamilton, a married man with eight children and a wealthy, socially respected wife who adored him, issued a written statement admitting the extramarital affair but denying any corrupt dealings in securities. This admission haunted Hamilton for the rest of his life by providing fodder for his critics, especially in light of his own out-of-wedlock birth.

Following a stint working for the *Aurora* in Philadelphia during 1798 and a brief hiatus fleeing from prosecution for sedition there, Callender surfaced in Virginia as a writer for the Richmond *Examiner*. His vitriolic assaults on Adams boosted the *Examiner*'s circulation and were reprinted in other Republican newspapers. Jefferson, Madison, and Monroe took an interest in Callender's work and supported it. With funds secretly provided by Jefferson, Callender revised and expanded his articles on Adams into *The Prospect before Us*, which appeared early in 1800. When Jefferson saw an advance copy, he congratulated Callender, "Such papers cannot fail to have the best effect."

Although it exposed no private scandals, the 183-page pamphlet restated the standard Republican charges against Adams's intemperate behavior and imprudent policies in the most caustic terms to date. "The reign of Mr. Adams has, hitherto, been one continued tempest of *malignant* passions," Callender wrote, resulting in a costly war with France solely "for the sake of yoking us into an alliance with the British tyrant." Onerous direct taxes, a soaring national debt, and "profligate expenditure of public money" have resulted, he claimed. "Take your choice," Callender advised readers, "between Adams, war, and beggary, and Jefferson, peace, and competency!" Abigail Adams soon denounced "all the host of Callender's lies."

On May 21, Samuel Chase descended on Richmond in pursuit of Callender. "Judge Chase," the *Aurora* taunted, "the *pious* and *religious* Judge Chase, is going to Virginia where, he says, if a *virtuous* jury can only be collected, he'll punish CALLENDER with a vengeance." At the time, federal courts did collect jurors rather than choose them at random, with the local federal marshal able to handpick individuals for the jury pool. The marshals themselves were political appointees of the President and invariably party loyalists. Republicans charged with sedition never had a chance with a jury composed of local Federalists, especially with Chase on the bench. Washington had appointed Chase to the Supreme Court in 1796, but he was loyal to John Adams and partisan in the extreme. Even after being named to the High Court, Chase continued to campaign for Federalist candidates in his home state of Maryland and publicly endorsed Adams over Jefferson in 1800.

Chase acted virtually as judge, jury, and prosecutor in Callender's highly publicized trial. The indictment accused Callender of maliciously defaming the President. As Chase interpreted the Sedition Act, Callender could escape conviction only by proving the truth of his malicious, defamatory assertions about Adams, many of which were simply matters of opinion. "Can any man of you say that the President is a detestable and criminal man . . . [and] excuse yourself by saying it is but mere opinion?" Chase rhetorically asked defense counsel, which featured three of Virginia's leading Republican lawyers—including the state's attorney general and assembly clerk—all serving without pay. Yet, when Republican Senator John Taylor tried to testify that Adams avowed aristocratic principles much like Callender claimed, Chase barred Taylor's testimony because it did not precisely track Callender's assertions. The appearance of Taylor and Virginia's top Republican lawyers at the trial underscored its partisan nature.

In a public and probably planned protest, Callender's lawyers withdrew from the case after Chase refused to allow them to challenge the constitutionality of the Sedition Act before the jury. Chase called their argument "irregular and inadmissible" in so far as it was directed to a jury rather than the judge. The defense maneuver left Callender visibly at the mercy of Chase, who was predisposed to show no mercy. After the jurors duly convicted Callender pursuant to the judge's instructions, Chase congratulated them on showing "that the laws of the United States could be enforced in Virginia, the *principal object of this prosecution.*" He sentenced Callender to nine months in the Richmond jail, which would keep him behind bars until after the election.

The conviction backfired. The national government had no prisons at the time, and Virginia jails did not harshly confine Sedition Act violators. Portraying himself as a victim of Federalist tyranny, Callender published various attack articles and a second volume of *The Prospect before Us* from jail. Defiantly titling one chapter of the new book "More Sedition," Callender depicted the President as "insolent, inconsistent, and quarrelsome to an extreme. . . . *Every inch which is not fool is rogue.*" In addition, the Republicans turned Chase's bullying tactics at Callender's trial into an effective campaign issue. "The judge spoke of Mr. Callender in the most contemptuous manner," one partisan newspaper reported, "and made many remarks which proved that he was much better qualified to act as *prosecutor* than to act as an impartial judge." Government officials never brought another indictment under the Sedition Act: Apparently they learned not to make writers into martyrs.

Ironically, Jefferson later felt Callender's sting, when, two years after the election, the acerbic writer broke the story that Jefferson kept his slave, Sally Hemings, as a mistress. "Human nature in a hideous form," Jefferson wrote to Monroe in 1802 about Callender, whose body was found floating in Virginia's James River a year later. An inquest ruled that Callender had drowned accidentally while bathing drunk. Unlike Hamilton in the Reynolds affair, Jefferson never publicly admitted to the relationship with Hemings, which remained simply a persistent rumor until the advent of DNA testing two hundred years later.

By the end of May, roughly the midpoint between the effective beginning of the presidential campaign and the December date fixed for voting by electors, the Federalists were unnerved. Virtually nothing had gone their way. Their most respected leader, Washington, had died. Republicans had won critical state elections in Pennsylvania, Virginia, and New York. Without yet producing any diplomatic results, Adams's peace mission to France had dissipated the war fever that once had drawn voters to the Federalist banner. The Additional Army was disbanding. The Sedition Act was discredited. Americans everywhere complained about high taxes and the rising national debt. Worst of all for the Federalists, their party unity was shattered by the caucus decision urging electors to vote equally for Adams and Pinckney, and by Adams's subsequent dismissal of High Federalists from the cabinet. Meanwhile, the Republicans appeared united behind Jefferson for President and Burr for Vice President. As if to symbolize the shift in party fortunes, after Congress adjourned in May 1800, the nation's capital moved from Federalist-friendly Philadelphia to the new town named for Washington just across the Potomac River from staunchly Republican Virginia.

"The Fed[eralist]s have split," the President's youngest son, Thomas

Boylston Adams, wrote to a friend on the last day of May 1800. "Some are resolved to abandon the present leader while some abide by him. . . . General Pinckney will run as V.P. in several eastern states and as President in the Southern [ones], which according to some calculations will put him into the [presidential] chair. All the opinion I can give at present is that the Federal[ist] candidate will not prevail."

His father had not given up, though. Sixty-five years old and toothless but with the energy and emotions of a much younger man, Adams resolved to rally his old supporters one last time. Jefferson had trusted allies in Madison and Monroe; except for his beloved wife, Adams felt alone and embattled. But he soon made a bold move to reinvigorate his prospects. For the first time in American history, a presidential candidate took his campaign on the road.

CHAPTER SIX

A NEW KIND OF CAMPAIGN

*T*HE FUTURE District of Columbia was virtually a wilderness in 1790, when Jefferson bargained with Hamilton to make it the nation's permanent capital. As the sitting Treasury Secretary, Hamilton wanted the national government to assume the states' unpaid Revolutionary War debts. By this, he hoped to give wealthy creditors further reason to support the new Constitution and to facilitate banking and commerce generally. Hamilton's critics savaged the plan as a costly boon to speculators who had bought unpaid war bonds at a discount and done little for the patriot cause. As the Secretary of State with a following among the emerging Southern Republican faction in Congress, Jefferson (working with Madison in the House of Representatives) could supply the votes needed to pass Hamilton's debt-assumption bill. In return, however, he wanted the capital in or near Virginia. They struck a deal: Southern Republicans would vote for debt assumption if Northern Federalists voted for a capital on the banks of the Potomac River, within an easy ride of Washington's Mount Vernon plantation. Congress named the new city for the nation's beloved leader, who took a fatherly interest in its planning throughout the remainder of his life.

For a decade, the government sat first in New York and then in Philadelphia while architects and builders struggled to transform the District's wooded hills and swampy thickets into a capital city of broad avenues and impressive edifices. Local officials renamed diminutive

Goose Creek after Rome's Tiber River in a widely ridiculed effort to lend some classical dignity to the place. Congress counted on the sale of private building lots to supplement meager national appropriations and state funds from Maryland and Virginia to finance the city's construction—but enough never came from any source to meet the needs. The town of Alexandria, Virginia, lay across the Potomac from the main development site, and tiny Georgetown, Maryland, stood upstream, on the far side of Rock Creek, but otherwise the area presented a nearly virgin landscape for a people accustomed to staking their future on the frontier.

"No stranger can be here a day and converse with the proprietors without conceiving himself in the company of crazy people," Treasury Secretary Oliver Wolcott observed upon his arrival in 1800. "Their delusions with respect to their own prospects are without parallel." Speculators all, local boosters talked of the Potomac becoming a major avenue of trade to the west and touted Washington as a future center of commerce. The river's Great Falls above Georgetown and its twisted course frustrated such developments, however. Unlike most other world capitals, Washington remained a one-industry town: the seat of government only.

The architectural plans remained more vision than reality in 1800, when Congress determined nevertheless to transfer the seat of government to Washington. One correspondent wrote in 1800 of it "resembling more the encampment of hunters than a city," and commented on its "few scattering houses, without doors, yards, gardens, streets, or enclosures (there being not one foot of fence to be seen from the Capitol)." Another observer rapped poetic in ridicule:

> *Where tribunes rule, where dusky Davi bow,*
> *And what was Goose Creek once is Tiber now:*
> *This embryo capital, where fancy sees*
> *Squares in morasses, obelisks in trees.*

This critic reported finding only woods to see "Where streets should run and sages ought to be." Only a few public buildings were ready for use by 1800, and only one wing of the Capitol.

The administration moved first, soon after Congress adjourned in May. "Notice. The Office of the Department of State will remove this day from Philadelphia," a paid announcement in the *Aurora* stated on May 28, 1800. "All letters and applications are therefore to be addressed to that Department at the City of Washington from this date." The ad could not supply an exact address because the State Department's building simply did not exist. For now, the department's small staff would borrow space in other structures. The graceful sandstone north wing of the Capitol, along with framework for its south wing, rose on a low hill near the planned city's center surrounded by a small cluster of privately owned structures. On high ground a mile and a half west of the Capitol stood the completed two-story Treasury building, the exterior walls of the War Department offices, and the imposing outer shell of the unfinished Executive Mansion—the future White House. "I cannot but consider our presidents as very unfortunate men if they must live in this dwelling," Wolcott noted. "It was built to be looked at by visitors and strangers," not to be lived in comfortably. The older shops and houses of Georgetown lay two miles farther to the west, across the Rock Creek ravine, on a steep bank above the Potomac.

In May 1800, tree stumps lined the dirt path running from Capitol Hill to the Executive Mansion, with much of the route becoming a muddy swamp in wet weather. Washington did not yet have its own newspaper, though preexisting publications in both Alexandria and Georgetown claimed to serve the new capital too. The town's first bookstore and theater opened later in the year. In the meantime, taverns provided the only public entertainment.

Seven packing crates sufficed to cart the entire archives of the executive branch from Philadelphia to Washington during May and early June. Congress followed when it reconvened in November, while the Supreme Court did not sit in the new capital until 1801. Both houses of Congress and the Court initially squeezed into the Capitol's completed north wing. Lodging was so scarce that members of Congress had to share rooms in local boardinghouses. Wolcott predicted that they would "live like scholars in a college, or monks in a monastery, crowded ten or twelve in one house."

When the First Lady arrived in November to take up residence in the cavernous but still incomplete Executive Mansion, she lamented about the town, "If the twelve years in which this place has been considered as a future seat of government had been [well used], as they would have been if in New England, very many of the present inconveniences would have been removed." Abigail Adams saw beyond the discomforts, though. "It is a beautiful spot and capable of every improvement," she added. "The more I view it, the more I am delighted with it." Clearly, she hoped to stay. Her husband's political fortunes would decide that matter, however, and they were seriously in doubt.

During his twelve years as President or Vice President, John Adams returned to his Quincy, Massachusetts, farm whenever Congress stood in prolonged recess, which meant most of the time. He then conducted the nation's business from home. Washington had established a similar routine during his two terms as President. In May 1800, however, after seeing his wife off to Quincy, purging his cabinet, and pardoning Fries, Adams followed his administration south to Washington for a few weeks before returning north to Massachusetts for the summer and early fall.

The trip was largely ceremonial—Adams did not perform any official duties at the new capital. Rather than go directly from Philadelphia to Washington, however, Adams first went west through Lancaster and York, Pennsylvania, then east through Frederick, Maryland, and south to Washington, before passing through Baltimore and Philadelphia on his way back to Massachusetts, where he remained until November. This took him through Federalist regions of two major states still in play for the election—Pennsylvania and Maryland.

Large crowds and official receptions greeted the President at every stop in both states. Although presidential candidates had never publicly campaigned for election before 1800, Adams desperately needed electoral votes from these states to win. Maryland remained one of the few states where voters chose electors by districts; Pennsylvania might still opt for a popular vote for presidential electors too, if the state's Republican governor and Federalist senate could ever agree on the process. Due to the District of Columbia's unresolved legal status, Washington and Georgetown voters could still participate in Maryland elections. In effect, Adams's month-long journey to the nation's capital became the first presidential campaign trip in American history. It visibly boosted the President's sagging spirits.

"Is gone—what! Gone? Yes! Dead? Mortally, *no*; politically, *aye*? But he has left town. How? In his coach and four with the blinds up," the *Aurora* reported on Adams's departure from Philadelphia on May 27. "Are the blinds to be kept up or down on the way? Out of Philadelphia by all means an open carriage—that the swinish multitude may see who has been in the president's chair four years." The Republican newspaper thus sought to demean the President for reaching out to the people only now, when he needed their votes.

Adams traveled with his wife's nephew, William Shaw, who served as his private secretary, two footmen, and a driver. They stayed in public houses along the way. "Remarkably cheap," Shaw wrote to his aunt about the accommodations, "between two and three dollars at noon and seven and eight at night have been the amount of our bills." Civic leaders and local militia turned out at every community to greet the presidential coach and escort it into and out of town with great fanfare. Bands played, church bells rang, and bonfires lit up villages at night as the President passed through. Adams loved it, and the people loved him. He became once again the Revolutionary War hero of '76 rather than the harried politician of the past four years. Suddenly this often sour, sixty-five-year-old man saw nothing but fertile fields, burgeoning industry, and bright prospects for himself and his country.

"In re-visiting the great counties of Lancaster and York after the interval of three and twenty years," Adams addressed the crowds in Pennsylvania, "I have not only received great pleasure from the civilities of the people, . . . but a much higher delight from the various evidences of their happiness and prosperity." Adams's previous visit came during the American Revolution, when the Continental Congress met in York during the British occupation of Philadelphia. His remarks reminded townspeople of his patriotic service during those dark days of British oppression, and how far they had come under his leadership during the intervening years. Adams spoke glowingly of "the multiplication of inhabitants; the increase of buildings for utility, convenience, and ornament; and the extensive improvements of the soil" since his earlier visit.

His brief address made the case for his reelection, and his listeners got the message. "Your presence strongly renews in our grateful remembrances your many, faithful, and important public services," York's mayor observed on behalf of the citizenry. "As your past life has been so successfully devoted to the service of the American people, it is our fondest hope that heaven may long continue it to add still more to the happiness and respectability of the republic."

In Maryland too, the newspapers reported, Adams "was received with every demonstration of joy." At a public reception in Georgetown, for example, the host formally toasted Adams as "the early, the uniform, the steady and unshaken friend of his country." Other townspeople picked up various Federalist campaign themes, with one publicly toasting "the triumph of religion and order over infidelity and confusion"; another hailing "the Navy and the Army"; and a third raising his glass to Massachusetts, "the nurse of patriots." For his part, Adams toasted the prosperity and enterprise of Georgetown and its inhabitants. "The utmost harmony and conviviality prevailed," a local newspaper reported.

During this trip, Adams spoke from the heart about his impressions of bounty under Federalist rule. "Every inch of the land from Philadelphia to Frederick Town is a perfect garden, luxuriant as any in the world and only equaled, the President thinks, in Flanders and England," Shaw wrote privately to the First Lady. "Our eyes have been delighted throughout the whole journey with cultivated fields and prospects of a fruitful harvest. . . . The people are prosperous and, of course, ought to be happy." Adams viewed America through partisan eyes and believed that what he saw fully justified his continuance in office. Republicans, in contrast, saw high taxes, protective tariffs, and unresolved trade disputes with France and Britain holding back the economy. The reality lay in between. By 1800, the national recession that had marked the early years of Adams's presidency was finally giving way to economic expansion. Regarding the public response to Adams's visit, Shaw simply noted that "the President has been highly gratified."

Raw and unfinished, Washington proved the ultimate test of the President's rosy new view—but it passed. "I have seen many cities and fine places since you left me," he wrote to his wife from the nation's new capital. "I like the seat of government very well and shall sleep or lie awake next winter in the President's house." This future prospect cheered Adams even though, due to the Executive Mansion's incomplete state, on this trip he stayed in a local hotel with his new Secretaries of State and War. "Oh! That I could have a home," he exclaimed to his wife, thinking perhaps of living in the Executive Mansion for the next four years. Whatever happened in the election, Adams would reside in Washington from the time Congress reconvened in November 1800 until the end of his current term in March 1801. Knowing that the Executive Mansion would still remain under construction, several local citizens offered to rent their houses to Adams for that period, but he declined. He decided to move into the unfinished Mansion instead. Adams wanted to reside where his successors would live, even if only for a few months. He had a deep sense of history.

The President crossed the Potomac to make a courtesy call on Martha Washington at Mount Vernon—his first trip to a southern state—and received a surprisingly warm welcome in Republican Virginia. A crowd described by newspapers as the largest ever assembled in Alexandria turned out to greet him. "There was not a man in Alexandria who was not disposed, on the arrival of the President, to treat him with every remark of respect and attention to which, as chief magistrate, he is entitled," one Republican observer noted. Adams used the occasion to speak of both his Revolutionary War service defending Americans from British "injustice" and the "enviable tranquility and uncommon prosperity" that the country had enjoyed ever since. "We are grown a great people," he concluded. "May no error or misfortune throw a veil over the bright prospect before us."

In an address calculated to assert Adams's political independence, this concluding phrase held special meaning. Speaking in the very state where the prosecution occurred, Adams had coopted the title of Callender's scandalous book, *The Prospect before Us*, only eight days after its author had been convicted in a show trial staged by Adams's own administration. The President sought to turn the tables on the Republican attacks against him. Regardless of what his critics might claim, Adams told Virginians, *the prospect before us* is bright.

Having perceived the enduring appeal of his role in the Revolution, Adams determined to fight for reelection by reminding Americans of his patriot credentials, centering himself between the Republicans and High Federalists, and distancing himself from the recent partisanship that he abhorred. At the same time, with his new Secretary of State from Virginia at his side, Adams distinguished himself from the pro-British Hamiltonian wing of his own party by speaking of past British "indignities" rather than recent French ones. After heading an administration seemingly bent on war with France and alliance with Britain, Adams now campaigned on a platform of peace through neutrality. His words, which were widely reported in newspapers across the country, exasperated High Federalists. One of their leaders accused Adams of "rousing the spirit of animosity against the English" to bolster his own position at the expense of the party's so-called British faction, which followed Hamilton and favored Pinckney.

The scene repeated itself when Adams reached Baltimore. The mayor praised the President for his "eminent and long services . . . [that] have so largely contributed to establish us as an independent nation." Adams accepted credit for his past services and hailed the city's burgeoning prosperity. "I wish a continuation in future of rewards to your enterprise, industry, and faculties, in proportion to those which have attended you for the last three and twenty years," he observed. As at earlier stops, Adams urged citizens to stay the course. The *Gazette of the United States*, which spoke for Adams's wing of the Federalist Party, concluded, "The very affectionate reception and respectable addresses which have everywhere met our venerable and vigilant President on his tour to and from Washington has [*sic*] greatly increased the malignity and chagrin of the Jacobins."

Accounts of the President's speeches and the public responses to them appeared in Federalist newspapers across the country, allowing Adams to reach his supporters everywhere and solidify his popular base with his patriotic rhetoric. Of course, state legislators picked electors in ten states, but the people—or, more properly, free, adult, male landowners—voted directly for electors in some states, and popularly chosen electors in Rhode Island, Maryland, and North Carolina could supply the margin of victory in a close contest. Further, even in states where legislators selected electors, the President's popularity could help to elect Federalist legislators who would choose pro-Adams electors. Several states—most notably New Jersey, Pennsylvania, Delaware, and South Carolina—still had state legislative elections scheduled prior to the naming of electors.

The challenge, however, was formidable, and the split within his own party was a vexing problem undermining his efforts. Indeed, Adams's actions during May and June—from his cabinet shake-up through the Revolutionary rhetoric in his stump speeches—excited extensive public speculation about the state of affairs within the Federalist Party. Despite the positive receptions that Adams received on his trip, observations and predictions concerning the apparent intraparty split dogged him along the way. "It appears now certain that the Federalists are determined to drop John Adams: they find him too much of a 'dead lift' to rise to the presidential chair," a local Pennsylvania newspaper commented as the President passed through the state. Newspapers in both Alexandria and Baltimore reprinted an article from the *Trenton*

Federalist claiming that Adams and Jefferson "have come to an agreement on certain *equivalents* to produce a *common interest*, which shall place them again in the seats of magistracy and produce a neutralization of the two great contending parties." Each candidate would discard extremists from his camp and the two would rule together from the center, the article stated. Another Maryland newspaper countered "that Mr. Adams will not be the next president but General Charles Cotesworth Pinckney shall be the man."

At about this time, various newspapers started running periodic projections of the probable electoral-vote count, with some listing Adams, Jefferson, and Pinckney separately, as if in a three-person race. Burr typically was not listed in these tabulations or was named along with Jefferson. During Adams's visit to Baltimore, for example, the city's conservative *Federal Gazette* published a state-by-state analysis projecting that Pinckney would edge out Jefferson in the electoral-vote count, 77 to 70, with Adams coming in a close third with 65 votes. The two Federalist candidates would sweep New England, New Jersey, and Delaware according to this tally. Jefferson would carry New York, Virginia, Kentucky, and Tennessee. The parties would split the three middle- or upper-South states expected to use district voting: Pennsylvania, Maryland, and North Carolina. The *Federal Gazette* gave Pinckney the nod by predicting that independent electors in South Carolina and Georgia would vote for Pinckney along with Jefferson.

Tabulations appearing in Republican newspapers tended to predict a win for Jefferson by projecting that South Carolina electors would vote for the two Republican candidates and that Pennsylvania would either go Republican or not vote. Otherwise, the tallies of all papers were remarkably similar, with partisans on both sides projecting that virtually all electors from New England, New Jersey, and Delaware would vote for Adams and Pinckney, while the lion's share of electors from southern and western states would vote for Jefferson and Burr. With few exceptions, most calculations suggested that the contest remained extremely tight. With New York already decided by a close but conclusive election, most prognosticators suggested that the outcome would likely turn on Pennsylvania, Maryland, and the Carolinas.

Betraying just how set against him so many leaders in his own party had become, when Adams passed through High Federalist strongholds in the Northeast on his journey home to Massachusetts, he received a chillier greeting than in the contested middle states. In Newark, New Jersey, for example, where local party leaders typically staged a formal welcome whenever the presidential party passed through, they did nothing to mark the occasion. "Their silence and quietude at this time," the *Aurora* reported, "is an implied acknowledgment of their disapprobation of some of his late transgressions," notably dismissing Pickering, disbanding the Army, and pardoning Fries. Adams nevertheless continued to defy the High Federalists by seeking center ground even on their home turf. Speaking at an official reception in New London, Connecticut, Adams pointed to his part "in our important and glorious revolution." At a formal dinner at Boston's Faneuil Hall, Adams toasted "the prescribed patriots, [John] Hancock and Samuel Adams"—two popular Anti-Federalist former Massachusetts governors. High Federalists reportedly boycotted the Boston dinner and became enraged upon learning that Adams had toasted their former political foes. "The man that would give that toast ought to be d——d, and kick'd out of the Hall," a local partisan allegedly declared. "Has he turned Jacobin?"

In Massachusetts, certain prominent High Federalists with ties to Essex County—a wealthy center of commerce near Boston—were known derisively as the "Essex Junto." John Hancock had coined the term in 1778 to label those he viewed as his most reactionary opponents—and it stuck. The core group included Ames, Pickering, Senators George Cabot and Benjamin Goodhue, and Theophilus Parsons. Adams now began using this old term to attack his new opponents within the party. In a letter dated July 19, Cabot complained of Adams having denounced "High Federalists as 'a Junto of incorrigible Aristocrats'" and expressed his hope that the President's Faneuil Hall toast would turn "judicious and discerning men" against him. Ames also criticized Adams's toast: "The great man has been south as far as Alexandria making his addressers acquainted with his revolutionary merits. . . . He inveighs against the British faction and the Essex Junto like one possessed." Cabot and Ames had regularly dined with Adams in the past, but snubbed him now. "It would be embarrassing to know what to say," Ames noted. In July, Goodhue wrote of "Mr. Adams' insufferable madness and vanity."

As much as it infuriated High Federalists, the public display of his Revolutionary Era credentials served Adams well in his contest with Jefferson. Adams was an early advocate of American independence, a leader in the patriot cause, and an ardent nationalist. Although he admired its balanced system of government, Adams hated Britain and distrusted its leaders. Reminding voters of these aspects of his service and character acted as a perfect foil to Republican attacks on him as a pro-British monarchist. The approach had struck a responsive chord with citizens during his June trip through the battleground states of Pennsylvania and Maryland, and Adams continued using it into the summer and fall. In response to a midsummer testimonial from citizens in North Carolina, for example, Adams referred to his forty years in public service. "No man ever served his country with purer intentions or for more disinterested motives," he boasted. Distinguishing himself from the faction within his own party that supported the Additional Army and opposed peace with France, he added, "I never shall love war or seek it for the pleasure, profit, or honor of it."

In a tactical victory for Adams, his natural supporters—the moderates in his party—began taking a similar tack to their President's. In an open breach with High Federalists, they joined Adams in embracing the decision to resume negotiations with France, and made it a major campaign issue. Adams referred to his peace mission as "the most glorious act of my life," Fisher Ames complained bitterly in September. "His partisans boast of its popularity and that only a few like Hamilton and the Essex Junto condemn it." Throughout the summer, Adams anxiously awaited word from his negotiators, hoping that reports of success might brighten his election prospects. The intelligence that he received remained encouraging but inconclusive.

Leading High Federalists monitored Adams's words closely throughout the summer and perceived that they were directed as much against Hamilton and Pinckney as against Jefferson. "He everywhere denounces [High Federalists] as an oligarchish faction [that is] combining to drive him from office and to appoint Pinckney," House Speaker Theodore Sedgwick complained. Adams's whole plan, Ames warned in August, "is, by prating about impartiality, Americanism, liberty, and equality, to gull the weak among the Feds" and turn them against Hamilton, Pinckney, and the Essex Junto. Some leaders on both sides of the Federalist divide openly discussed breaking the party into two—one archconservative, one pragmatic. Inevitably they concluded that the American political system could not sustain a third party, however. The factions would fight for the party's soul and unite to battle the Republicans. "Perhaps a party, whenever it thinks itself strong enough, naturally splits," Ames mused. "Nothing but dread of its rival will bind it firmly enough together."

As a warm spring turned into a hot summer, more Federalists took sides in their party's increasingly bitter and public breakup. On the one side, many Federalists rallied to their embattled President as he defended his pragmatic course and reminded Americans of his long, patriotic service to the country. Even if they did not like him, Federalist leaders could not deny that Adams remained the party's only viable popular candidate. Pinckney could win only by bootstrapping on to Adams in the North and capturing a few additional votes on his own in the South. "If under the present administration the country has prospered;" the High Federalist Congressman Robert Harper now wrote in an open letter to his constituents, "if peace has been preserved with honor during a conflict which has involved almost every nation except ourselves; if commerce has been protected, industry been made to flourish, public credit maintained, tranquility preserved at home, and the character of the nation raised abroad; I ask, what more could any administration have done? Where is the need for change?"

Harper may have simply been trying to preserve the façade of Federalist unity, but New York Governor John Jay and the respected Maryland jurist and former governor Thomas Johnson unequivocally took Adams's side. "It really appears to me that the mission of our envoys to France has been treated with too much asperity," Jay wrote in defense of Adams. "His attachment to the dictates of honor and good faith, even supposing it to have been too scrupulous, is amiable and praiseworthy."

On the other side, more High Federalists began speaking out against Adams even at the risk of losing the presidency. "The public feeling is opposed to the censure of Mr. Adams in this quarter," Cabot wrote from Massachusetts in July. "It is impossible, however, that Mr. Adams should govern as a Federal man and this must be seen presently by all sagacious men."

Cabot and his crowd never cared about following public opinion; they wanted to lead it. As High Federalists, they sought to purge the party of Adams despite—indeed, perhaps in part because of—his popularity. In some respects, he represented a greater threat to them than Jefferson: Better the devil without than the devil within. In a letter that laid bare the High Federalists' election strategy, Cabot had reminded Wolcott several months earlier about the "great pains" that leaders in their party had taken "to make it believed that the French revolutionary system was a war against real liberty and legitimate property in every country." The strategy had helped the Federalists get elected and enact their policies. But following Adams's peace overture, Cabot noted, "It is asked now, if this were true, would the heads of our nation be seen negotiating with France?" Federalists could not effectively invoke revolutionary France as a boogeyman if their own President was reaching out to its leaders. Expressing his final break with the President, Wolcott now wrote back to Cabot, "If General Pinckney is not elected, all good men will find cause to regret the present inaction of the Federal Party" against Adams.

Hamilton, who by this time wanted nothing more than to unseat Adams, saw the political landscape in much the same way as Cabot. Throughout New England, Adams remained popular with Federalists "of the second class," as Hamilton contemptuously referred to those he deemed lesser lights within his own party. "The leaders of the first class" know better, he maintained in a letter to Wolcott. This state of affairs posed a problem for Hamilton's plan of swinging the election to Pinckney through a combination of Federalist votes from the Northeast and favorite-son votes from South Carolina. If New England electors abandoned Pinckney to save Adams by casting their second votes for someone like John Jay, as happened to Pinckney's brother in 1796, then either Jefferson or Adams would prevail. To prevent this from happening again, Hamilton decided to meet with leading New England Federalists and urge them to stick with Pinckney even at the risk of Adams's loss.

Making the most of the short time remaining in his tenure as Inspector General of the Additional Army, Hamilton set out in June to bolster Pinckney and undermine Adams among potential Federalist electors in New England during a four-state tour ostensibly designed to bid farewell to the disbanding troops. Traveling in full military regalia, Hamilton planned to meet with Federalist leaders throughout the region. Surely they still deferred to him, he believed, even if Adams did not.

Any military purposes for Hamilton's trip took a backseat to political ones. "The General did not come to disband the troops," Abigail Adams explained in a letter to her son, Thomas. "His visit was merely an electioneering business, to feel the pulse of the New England states, and to impress those upon whom he could have any influence to vote for Pinckney and bring him on as president." Her husband had heard as much from several of those subjected to Hamilton's pleas. By this time, the First Lady was referring to Hamilton as "the little cock sparrow general" and Fisher Ames was mocking her as being "as complete a politician as any lady in the old French court."

The General did review the troops at Oxford, Massachusetts—the

Army's northern base. The much-maligned soldiers mustered in dress parade to hear Hamilton deliver an emotional speech that some observers compared to Washington's legendary farewell address to the Revolutionary Army—a tribute they scarcely deserved if even half of the stories about them had any merit. According to widely reported Republican accounts, these full-time soldiers had used their idle time to prey on the local citizenry without serving any meaningful purpose in the Quasi-War with France. Addressing the soldiers, however, Hamilton blamed their dismissal solely on Adams.

Hamilton's other stops had purely political purposes. Adams could not win, Hamilton told Federalists in Connecticut, Massachusetts, New Hampshire, and Rhode Island. Only a solid vote for Pinckney could hold the presidency for the party. Some listened; others balked. The high point for Hamilton surely came when the Essex Junto turned out in force for a gala banquet in his honor at Boston's elegant Concert Hall. "At no public feast ever prevailed greater harmony, good humor, and public spirit," one High Federalist newspaper reported. Hamilton hit the low point, however, when he tried to lobby Rhode Island Governor Arthur Fenner. "I then asked him what Mr. Adams had done that he should be tipped out the tail of the cart," Fenner recalled telling Hamilton, adding "that my attachment for Mr. Adams was much greater now . . . that he had sent envoys to France . . . [and] had disbanded an unnecessary army." When pressed by Hamilton, Fenner reported saying that he preferred *even* Jefferson to Pinckney, "for the British yoke I abhorred." The Republican campaign to link High Federalists such as Hamilton and Pinckney with the British was working; at least Fenner seemed to believe the charge.

Ultimately, Hamilton's trip did little more than harden positions within both Federalist camps. "I yesterday returned from an excursion through [four] of the [five] eastern states," Hamilton wrote on July 1. "The greatest number of strong minded men in New England are not only satisfied of the expediency of supporting Pinckney, as giving the best chance against Jefferson, but even prefer him to Adams; yet in the body of that people there is a strong personal attachment to [the President]." If by New England's "strong minded men" Hamilton meant the Essex Junto, then he was probably right—but in general New Englanders and their elected leaders were determined to stick by Adams.

Despite the division between High Federalists and moderates that threatened to tear apart their party from the top down, most New Englanders remained loyal to both the Federalist Party and Adams. High Federalists may have best represented their commercial and maritime interests in the national government but New Englanders had also grown to trust and respect Adams despite his quirks. He was their region's hero of the Revolution and nothing that Hamilton could say about him would tarnish that reputation. The structure of Federalism in New England, complex as it was, simply rested on too firm a foundation for Hamilton's gusts to shake it even as they wreaked havoc elsewhere. Certainly his belligerent style played poorly in the region. He bullied local leaders and belittled those who disagreed with him. "Electioneering topics were his principal theme," one Adams supporter said of Hamilton's visit. "In his mode of handling them, he did not appear to be the great general which his talents designate him." Even Ames now conceded about Hamilton, "You know he is the most frank of men."

As Adams, Hamilton, and their respective factions struggled for pre-eminence within Federalist ranks during the summer of 1800, Jefferson and his supporters brought added discipline to the Republican camp. Overturning the established political order by unseating an incumbent President in times of relative peace and prosperity required a concerted, committed effort by the opposition. Republicans' shared dread of continued Federalist rule bound them ever more firmly together as the year progressed.

In private letters, Jefferson assessed his prospects. He felt buoyed by growing public disillusionment with Federalist policies. "The Alien and Sedition Acts have already operated in the south as powerful sedatives of the XYZ inflammation," he wrote in 1799 to maverick politician Elbridge Gerry of Massachusetts. "In your quarter, where violations of principle are either less regarded or more concealed, the direct tax is likely to have the same effect and to excite inquires into the object of the enormous expenses and taxes we are bringing on."

Despite all the good news for his party, however, in the late summer of 1800, when Jefferson projected the probable electoral votes of the various states, victory was still far from certain. "I have a letter from [Senator Pierce] Butler in which he supposes that the Republican [electoral] vote of North Carolina will be but a bare majority" of the state's total, he wrote to Madison. North Carolina, with its district voting for electors, could split its vote between the parties. "South Carolina," Jefferson continued, will be "unanimous either with them or against them, but not certainly which. Dr. [Benjamin] Rush and Burr give favorable accounts of Jersey. [Connecticut Republican leader Gideon] Granger and Burr even count with confidence on Connecticut, but that is impossible." With New England in the Federalist column, the middle states split, and the Carolinas still in play at least for Pinckney, Jefferson could not count on discontent with Federalist policies translating into victory for him. "The unquestionable Republicanism of the American mind will break through the mist," he assured Gerry, but it might take time.

In an overt gesture at active campaigning of the type that he regularly engaged in during the run-up to the election, in this same letter to Gerry, Jefferson set forth the "principles" that would guide his presidency. It offered a virtual election platform for the Republican ticket, various planks of which he regularly repeated in other letters during the course of the campaign. These principles, which Jefferson called "my political faith," fit into three basic categories: restoring civil liberties; curbing the excessive growth and power of the national government, particularly of its executive branch; and protecting states' rights. They became the chief Republican campaign themes. In announcing them, Jefferson sought to rebut Federalist charges that he would overturn the constitutional and religious order.

Jefferson began his letter with a vow: "I do then, with sincere zeal, wish an inviolable preservation of our present federal Constitution according to the true sense in which it was adopted by the states." Federalists had violated the Constitution, Jefferson implied, and he would defend it. His presidency would rest on principles, while the Federalists simply sought power and their own economic gain. From this starting point, Jefferson went on to state his principles in stark, dramatic terms.

"I am for freedom of religion and against all maneuvers to bring about a legal ascendancy of one sect over another," Jefferson wrote, "for freedom of the press and against any violations of the Constitution to silence by force and not by reason the complaints or criticism, just or unjust, of our citizens against the conduct of their agents." The former principle neatly distinguished Jefferson from New England Federalists, including Adams, who defended the established churches in their states against challenges from a growing body of ecclesiastic dissenters ranging from Baptist revivalists to avowed secularists. Voters knew that Jefferson authored his state's 1786 Statute for Religious Freedom, which disestablished the Episcopal Church in Virginia. Whether or not it reflected Jefferson's actual motives, casting the Statute as a hammer blow for the religious liberty of dissenting Christians rather than for a secular society put Jefferson's position in its best light for America's Christian majority. The latter principle reasserted Jefferson's repudiation of the Sedition Acts and placed that opposition in hallowed Constitutional terms. Jefferson stood for civil liberties, Republicans asserted, and would rule on behalf of the people rather than for the special interests.

"I am for a government rigorously frugal and simple, applying all the possible savings of the public revenue to the discharge of the national debt," Jefferson added. "I am for relying, for internal defense, on our militia solely, till actual invasion . . . and not for a standing army in time of peace, which may overawe the public sentiment." He chose his words carefully. Jefferson opposed both the direct tax imposed by the Federalists in 1798 to finance the military buildup and the Additional Army, which he viewed as unnecessary and potentially dangerous. The national government also used tax revenue to repay its credi-tors, including bond speculators profiting from Hamilton's controver-sial program of state-debt assumption by the federal government. To reassure these speculators—and Gerry, who had supported Hamilton's program—Jefferson added about debt-assumption that "from the moment of its being adopted by the constituted authorities, I became religiously principled in the sacred discharge of it to the uttermost far-thing." As President, Jefferson promised to eliminate the need for the direct taxes by cutting future spending, especially on a standing army, rather than by reneging on prior government commitments. The elec-tion of 1800 would not overthrow property rights, he as much as assured Gerry.

"I am not for transferring all the powers of the states to the general government, and all those of that government to the executive branch," Jefferson stressed. "Our country is too large to have all its affairs directed by a single government," he explained in a subsequent letter. "I do verily believe, that if the principle were to prevail of a common law being in force in the United States (which principle . . . reduces us to a single consolidated government), it would become the most corrupt government on the earth."

For Jefferson and the Republicans, the primary threat of govern-ment corruption lay in an all-powerful presidency immune from the checks and balances of congressional and state authority. They saw popular elections as a bulwark for freedom and never tired of remind-ing voters that, in his earlier writings, Adams had expressed admiration for the British system of a constitutional monarchy and hereditary House of Lords. "I am opposed to the monarchizing" of government, Jefferson wrote to Gerry, "with a view to conciliate a first transition to a President and Senate for life, and from that to an hereditary tenure of these offices." Even though Adams never proposed anything so dras-tic for the United States, Hamilton and some High Federalists had. Relentlessly attacking the most extreme elements of Federalism, Republicans ran as states'-rights democrats and portrayed their oppo-nents as power-hungry monarchists.

"These, my friend, are my principles," Jefferson concluded. "They are unquestionably the principles of the great body of our fellow citizens." While acknowledging his support for republican rule in France, Jefferson took pains to deny having undue allegiance to any foreign government. "The first object of my heart is my own country," he told Gerry. "I have not one farthing of interest nor one fiber of attachment out of it, nor a single motive of preference of any one nation to another but in proportion as they are more or less friendly to us." Although Jefferson typically urged recipients of his political correspondence to keep the contents in strict confidence, he placed no such restriction on Gerry regarding the principles set forth in this letter. These, he wrote, "I fear not to avow."

Unlike in 1796, when Jefferson remained aloof from the politicking on his behalf, four years of Federalist rule under Adams convinced him that Republicans must win in 1800. Consequently, despite his personal distaste for campaigning, Jefferson supported Republican polemicists, distributed partisan literature, and wrote a steady stream of highly political letters. "Politics are such a torment that I would advise every one I love not to mix with them," he wrote to his daughter, Martha, early in 1800, yet he was already deeply engaged in the presidential campaign. His involvement in it only deepened as the election approached.

When Congress recessed in May, Jefferson offered to make a campaign stop in Richmond, Virginia, on his return trip to Monticello—but Governor Monroe waved him off. Any direct campaigning by Jefferson might lead the new Secretary of State from Virginia, John Marshall, to respond in kind on behalf of Adams, Monroe warned, "whereby you would be involved in a kind of competition." Better to leave well enough alone, the governor reasoned. Jefferson's formidable communication skills lay in writing, not public speaking, and he never again proposed making a campaign appearance. He remained at Monticello for the summer, writing and receiving letters. "Rally round the Constitution," he urged in an August letter to a Connecticut Republican, "rescue it from the destruction with which it has been threatened."

*   *   *

While Jefferson therefore returned to Monticello to campaign quietly during the summer of 1800, Burr was as hyperactive as usual. He "is intriguing with all his might in New Jersey, Rhode Island, and Vermont," Hamilton warned in August, "and there is a possibility of some success to his intrigues."

Burr made a late summer trip through New England to meet with potential electors and urge them to vote Republican. It was a futile effort, but he nevertheless sounded optimistic about the prospects for Jefferson in the region. "He will have all the votes of Rhode Island," Burr assured Madison about the only New England state that would choose its electors in a direct popular election. "Nothing can be pronounced of [New] Jersey, but everything may be hoped," he added about a state that had not yet elected the legislators who would choose its electors. Burr had already written to Jefferson promising him votes from Connecticut, where the legislature was also still to be elected. Burr hinted that these Northeast electors might vote for Jefferson in place of Pinckney rather than vote a strict Federalist Party ticket. This, he suggested, would give the Virginian a comfortable margin of victory over all three national candidates in the final tally. It was all fancy, but perhaps not folly.

Critics later charged Burr with deliberately misleading Southern Republicans about the situation in the Northeast. He did so, they claimed, so that Republican electors in the South would feel free to vote unanimously for him and Jefferson, not dropping any votes, without fearing a tie between the two Republican candidates. Although no hard evidence supports this charge, Burr's leading biographer concluded that "the logic of it is hard to ignore."

Burr was not the only one drumming up votes for Republicans. During the summer, Virginia became a hotbed of Republican Party activity. In 1796, one Virginia electoral district had chosen a Federalist elector, who duly voted for Adams and Thomas Pinckney. This time, the state's Republican Party leaders were determined to shore up all of the state's electoral votes for Jefferson and Burr.

They had already successfully replaced district voting with a general ticket as Virginia's method of choosing electors. Under the new rules, candidates for elector ran statewide, and the top twenty-one finishers served as electors. With the general population of the state heavily Republican, this system strongly favored a Republican sweep, though it did not guarantee it. Virginia Federalists countered by challenging the equity of the election-law change. Fairness demanded that each party receive electoral votes roughly proportional to its strength in the state, Federalists claimed, which was more likely to happen under the old rules of district elections than under the new general-ticket law. With the Republicans firmly in control of the state legislature, Federalists could not hope for a change in the law. Nevertheless, their pleas for equity might peel off enough votes for at least some of their candidates to finish among the top twenty-one. Presumably to bolster the chances of this outcome, Federalists in the state ran on the "American Republican Ticket," as opposed to Jefferson's regular "Republican Ticket." Adding to the confusion, Federalists also nominated one candidate with the same first and last name as that of an opponent, forcing Republican voters to identify their candidate's middle initial when voting.

To enhance their prospect of winning all of Virginia's electoral votes, Republicans nominated stellar candidates known throughout the state. Revered Revolutionary Era leaders George Wythe and Edmund Pendleton—both in their midseventies—topped the ticket, which also included Madison, over a half-dozen former or future governors or members of Congress, three state militia generals, and representatives from several of the first families of Virginia. This ticket, which probably constituted the most illustrious slate of electors ever offered in any state, demonstrated the commitment of Virginia's political elite to the Republican cause. An official Federalist circular, issued in late May, resorted to the bizarre charge that Republicans sought to influence voters by nominating candidates with "great and imposing names." The circular described Federalist candidates as "common" men "like yourselves"—an ironic boast for an elitist party. A midsummer Republican circular responded in defense of its candidates, "There is indeed an influence in their names: an influence which we dare to avow: an influence in which we glory." A party leader wrote to Jefferson, "I cannot but augur well of a cause which calls out from their retirement such venerable patriots as Wythe and Pendleton."

Watching the aristocracy of Washington's home state fall in line behind Jefferson stunned High Federalists. Calling them "fools in earnest as to democracy," Fisher Ames denounced the "extreme sensibility of the good men of Virginia to silly principles and silly people." Jefferson, he noted, "wrote some such stuff about the will of majorities" that would cause a New Englander to "lose his rank among men of sense." In a similar vein, Hamilton observed early in the campaign, "The spirit of faction . . . is more violent than ever" in Virginia. However much they hated and feared Virginia's aristocratic Republicans, however, these and other prominent High Federalists recognized them as able political adversaries. Without them, Republicanism would be leaderless; with them, it represented a formidable foe to Federalism.

Indeed, Virginia's Republican leaders took a decisive step during the campaign toward the formal institutionalization of their party. For the first time by members of any state party, Republicans in Virginia named a general committee and county committees. This structure, which was in place by the summer, enabled state Republicans to disseminate information and organize voters. According to the official record, these county committees were directed "to receive all communication from the general committee, and to send to [it] such information as they shall deem necessary to promote the Republican ticket."

The general committee's chairman soon wrote to Jefferson, "We have begun our correspondence with the [county] committees, and mean to keep up a regular intercourse upon the subjects which may seem to require it." This included distributing a midsummer circular designed to counter Federalists' appeals to Virginians' loyalty to George Washington and his party. "Let the contest be considered as it really is, between Thomas Jefferson and John Adams," the circular asserted. "Consummate your reverence for the memory of Washington, not by employing it as an engine of election, but by declaring that even his name shall not prevent the free use of your own understandings. As a friend to liberty, we believe Jefferson second to no man, and the experience of no man has afforded better lessons for its preservation." Most critically, the general committee worked through the county committees to distribute handwritten cards listing the entire slate of Republican candidates that voters could sign and deposit in the ballot box on Election Day. Voting was done by signed ballots in Virginia, but voters needed to supply their candidates' names.

Even as Republican leaders in Virginia tried to stir up voting for their party's ticket, they tried to damp down partisan protests. Indeed, they worried that violence would erupt as tensions rose during the run-up to the election. In particular, Madison and Monroe feared that the administration might seek to incite violent protests by enforcing the hated Sedition Act in Virginia, and thereby make the Virginia Republicans look like French Jacobins. They interpreted the May 1800 prosecution of Republican scandalmonger James Callender in Richmond—the only such trial ever held in Virginia—in this light and sought to reduce the public outrage against it. By this time, they saw every act in a partisan context, even a criminal prosecution.

As the trial approached, Monroe sent out word to Richmond-area Republican leaders to keep their partisans calm. If the Federalists expected to incite a violent Republican reaction to the prosecution, Monroe wrote to Madison at the time, "they are deceived as . . . an attempt to excite a hot water insurrection will fail." In his reply, Madison expressed his approval of this course of action, noting that it seemed especially wise at a time when the Federalist Party, by its extreme actions in enforcing the Sedition Act, seemed "so industriously co-operating in its own destruction." Virginians would submit to the law, Monroe assured Jefferson on the eve of Callender's trial, "and give no pretext for comment to their discredit."

More than ever, Virginia Republicans did not want to act like French Jacobins or give any justification for the Federalists' domestic-security measures. With the collective fears inspired by the XYZ Affair and Fries's Rebellion finally easing—due in part to Adams's handling of them—any new threat of disorder would play into Federalists' hands. In 1799, Jefferson had expressed concern that, by their repressive acts, the administration might attempt to "force a resistance which with the aid of an army may end in monarchy." As the election approached, Republican leaders called for peace in Virginia and used the new party structure to foster it. The trial, which passed without incident, became a testament to Federalist oppression rather than Republican reaction.

By midsummer, Americans were watching a new form of campaign for the presidency. Adams had traveled through the middle states, appealing directly to potential voters. With this trip, and a series of policy adjustments, he had rallied his supporters, fended off the High Federalists' effort to oust him from the ticket, and secured his position as the party's principal nominee. Meanwhile, perhaps inspired by Burr's success in building a political machine in New York, Virginia Republicans organized themselves to deliver votes for their party's candidates. In some other states holding elections in the fall, such as Maryland and New Jersey, similar party organizations soon appeared. For the first time, the outlines of a modern presidential campaign took shape in various places across the country focused on a series of state elections in Rhode Island, New Jersey, Pennsylvania, Maryland, Virginia, and the Carolinas—some for legislators, others for electors—scheduled for the fall. Everyone now knew that these elections would decide the presidency.

CHAPTER SEVEN

FOR GOD AND PARTY

SUMMER was a quiet season in the American political calendar during the early national period. Legislatures traditionally convened in the winter and spring, drawing public attention to political matters. Adding to the interest, some places held town meetings or local and state elections in the late winter or early spring. Politicians used this time to plot and posture with an eye toward the fall, when most elections occurred. When summer came, legislators went home, and other concerns took precedence over politics. Farmers would tend to their fields and flocks, the rich might move to their summer homes, and everyone would complain about the heat. Epidemic diseases, particularly cholera and malaria, became a threat in some urban areas. Life slowed, and only extreme partisans showed much concern about politics. Campaigns stalled and candidates struggled to get attention or simply took a break themselves.

Despite the heightened level of partisanship that marked the year, political issues lost traction during the summer of 1800 as well. Even Adams and Jefferson settled into something akin to their customary summer routines at home. With no critical elections scheduled for the summer, observers and participants had time to assess the state of play, which was so much in flux.

The spring elections in New York were touted as decisive before they occurred, and they might have been if Federalists had won them.

For Jefferson to prevail in the final count, however, Republicans still needed at least a half-dozen more electoral votes from northern or middle states than New York's twelve to supplement those expected to come their way from southern and western states, and even more to offset any votes for Adams or Pinckney from the Carolinas. Pennsylvania with its fifteen electoral votes could supply them all if Federalists in the State Senate either gave in to the will of the governor and the State Assembly or lost their slim majority after the October elections. Alternatively, if Federalists could keep Pennsylvania from voting or split the vote there, then a Federalist sweep in Maryland could supply the margin of victory for Adams or Pinckney. If these two contested middle states broke about evenly, New Jersey stayed in the Federalist column, as was expected, and North Carolina voters chose at least some Federalist electors in their district elections, as even many Republicans conceded, then South Carolina legislators would decide the presidency with the selection of their eight electors. No one could know what they would do until they did it.

As the overall debate quieted considerably with legislators and the candidates headed home for the summer, in its place issues of extraordinary concern to select groups of voters rose to the fore. One issue that gained particular attention was the supposed scandal regarding Jefferson's religion.

Federalists hoped that concerns about Jefferson's views on religion and its relationship to government would rally Christians to their side. In 1800, the United States remained a fundamentally Christian nation even as the nature of its religious establishment was evolving. Before the Revolution, colonies typically provided government support for one favored denomination—usually the Church of England or, in New England, the Congregational Church—and required officeholders to profess their faith in Jesus Christ as God and savior. During the Revolution, the Church of England in America renounced the English King's leadership and became the Episcopal Church, but still it lost its established status in most states. Dissenting sects—particularly the Baptists and the Methodists—flourished among the people as revivalism spread.

Many Revolutionary Era leaders gravitated toward various forms of Deism or Unitarianism that acknowledged God as the Creator of nature and nature's laws but denied that God intervened in natural processes through miracles and viewed Jesus as simply a great moral teacher. Among statesmen, Franklin, Jefferson, and Thomas Paine publicly supported this movement, but Washington, Adams, and even Hamilton privately drifted in the same direction even as they endorsed public displays of conventional religiosity. As political conservatives, Federalists tended to value religion, tradition, and family authority as means of fostering social, economic, and political order. In contrast, Jefferson and many Republicans saw religion as a personal matter and denounced established churches as fetters on freedom.

Pushed by an unlikely coalition of dissenting Christians and principled secularists, many states shifted from establishing only one denomination to authorizing government support for all churches—though in practice those funds either dried up or continued flowing along traditional channels. Presbyterians in particular vied with Episcopalians and Congregationalists for cultural authority in many places. Members of these mainstream denominations felt that their traditional religious beliefs and practices were under siege from the forces of Enlightenment secularism on the one side and evangelical revivalism on the other. There were Deists and secularists in the uppermost echelons of both parties, but the issue of religion had become increasingly partisan in the wake of the French Revolution, in which the Jacobins had moved so abruptly and violently to break the back of church authority. Republican support for the revolution in France was portrayed by many Federalists as opposition to Christianity. They pointed to what Jefferson had done in Virginia and drew extravagant parallels between it and recent developments in France.

In 1786, Virginia had leapfrogged other states by enacting Jefferson's Statute of Religious Freedom. By law, the state had established the Episcopal Church since colonial days, but in one jump, this land-mark legislation repealed that law and provided instead that "no man shall be compelled to frequent or support *any* religious worship, place, or ministry whatsoever." Further, it abolished a religious test for pub-lic office by adding "that our civil rights have no dependence on our religious opinion any more than our opinions in physics or geometry."

For Jefferson and Madison, who led the fight for the law's enact-ment, those two principles—no state support for religion and no reli-gious test for civil rights—constituted fundamental freedoms endowed by the Creator. "Whereas, Almighty God hath created the mind free," the statute declared in a ringing affirmation that has echoed through the centuries, "all attempts to influence it by temporal punishments and burthens, or by civil incapacitations, tend only to beget habits of hypocrisy and meanness, and are a departure from the plan of the Holy author of our religion." As Jefferson saw it, state churches in Europe, stereotypically with bloated, corrupt hierarchies, invoked irrational superstitions to oppress people and support despots. Through his Statute of Religious Freedom and similar laws, he hoped for the free-dom from religion as much as the freedom of religion.

At the national level, the Constitution soon followed Virginia in pre-cluding a religious test for public office and, with the ratification of the First Amendment in 1791, barring a national establishment of religion. Some states continued to provide public funds for churches into the 1800s, however, and to require that government officials profess faith in Christ or, more generally, in God. Many Americans believed that, in order to act right, people needed the precepts of religion backed by the promise of Heaven and the threat of Hell. They viewed Jefferson's sup-port for the separation of church and state as reckless. For some, the Vir-ginian's apparent rejection of core Christian doctrines simply made matters worse. A leader should rely on God, Christ, and the Bible, they believed. In 1800, Federalists could point to the terrors of Jacobin France as the logical consequence of trying to rule without religion.

Two years before the election, Timothy Dwight, America's leading evangelical minister and a virtual institution in his home state of Connecticut, laid down the gauntlet against Jeffersonian secularism in a published Fourth of July patriotic oration. He took a biblical passage from the Revelation of John as his text:

> *And the sixth angel poured out his vile [of God's wrath]. . . . And I saw three unclean spirits like frogs come out of the mouth of the dragon, and out of the mouth of the beast, and out of the mouth of the false prophet. For they are the spirits of devils, working miracles, which go forth unto the kings of the earth, and the whole world, to gather them to the battle of . . . Armageddon.*

Biblical prophecies about the end of time loomed large in Dwight's theology and they inevitably influenced his political philosophy. A Calvinist, he believed that the state needed the church and political leaders needed Christ.

Interpreting this biblical prophecy from John's Revelation, Dwight posited that Americans were living under the outpouring of the sixth vial of God's wrath, when the Antichrist's empire crumbled and humankind embarked on what he called "a professed and unusual opposition to God" leading directly to the Final Judgment. Dwight saw the crumbling of the Antichrist's empire in the collapse of Roman Catholicism before the revolutionary armies of France and marked opposition to God in the rise of Enlightenment naturalism. Deluded by French philosophy, princes and teachers in Europe had become proponents of "irreligion and atheism," Dwight asserted. "The being of God was denied and ridiculed," he added. "Chastity and natural affection were declared to be nothing more than groundless preju-dices." Spiritual and social ills merged in his conception of them, with their common root in demonic forces allegedly channeled through the secret Society of the Illuminati in Europe.

In Dwight's mind, Jefferson and the Republicans, as proponents of French secularism in America, served as the unwitting link between this vast satanic conspiracy and the United States. "The great bond of union to every people is its government," Dwight declared. Without

Christian rulers, "there is no center left of intelligence, counsel, or action; no system of purposes or measures; no point of rallying or confidence."

Secular chaos had replaced Christian order in France, he observed, and it could happen in the United States too if anticlerical leaders like Jefferson took power. "For what end shall we be connected with men of whom this is the character and conduct?" Dwight asked. "Is it that our churches may become temples of reason? . . . Is it that we may see the Bible cast into a bonfire? . . . Is it that we may see our wives and daughters the victims of legal prostitution?" All these acts had become commonplace in France, he claimed. "Shall our sons become the disciples of Voltaire . . . or our daughters the concubines of the Illuminati?" Only Christian leaders can foster ordered liberty, Dwight maintained. "If our religion were gone, our state of society would perish with it, and nothing would be left which would be worth defending."

Dwight's words carried weight. Dubbed the "Pope of Connecticut" by his detractors, Dwight served as president of Yale College from 1795 to 1817. From that post, he shepherded both his state's Federalist Party and its established church. His brother represented Connecticut in Congress. Grandson of the legendary evangelical theologian Jonathan Edwards and first cousin of Aaron Burr, Dwight was an ordained minister in the state-supported Congregational Church. In books, sermons, lectures, and even poems, he used his keen intellect and sharp wit to promote his views of politics and religion.

"Will you trust philosophers?" Dwight asked in his July 4 oration. "Men who set truth at nought, who make justice a butt of mockery, who doubt the being and providence of God?" Widely known for his interest in philosophy and science, Jefferson bore the brunt of Dwight's assault. On the eve of the 1800 election, an appreciative Federalist leader in Massachusetts wrote, "Dr. Dwight is here stirring us up to oppose the Demon of Jacobinism." By then, however, Dwight was not alone in this religious crusade.

During the anxious months leading up to the presidential election, countless tracts, essays, and sermons damned Jefferson as a Deist or worse and called on Christians to oppose his candidacy. The flurry of activity bore the hallmarks of a coordinated campaign, but may have simply emanated from the collective angst of countless Christians, especially from the established churches of the Northeast, confronted with the prospect of something new: a President who did not defer to their beliefs. In their official capacities while President, Washington and Adams had publicly acknowledged God's sovereignty and Christianity had flourished. Its prospect under Republican rule looked less certain.

Dwight's public airing of Illuminati conspiracy theories and invocation of obscure biblical prophecies evoked ridicule from the Republican press, even in Connecticut. "His overheated imagination adopts chimeras for reality," an article in the New London *Bee* observed. "This perversion of the prophecies of revelation . . . increases and confirms the disciples of deism." By 1800, Christian critics tended to take a subtler approach in their published attacks on Jefferson. In his words and deeds, Jefferson renounced the basic tenets of Christianity, they argued, and voters, as God's anointed means of choosing America's political leaders, therefore should reject his bid to become President. Rulers needed the wisdom that comes from faith in Christ and reliance on scripture, some Christians maintained. Although the Constitution permitted non-Christians to hold public office, they conceded, the people should impose their own religious test on candidates.

In late-eighteenth-century America, most Deists and atheists kept their religious opinions private. Those who did not, such as patriot pamphleteer Thomas Paine in his 1795 book, *The Age of Reason*, were widely ostracized for their views. Indeed, in their zeal to expose error and attract followers, evangelical Christians probably exaggerated the extent of disbelief in the post-Revolutionary War period.

Jefferson never publicly professed either Deism or atheism, even though critics regularly accused him of holding such views. When asked about the subject at this time, Jefferson later recalled, "My answer was, 'say nothing of my religion. It is known to my God and myself alone'"—which was hardly the response of either a Deist or an atheist. They would not speak of God knowing or caring about their religion: A personal God played no part in their thinking.

Although Jefferson may have been a Deist at one time, by 1800 he probably was a Unitarian. His private writings from the period reveal a profound regard for Christ's moral teachings and a deep interest in the gospels and comparative religion. "I am a Christian," Jefferson confided to Benjamin Rush in 1803, "in the only sense that [Jesus] wished any one to be; sincerely attached to his doctrines, in preference to all others; ascribing to himself every *human* excellence; and believing he never claimed any other." As Jefferson read the Bible, Jesus never professed to be God. Although his private denial of Christ's divinity separated him from trinitarian Christians, his public statements and writings did not clearly betray the extent of his heterodoxy. To use it against him in 1800, Federalists needed to draw on circumstantial evidence. Jefferson was too circumspect a politician and Virginia gentleman to have published his innermost religious thoughts to the world.

As the election approached, Federalist orators and pamphleteers endlessly repeated the same few hints of heresy drawn from Jefferson's words and actions. *Notes on the State of Virginia*, written by Jefferson nearly two decades earlier, provided most of the fodder for his opponents. In it, for example, he defended his position on the separation of church and state by observing, "The legitimate powers of government extend to such acts only as are injurious to others. But it does me no injury for my neighbor to say there are twenty gods or no god. It neither picks my pocket nor breaks my leg." No one would make such claims who believed in God or appreciated religion's role in maintaining ordered liberty, Federalists charged. "Ponder well this paragraph. Ten thousand impieties and mischiefs lurk in its womb," the Reverend John Mason of New York warned in a partisan sermon published as a campaign pamphlet in September 1800. "I will not abuse you by asking whether the author of such an opinion can be a Christian? Or whether he has any regard for the scriptures which confine all wisdom and blessedness and glory . . . to the fear and the favor of God?" Another New York minister, William Linn, noted in his popular pamphlet, also published in 1800, "Let my neighbor once perceive himself that there is no God, and he will soon pick my pocket and break not only my *leg* but my *neck*."

Three other passages in *Notes on the State of Virginia* caught the eye of election-year religious inquisitors. First, Jefferson denied that the flood of Noah's time, described in the Bible as covering all the earth, could have submerged Virginia's mountains. Second, he suggested that the various human races had separate origins, which allegedly contradicted the biblical account of Adam and Eve as the first parents of all people. Third, he proposed that public-school students learn history rather than study the Bible "at an age where their judgments are not sufficiently matured for religious enquiries." Some Federalists openly asserted that such a critical approach toward scripture disqualified Jefferson for the presidency. He failed their religious test for public office. "On account of his disbelief of the Holy Scriptures, and his attempts to discredit them, he ought to be rejected for the Presidency," the Reverend Linn concluded in his pamphlet. "Would Jews or Mahometans, consistently with their beliefs, elect a Christian? And should Christians be less zealous and active than them?" At the time, most readers of popular pamphlets and newspaper articles lacked access to Jefferson's published writings, and so could not evaluate the accuracy of the claims made about them.

In their public attacks, Christian critics drew on evidence from Jefferson's private and public life to complete their picture of him as an infidel. Jefferson rarely attended church services, they noted. He desecrated the Sabbath by working and entertaining on Sunday. He did not invoke biblical authority or acknowledge Christ in the Declaration of Independence. When a foreign visitor to Virginia commented on the shabby condition of local churches, Jefferson reportedly replied, "It is good enough for him that was born in a manger!" Federalists eagerly repeated the visitor's conclusion: "Such a contemptuous fling at the blessed Jesus could issue from the lips of no other than a deadly foe to his name and his glory."

A campaign tract addressed to Delaware voters by a self-proclaimed "Christian Federalist" put the issue in blunt terms. "If Jefferson is elected and the Jacobins get into authority," it declared, "those morals which protect our lives from the knife of the assassin, which guard the chastity of our wives and daughters from seduction and violence, defend our property from plunder and devaluation, and shield our religion from contempt and profanation, will be trampled upon and exploded." With Republicans in power, this Christian warned, America would follow France into the moral and political abyss where the people turned "more ferocious than savages, more bloody than tigers, more impious than demons."

In a boldface notice captioned "THE GRAND QUESTION STATED" and reprinted almost daily during September and October, the *Gazette of the United States*, the nation's premier Federalist newspaper, starkly presented the choice facing Christian voters in austere terms. "At the present solemn and momentous epoch," it declared, "the only question to be asked by every American, laying his hand on his heart, is, 'Shall I continue in allegiance to GOD—AND A RELIGIOUS PRESIDENT; or impiously declare for JEFFERSON—AND NO GOD!!!'" Stated this way, the choice seemed easy.

Although Jefferson privately denounced the "lying pamphlets" and "absolute falsehoods" of his Christian critics, he feared that responding to them publicly would make matters worse. "As to the calumny of atheism, I am so broken to calumnies of every kind . . . that I entirely disregard it," Jefferson wrote to James Monroe in May 1800. "It has been so impossible to contradict all their lies that I have determined to contradict none; for while I should be engaged with one, they would publish twenty new ones." Nevertheless, assaults on his personal beliefs wounded Jefferson deeply. "I have a view of the subject which ought to displease neither the rational Christian nor Deists," he assured Benjamin Rush in September 1800. "I do not know that it would reconcile the [irritable race of critics] who are in arms against me." These critics opposed him because they believed that he would scuttle their schemes to establish their religion through law, Jefferson claimed. "And they believe rightly," he added, "for I have sworn upon the altar of god, eternal hostility against every form of tyranny over the mind of man." Clearly, Jefferson saw himself as the righteous party in this dispute.

While Jefferson remained publicly above the fray, Republicans rushed to his defense. In separate pamphlets, longtime Republican propagandist John Beckley characterized Jefferson as "an adorer of our God" and George Clinton's nephew, the rising New York politician DeWitt Clinton, hailed him as "a real Christian." In their hands, *Notes on Virginia* became an epistle of orthodoxy. Both pamphlets circulated widely, with Beckley boasting in August that his work had gone through five printings in four different states of one thousand copies each. "It will, I trust, do some good," he wrote in a letter to Monroe enclosed with a bundle of the pamphlets for distribution in Virginia.

Republicans everywhere wooed Baptists, Methodists, and local members of smaller denominations by contrasting Jefferson's support for religious liberty in Virginia with Adams's deference to an established church in Massachusetts. Jefferson supported the "sound practical equality of the Quaker," Pennsylvanians heard. He "does not think that a Catholic should be banished for believing in transubstantiation, or a Jew for believing in the God of Abraham," a New Jersey Republican leader proclaimed. "The fact is, Mr. Jefferson is entitled to the applause of every sect of Christians throughout the United States," a partisan essayist concluded. "He is a friend to *real religion*, which consists of this, that every man worships God agreeable to the dictates of his conscience."

Turning the tables on their accusers, Republicans also questioned the piety or religious orthodoxy of many leading Federalists. In an obvious reference to Hamilton's admitted extramarital affair, for example, one partisan essayist asked smugly, "Mr. Jefferson stands preeminent for his political, social, moral, and religious virtues. He is in fact what his enemies *pretend to be*. But what shall we say of a faction who has at its head a confessed and professed adulterer?" Yankee Federalists countered with scandalous stories about the sex lives of Southern slaveholders but did not yet connect Jefferson with any one particular Black mistress.

Other Republican writers took on Adams and Pinckney. Despite his bow to civil religion by participating in public worship and proclaiming national days of prayer and fasting, Adams privately differed little from Jefferson in his personal beliefs about God. Both men inclined toward Unitarianism, though Adams kept it under wraps better than Jefferson did and regularly attended conventional Christian church services during his presidency. This led some partisans to accuse Adams of hypocrisy. In their publications, Republicans also alluded to unfounded rumors about Pinckney's reputation as an impious libertine. "I have always understood that Mr. Jefferson belonged to the Episcopal Church," DeWitt Clinton wryly noted in his pamphlet. "How often he attends it I have not enquired, but I believe he does with as much sincerity as Mr. Adams and fully as frequently as Mr. Pinckney." Partisan critics made taunting references to a 1788 satirical poem by Timothy Dwight, *The Triumph of Infidelity*, in which a profligate, prideful Deist, supposedly based on Pinckney, boasted of being "the first of men in the ways of evil" with "two whores already in my chariot." The latter line alluded to Pinckney's purported amorous affairs while an American diplomat in Paris.

With all the candidates sullied, some partisans descended to the level of debating the relative merits of a pious hypocrite versus a known infidel as President. In a long newspaper essay, for example, a Republican wrote, "Now I don't know that John Adams is a hypocrite, or Jefferson a Deist; yet supposing they are, I am of the opinion the last ought to be preferred to the first [because] a secret enemy is worse than an open and avowed one." Even if Adams was a religious hypocrite, a Federalist pamphleteer shot back, "Your President, if an open infidel, will be a center of contagion to the whole continent." Writing for the *Carolina Gazette*, an exasperated commentator reached a similar conclusion. "Mr. Adams *may* have no more real religion than my horse," he declared, but in a contest with an open infidel, "all serious men would prefer the one who acknowledges his respect to his Maker."

For the most part, however, Christians on both sides probably accepted the professions of faith made on behalf of their party's candidates and voted accordingly. Federalists proudly pointed to Adams's public support for religious institutions: The President attended church, invoked God's name in his speeches, and declared days of prayer and fasting. Republicans countered by noting Jefferson's passion for religious liberty: He authored the Virginia Statute of Religious Freedom. Both political parties took Christian voters seriously.

Mainly, however, Jefferson's supporters simply urged voters to reject the concept of a religious test for public office and denounced Federalists for invoking one. Republican newspapers increasingly pushed this theme as the election approached. "No people differ more in their religious opinions than the people of the United States," an editorial in Washington's *National Intelligencer* noted, and therefore "religion ought to be kept distinct from politics." The bellwether Republican *Aurora* presented the choice as one between "an established church, a religious test, and an order of priesthood" with the Federalists or "religious liberty, the rights of conscience, no priesthood, truth and Jefferson." Given this choice, *Aurora* editor William Duane safely assumed that his readers would favor liberty.

Adams never joined in denouncing Jefferson's religion and thought that the tactic backfired badly. Indeed, according to Fisher Ames, the President privately expressed "indignation at the charge of irreligion [brought against Jefferson], asking what has that to do with the public and adding that he is a good patriot, citizen, and father." Nevertheless, Adams publicly did nothing to protect Jefferson or to reign in the Federalist press, not even the proadministration *Gazette of the United States*.

By his response, Adams left himself open to charges of complacency in promoting a state religion, which played into the hands of the Republicans. Having won their independence from a tyrannical monarchy, Americans cherished their political, economic, and religious freedom. In the American mind, every king had fawning nobles, a standing army, and corrupt priests lording themselves over oppressed subjects burdened with heavy taxes to pay for a regime they did not support and churches they did not attend. During the campaign of 1800, Republicans saw themselves as defenders of national independence and individual liberty, which Adams and the Federalists had betrayed by Jay's Treaty, a standing army, and the Sedition Act. Casting the Federalists also as proponents of an established church and a religious test for public office fit neatly into the larger Republican assault against them as crypto-monarchists and British lackeys.

By their deft handling of religious issues during the campaign, Republicans not only defended Jefferson. They also put their opponents on the defensive by linking Adams's public support of civil religion to popular concerns over the authoritarian tendencies of Federalists generally. Late in the campaign, Adams complained privately that, by its overzealous attacks, which often invoked religion, the Federalist press had "done more to shuffle the cards into the hands of the Jacobin leaders than all the acts of the administration and all the policy of [the] opposition." In later years, Adams came to see his party's visible association with members of politically active church groups—particularly Presbyterians, who lobbied for national days of prayer and fasting—as an undeserved blackball against him in 1800. "The secret whisper ran through all the sects, 'Let us have Jefferson, Madison, Burr, anybody, whether they be philosophers, Deists, or even atheists, rather than a Presbyterian President,'" he wrote, referring to a denomination he never joined but that had many Federalist members.

Just as Federalists used selected excerpts from *Notes on the State of Virginia* to paint Jefferson as a Deist, Republicans drew on earlier political writings by Adams to tag him as a monarchist. The charge was old, but Republicans prosecuted it with renewed vigor as negative attacks intensified during the summer and fall. It was central to their campaign against Adams.

"The foundation of a monarchy is already laid," Republican orator Abraham Bishop proclaimed in a late-summer speech that quickly appeared as a popular pamphlet. He blamed Federalist policies. Exaggerated threats of danger from France justified a costly military buildup and repressive domestic policies; funding the state and national debt raised a class of indolent government creditors; high taxes burdened working Americans; a privileged class benefited from government programs; and a compliant church "pronounces a hardy amen," Bishop declared. "All of these aristocracies and measures which I have noticed correspond exactly with the systems of monarchical government," he observed.

"Do you ask me for proofs that [Adams] is a monarchist?" a Rhode Island pamphleteer asked. "Read his *Defense of the American Constitution* and his commentary on the *Discourses of Davila*. In both of these, he speaks with rapture, almost with rhapsody, of the hereditary senate and executive." Neither book actually called for an American monarch, but Hamilton had long favored life tenure for presidents and senators, and some High Federalists agreed with him.

A Republican pamphlet published in October under the pseudonym Marcus Brutus tied various Federalist initiatives together into a dark conspiracy. It claimed that Hamilton's funding system begot debt, which begot taxes, which begot corruption and intriguing officeholders, which begot a standing army, which would beget monarchy "and an enslaved and impoverished people."

Republican newspapers echoed these themes. The *Aurora* called "Federalism a mask for monarchy." The *Hartford Mercury* composed a satirical creed for High Federalists that played on their support for an established church. "I believe in Alexander Hamilton, the Creole, mighty and puissant general of the standing army," it affirmed. "And in Charles Cotesworth Pinckney, his friend and faithful follower, who

. . . was sent from heaven to save this hapless country from the calamities of a republican government, and to confer upon it the beauty, the
splendor, and the glory of monarchy." Completing the High Federalist trinity, the creed concluded, "I believe in the virtuous efforts of
Timothy Pickering to prevent a peace with France and to unite us
again with the English nation." This creed neatly encapsulated many of
the popular arguments against continued Federalist rule.

As these various pamphlets and publications suggested, while Federalists focused their fury on Jefferson, Republicans had difficulty
deciding whether to attack Adams, Pinckney, or Hamilton. The people
perceived Adams as the Federalist candidate for President and were
generally unfamiliar with Pinckney. If Hamilton and the High Federalists had their way, however, Pinckney would run ahead of Adams in
the electoral vote and win the presidency. Responding to this threat,
Republican pamphleteers and printers turned some of their fire on
Pinckney, whom they typically portrayed as little more than Hamilton's pro-British puppet. "Mr. Adams, it is said, though he writes and
speaks and acts in favor of a British government, is far behind the real
state of political activity," one Republican newspaper noted. "Mr.
Charles Cotesworth Pinckney will answer the purposes of British
design much better. The party has discovered he is less timid and that
his policies are much higher toned than those of Mr. Adams."

Republicans found their best material for attacking Pinckney in a
1792 letter from Adams to Tench Coxe, a former Hamilton aide. Coxe
had turned Republican and given the letter to Adams's opponents.
Commenting in it on the appointment of Thomas Pinckney to a diplomatic post in London, Adams criticized the British ties of "the two Mr.
Pinckneys" and cautioned, "Were I in any executive department, I
should take the liberty to keep a vigilant eye upon them." After alluding to its contents for months, the *Aurora* published the entire letter in
August 1800, and reprinted it weekly until the election. Other Republican newspapers published the letter as well. It cast both Federalist
candidates in bad light. Adams disputed the authenticity of the letter,
while Thomas Pinckney issued a public statement in September assert-

ing that, if genuine, then it "must have been founded on misapprehension of persons." Surely Adams meant to slur his Republican cousin, South Carolina Senator Charles Pinckney, Thomas Pinckney suggested. Reviewing the entire exchange in October, one Republican newspaper described it as "proof, strong proof, of Messrs. Adams, Pinckney, and Hamilton's attachment to royalism."

Monarchism may have been too strong a term for it, but Federalists did share a common vision of society and politics that many Republicans regarded as too hierarchical and authoritarian for America. Despite their intraparty differences, Federalists agreed that family values, cultural traditions, and private property provided the best foundation for a stable society and vibrant economy. They believed in deference to elite leaders. Guided by their common vision, Federalists had provided able, conservative leadership for the United States since the government's founding in 1789. "Our country is prosperous beyond all example," a midsummer essay in Baltimore's *Federal Gazette* claimed. "Why then should we wish a change?" Federalists stood on their record, which to them looked pretty good. "This is the 12th year of our government," a Delaware Federalist wrote in 1800, "and is it not as free and republican as it was the first year? If the Jeffersonians wish more republicanism, what must it result in? Not in the freedom of equal laws, which is true republicanism, but in the licentiousness of anarchy."

As adept as their opponents in exaggerating the negative traits associated with the other side, Federalists portrayed Republicans as violent levelers devoid of any principles except those that served their immediate self-interest. "They are composed of French intriguers, English fugitives from justice, and many of the worst sorts of Americans," one typical campaign address said of Republicans. The *Gazette of the United States* depicted Republican leaders as "chimney-sweeper politicians and scavenger statesmen" and characterized their followers as "the very *refuse* and *filth* of society."

A learned Virginia gentleman, Jefferson obviously did not fit these

characterizations. Federalists instead portrayed him as a dreamy idealist corrupted by French philosophy and utterly incapable of providing
practical political leadership. Whatever his personal and intellectual
virtues, should Jefferson gain office, Federalists feared that he could
never control the Republican rabble that would take power with him.
"The lower class of democrats and Jacobins would endeavor to render
the new administration violent and convulsive," Wolcott warned in
August. "The People are his Gods," the High Federalist *Philadelphia
Gazette* jeered about Jefferson. "May he not be driven to measures
which his own judgment would reject?" a prominent High Federalist
asked Hamilton in August.

Intellectual elitists themselves, Federalists appealed to antiintellec-
tualism in smearing Jefferson. His pursuit of natural science and interest in philosophy all but disqualified him for high office, they claimed.
"Science and government are different paths. He that walks in one
becomes, at every step, less qualified to walk with steadfastness or vigor
in the other," a Federalist pamphleteer charged against Jefferson. "O
that his friends were aware that to him the honorable station is a private one, that mankind would suffer his talents and energies to be
harmlessly exhausted in adjusting the bones of a *nondescript* animal, or
tracing the pedigree of savage tribes, who no longer exist." Jefferson
had published research along these lines in *Notes on the State of Virginia*,
which had earned him an international reputation in science.

Jefferson had also studied philosophy, which Federalists portrayed
as even more problematic than his work in natural science. "He is so
true a philosopher as to be above matters of fact," the *New England Palladium* reported. "Philosophers admire no governments that are practicable. . . . They trust no theory but such as are untried." Even the
highest of the High Federalists—elitists to the core—worried about
too much philosophy in government. "Mr. Jefferson's conduct would
be frequently whimsical and undignified," Wolcott wrote in August.
"He would affect the character of a philosopher [and] countenance
quacks." The aristocratic Charles Carroll of Carrollton, who lived like
a feudal lord on his Maryland manor, suggested that Jefferson should

try his experiments in government on the Lilliputian European republic of San Marino rather than the United States. "His fantastic tricks would dissolve this Union," Carroll warned. "Against the dangerous principle of Mr. Jefferson's philosophy," a North Carolina pamphleteer added in July, "I have only to direct your view to that ill fated country France and bring to your recollection the history of the horrid government of their philosophers, who professed similar principles."

Republicans defended Jefferson by praising his practical ability and political experience. "The philosopher is nothing more than a being . . . whose opinions are drawn from the convictions of truth and reason," a Kentucky essayist explained. Rather than inspire mad speculations and fanatical reforms, as some Federalists charged, this writer claimed that Jefferson's scientific reflections had "given to his mind a degree of philosophical tranquility infinitely superior to most of his contemporaries." During the campaign, no Republicans ever questioned Jefferson's ability to lead or challenged the direction in which he would take the country. They stood as united as their opponents were divided. With Adams rallying the middle and all Federalists conjoined at least in their scorn for Jefferson, Republicans knew that they must stand together or fail.

Four years earlier, a swing of only two electoral votes from Adams to Jefferson would have switched the outcome. If the 1800 election proved equally close, then any state could decide the whole. By summer's end, however, most close observers expected the outcome to turn on the results from Maryland, Pennsylvania, and South Carolina—the three remaining states that could plausibly give all their electoral votes to candidates from either party or split them among the contenders.

Without mass communication, people relied on private letters and local newspapers for word on political developments elsewhere. They pumped out-of-state visitors for news and endlessly rehashed available information. From his seat at Monticello, during the summer Jefferson sent and received a steady stream of letters speculating about the probable outcome in various states. In his letters, he typically projected falling just short, as if to goad his correspondents to greater effort. Hamilton conducted a similar correspondence within the nationwide network of High Federalists, always plugging for Pinckney. Adams also closely monitored election trends from his farm in Massachusetts. The Pinckneys of South Carolina, both Federalist and Republican, were convinced that the election would come down to their state's eight votes. Politicking in New York and the Northeast, Burr worried openly about the electoral count, remembering how Southern Republican electors had deserted him in 1796.

Having neither opinion polls nor any nonpartisan sources of political information to guide them, the pundits and participants made their best guesses about how each state would vote. By September, they had reached strikingly similar conclusions. Virtually everyone agreed that the Republicans would sweep New York, Virginia, Georgia, and the western states of Kentucky and Tennessee. The Federalists would carry Delaware and all of New England, with the possible exception of one or two electoral votes in Rhode Island, which conducted a statewide vote for electors. The New Jersey legislature would surely choose Federalist electors for its state unless Republicans managed to wrest control of the State House in the October legislative elections, which appeared unlikely.

Counting only these twelve seemingly certain states, Federalists held a slight edge in electoral votes, 48 to 44, with 70 needed to win outright. The apparent advantage for the Republicans lay in the other four states: Pennsylvania, Maryland, and the Carolinas. These states held 45 electoral votes, with Republicans expected to pick up most of them.

Of course, only Jefferson could count on securing votes from all his party's electors. Just as Burr worried about losing Republican electoral votes in the South, and even as Hamilton actively campaigned for Federalist electors to abandon Adams, Pinckney feared that some pro-Adams electors would drop him from their ballots, as they had done to his brother in 1796. Some contemporary accounts had Burr actively trying to garner potentially wayward Pinckney second votes from Federalist electors to pad his own total. Burr "is intriguing with all his might in New Jersey, Rhode Island and Vermont," Hamilton wrote in early August about his old rival. "He counts positively on the universal support of the [Republicans] and that by some adventitious aid from other quarters; he will overtop his friend Jefferson. Admitting the first point, the conclusion may be realized. And if it is, Burr will certainly attempt to reform the government *à la Bonaparte*. He is as unprincipled and dangerous a man as any country can boast."

Of the four states generally viewed as still hotly contested, during the late summer of 1800, national attention focused mostly on Maryland. North Carolina voters would choose their electors in district elections during the autumn. Most observers expected Republicans to win easily in most districts, but the exact number that would go Republican, and how many Federalists might take, was disputed. Some estimates suggested that Federalists might carry as many as four or five of the state's twelve electoral districts. In Pennsylvania, the deadlock persisted between the Republican governor and Federalist senate pending the outcome of state legislative elections in October. Given the small number of the state's senate seats at stake in 1800—only one-quarter of the total—almost all of which they held already, Republicans faced an uphill fight to win outright control of the legislature. Nevertheless, they hoped that a strong popular vote for their candidates might persuade senators to cooperate with assemblymen and the governor in choosing Republican electors. Sectional politics and family ties would figure into the choice of electors by the South Carolina legislature— with neither factor favoring Adams. In 1796, legislators had picked electors who crossed party lines to vote for the two Southern candidates—Jefferson and Thomas Pinckney—and they might do so again in 1800 with another Pinckney on the Federalist ticket. Certainly the Pinckney family wielded enormous influence in the state.

In Maryland, however, the contest for presidential electors was wide open. The state traditionally chose its electors in district elections, scheduled this year for November. Each party expected to win some of them. If Federalists retained control of the state legislature in the October state elections, as most observers anticipated, they promised to change the election laws so as to empower legislators to appoint Maryland's ten electors. Of course, they would pick Federalists. This gave Maryland voters two potential opportunities to weigh in on the presidential contest—first in the October legislative elections and, if Federalists failed to retain complete control of the State House, then in November district elections. Presidential politics consumed the state from midsummer through the autumn elections. Only five months earlier, New Yorkers thought that their state elections would decide the presidential contest. Now Marylanders claimed that distinction. "It is admitted," one Federalist candidate for elector noted in September, "that in all probability the election of president will depend on Maryland."

At the time, political campaigns in Maryland featured debates between candidates or their representatives. "These are always held," one observer noted in 1800, "where there is known to be a great concourse of people, [such as] at a horse race, a cock-fight, or a Methodist quarterly meeting." In Maryland during the summer of 1800, despite the lull in campaigning elsewhere, candidates for the offices of state legislator and presidential elector began making the rounds of these public gatherings and engaging their debating skills. Presidential politics dominated the debates, even those between would-be legislators, with the candidates offering themselves as loyal supporters of either Adams or Jefferson. Despite all the speculation about Pinckney and Burr by party insiders, the debaters rarely mentioned them. With the executive branch having moved to Washington during June, and that town still part of Maryland, some of the officials transplanted to the nation's new capital saw their first candidate debates that summer. Although a tradition in Maryland, open-air public debates between candidates did not then typically occur elsewhere.

"The candidates on both sides are now traveling through their districts soliciting the favor of individuals with whom they associate on no other occasion," Treasury Secretary Oliver Wolcott observed in August. "Men of the first [rank] condescend to collect dissolute and ignorant mobs of hundreds of individuals to whom they make long speeches in the open air." The President's son, Thomas, described the scene in a letter to his father's private secretary. "Here the candidates for political honors or preferment assemble with their partisans," he wrote. "They mount the rostrum, made out of an empty barrel or hogshead, [and] harangue the sovereign people—prais[ing] and recommend[ing] themselves at the expense of their adversary's character and pretensions." Steeped in politics, Wolcott and Thomas Adams clearly enjoyed the show.

The speakers gave voice to familiar arguments for and against Adams and Jefferson. Indeed, these debates showed just how universal the campaign themes had become. Despite the lack of mass media and national party organizations, virtually the same partisan messages reached citizens everywhere. In Maryland, newspapers captured the arguments as they were spoken rather than in the more studied formulation of a written essay or printed pamphlet.

The debate format facilitated a rapid exchange of views. Republicans pounded the Federalists' record of high taxes, rising national debt, a standing army and excessive navy, hostilities with France, and repressive domestic policies. They condemned the Sedition Act as unconstitutional and warned of monarchies afoot. "The measures of the present administration were conceived in wisdom and executed with firmness, uprightness, and ability . . . to ensure *justice* from abroad and *tranquility* at home," replied Supreme Court Justice Samuel Chase, a Maryland native who participated in local debates on behalf of his cousin, a Federalist candidate for elector. Appealing to moderates, Chase's cousin, the candidate, praised Adams as "a tried, firm, dedicated patriot [who will] resist the influence of party and will pursue that line of conduct which will best support the rights and liberties of the people." Times are good, various Federalists declared. "You may be certain never to be more happy than you have been under Mr. Adams's administration," one partisan declared. Not so, a Republican statement countered. "If ever an occasion justified public addresses and individual exertions to rouse the people to a sense of duty, the present is undoubtedly such an occasion," it claimed. "You will plainly see and feel that your *present rulers* have exercised unauthorized powers and undue influence over you."

Maryland Federalists faced their hardest task in selling voters on their proposal to have the legislature appoint the state's electors in 1800, rather than allow the people to elect them as before. Republican candidates for the state legislature characterized the proposal as an eleventh-hour power grab by desperate partisans. They made it their main issue in the campaign. It nicely reinforced the image of Federalists as monarchists. "The right of election is the very essence of our constitution," one Republican candidate declared. "Yet, . . . there are men among us who, to answer party purposes, are meditating a plan to deprive us of it."

Federalists persisted in supporting the election-law change despite the criticism because they saw it as essential for winning the presidential contest. The three or four electoral votes that Jefferson might win through district elections in Maryland would likely seal his victory, they reasoned. "I am aware of strong objections to the measure," Hamilton wrote to a worried Maryland Federalist in early August, "but if it be true, as I suppose, that our opponents aim at revolution and employ all means to secure success, the contest must be unequal if we *not only* refrain from *unconstitutional* and *criminal* measures, but even from such as may offend against the *routine of strict decorum*." Once again, as he had in New York, Hamilton urged using all necessary means to save the republic from the Jacobins.

During the campaign in Maryland, Federalist candidates struggled to put a democratic face on their undemocratic proposal. Virginia's move to a statewide election for its presidential electors would likely cost Adams at least six electoral votes and deprive him of the victory, they claimed. Legislative appointment of Maryland's ten electors would "counteract the policy of Virginia," one candidate explained in late July, "and give the state of Maryland its full weight and influence in the election of the president." In a joint statement issued in August, three other Federalists pleaded, "Equity among the citizens ought to be restored, and this can only be done by fighting Virginia with her own weapons." It hardly helped that Federalists vowed to restore the old method of district voting *after* the election. Every argument simply made matters worse.

The proposal proved disastrous for Federalists. In July, they confidently predicted that their candidates would retain control of the state legislature and use their majority to change the election law. By summer's end, they feared that Republicans would take control of at least one legislative chamber and block the change. "From present appearances," a state party leader concluded in September, "the choice of electors will be left to the people." Republicans viewed the situation similarly. In August, for example, Madison called "it more than probable" that Federalists would carry the legislative elections and immediately appoint Maryland's electors. A month later, he predicted a "Republican issue to the main question" of how the state chose electors. Maryland voters wanted to pick their electors and they would not willingly elect a legislature that would deprive them of that right, he concluded.

"It may be truly said that on the state of Maryland depends, in a great measure, the fate of America," an Annapolis Federalist, Charles Alexander Warfield, asserted in a September campaign address. By this time, partisans on both sides had convinced themselves that the outcome of the 1800 presidential election, which now hinged on electoral votes from Maryland, Pennsylvania, and South Carolina, could alter the course of American history. The French Revolution and America's reaction to it had made the choices appear stark to many: liberty or order. Extraordinarily able candidates and campaigners—Adams, Jefferson, Hamilton, Madison, Sedgwick, McKean, Jay, Monroe, three

Pinckneys, and a Burr, to name just a few—most of them already renowned for their roles in the American Revolution or founding the republic, played central parts again—in some cases for the last time. Partisan printers and pamphleteers had the means to reach Americans everywhere and the incentive to stir their passions. It made for a battle of titans.

The partisan rhetoric became severe. Republicans warned of monarchy if their opponents retained power. Federalists spoke of an atheistic, leveling revolution should the "Jacobins" take over. Many believed these words and feared the worst. Warfield closed his address with prayer: "May the Ruler of the Universe endow us all with wisdom to discern and with fortitude to act right on this truly momentous occasion!" He referred, of course, to the Maryland legislative elections, which he rightly viewed as Adams's last, best opportunity to secure reelection. If Federalists prevailed in those elections and went on to appoint ten of their own as electors, Adams would almost surely win another term in office. It seemed so simple. Even at this late date, no one could have foreseen the twists and turns that lay ahead before America finally chose its next President.

CHAPTER EIGHT

INSURRECTION

*G*ABRIEL was a large man with big plans. Like so many other Virginians in 1800, he dreamed of freedom. Born in 1776, Gabriel became a blacksmith and apparently worked at various sites in and around the state capital of Richmond. He stood well over six feet tall, had a powerful build, and commanded respect from his peers. Those peers, however, were African-American slaves, and Gabriel wanted more for them—and for himself—than bondage. As a semi-itinerant craftsman, he inevitably associated with free Blacks and white artisans. Most of his earnings however, went to his owner, Thomas Prosser, who engaged in the then-common practice of letting some of his skilled slaves work independently. The taste of personal liberty enjoyed by Gabriel may have increased his hunger for complete emancipation; it certainly allowed him to experience the election-year tumult in Virginia and to hear radical Republican calls for liberty.

One contemporary newspaper account described Gabriel as "a fellow of courage and intellect above his rank in life." He could read and write. He also had a temper. Caught in 1799 stealing a pig from a white overseer, Absalom Johnson, Gabriel bit off the pig owner's ear in the ensuing scuffle and was branded on the left hand for his crime. At some point shortly after this incident, Gabriel decided that he had had enough of slavery and scraping for food. He began plotting a massive insurrection designed to win freedom for himself and other slaves in southeastern Virginia. Events in revolutionary France and the wealthy French Caribbean colony of Saint-Domingue on Hispaniola Island—where slaves had taken over in 1793, and proclaimed their freedom—may have inspired him.

During the spring and summer of 1800, Gabriel conspired with other slaves in the region—probably too many—and became their general. Others served as captains and sergeants. Two radical white French immigrants and some free African-Americans allegedly also participated in the plotting. Gabriel forged swords from sickles for his men and made five hundred bullets for their few guns. He claimed that thousands of slaves would rise on his call and hoped that free Blacks and poor whites would rally to his banner. Inverting Patrick Henry's famous cry, Gabriel crafted a flag that read "Death or Liberty." According to courtroom testimony from participants, Gabriel at times demanded death for all the whites in the area except "Quakers, Methodists, and French people"—three groups widely perceived to oppose slavery. He spoke at other times of dining and drinking "with the merchants of the city" once they agreed to end slavery. In either event, Gabriel anticipated a bloody fight for freedom. "It is unquestionably the most serious and formidable conspiracy we have ever known of this kind," Governor James Monroe reported to Jefferson in September, after the plot became public.

The uprising might have succeeded up to a point had nature not intervened. The plan was as follows: During the evening of Saturday, August 30, the slaves around Prosser's plantation, six miles north of Richmond, would rise up; kill Gabriel's chief tormentors, Prosser and Johnson; and secure guns from a nearby tavern. Other slaves would join them for a midnight march on Richmond. Once in the city, some participants would set the warehouse district on fire to divert attention while others captured the state capitol, armory, treasury, and governor's mansion. They would use the state's guns as their weapons and distribute its treasure among their troops. Gabriel planned to take the governor hostage and bargain for emancipation. By some accounts, Gabriel harbored hopes that Monroe—who, as American ambassador in Paris, had once embraced the revolutionary regime in France—might prove cooperative. From this point on, Gabriel's plans become too vague to reconstruct. They went awry from the outset anyway.

"Upon that very evening" of August 30, Republican printer James Thomson Callender reported from his Richmond prison cell in a letter to Jefferson, "there came on the most terrible thunder storm, accompanied with an enormous rain, that I ever witnessed in this state." The road between Prosser's plantation and Richmond became impassable. Only a few local slaves turned out. "They were deprived of the juncture and assistance of their good friends in this city, who could not go out to join them," Callender noted. Gabriel postponed the uprising for a day and sent his followers home.

Rumors of a slave conspiracy had circulated in Virginia throughout the summer, but as governor, Monroe had dismissed and suppressed them. Republican leaders from Jefferson on down sought to discourage and deny threats of revolutionary activity at home during the campaign so as not to feed Federalist fearmongering on the issue of domestic security. They spoke and acted like moderate Federalists and appealed to their more radical supporters only for votes in contested elections. Threats of a slave revolt posed particular problems for Republicans. Southern Federalists had long warned that Republican calls for liberty and equality could stir up the slaves. In 1799, following the XYZ Affair, South Carolina Federalist Congressman Robert Goodloe Harper published an open letter to his constituents warning that France "was preparing to invade the southern states from St. Domingo with an army of [freed] blacks, which was to be landed with a large supply of officers, arms and ammunition, to excite an insurrection among the Negroes by means of missionaries previously sent, and first to subjugate the country by their assistance, and then plunder and lay it waste."

After the aborted rising on August 30, when it became clear that an insurrection might happen, Monroe responded swiftly, as if to reassure citizens that they could trust Republicans to maintain order. With critical state elections scheduled for October in the slave states of Maryland and South Carolina, Monroe would not run the risk of a violent insurrection by Blacks in Republican-ruled Virginia. "The scenes which are acted in St. Domingo," Monroe later wrote to his state military commander, "must produce an effect on all people of color in this and the states south of us, more especially our slaves, and it is our duty to be on guard to prevent any mischief resulting from it."

After Gabriel dismissed those few conspirators who managed to assemble at the appointed time despite the rain, one of them—perhaps unnerved by the delay—told his owner about the planned insurrection and its leader's name. That owner raised the alarm. Other owners soon heard about it from their slaves as well. Within hours, members of the county militia began hunting down the conspirators and Gabriel fled for the coast.

Word of these developments reached the governor in Richmond on August 31. He promptly moved the public arms to a secure location. As the full extent of the conspiracy became clear, Monroe called out various local units of the state militia and Richmond took on a military face. Soldiers began systematically rounding up slaves and arresting those thought to have joined the conspiracy. "There has been great alarm here of late at the prospect of an insurrection of the Negroes in this city and its neighborhood," the governor wrote to Jefferson on September 9. "About thirty are in prison who are to be tried on Thursday, and others are daily discovered and apprehended in the vicinity of the city. . . . It is the opinion of the magistrates who examined those committed that the whole, very few excepted, will be condemned." Monroe promised a $300 reward to anyone who captured Gabriel, plus a full pardon if an accomplice did the deed.

Under Virginia law, accused slaves appeared before a special court composed of five judges, all of whom had to agree on any punishment. Except for the governor's power to pardon, the court's decision was final. In cases of conspiracy, rebellion, or insurrection, the court could impose the death penalty and order an immediate public hanging. On the initial day of court proceedings, which occurred less than two weeks after the first arrests, the court sentenced all six defendants to die at dawn or noon of the next day. Nine more men were hanged the following week. At these executions, troops surrounded the scaffold to keep the hostile crowd from assaulting the convicted slaves before the executioners could kill them. "The whole state has been in consternation," a High Federalist commented smugly. "Courts are sitting, trials are taking place, and the gallows are in full operation."

By mid-September, Monroe began to question the wisdom of further reprisals and perhaps to fear a political backlash from too many hangings. "While it was possible to keep [the threat of an insurrection] secret, which it was till we saw the extent of it, we did so," he explained in a letter to Jefferson on September 15. "But when it became indispensably necessary to resort to strong measures with a view to protect the town, the public arms, the treasury, and the jail, which were all threatened, the opposite course was in part taken. We then made a display of our force." By the time Monroe wrote these words, the state had already executed ten conspirators. He predicted that up to forty more would hang unless he intervened with pardons. "When to arrest the hand of the executioner is a question of great importance," Monroe wrote to Jefferson. "I shall be happy to have your opinion on these points."

For Jefferson and Monroe, how to handle the conspirators was more than simply a moral or an ethical question. From a political standpoint, Virginia Republicans needed to display sufficient toughness to assure frightened citizens (particularly in key southern states) that a Jefferson administration would keep the peace and suppress leveling insurrections. At the same time, however, showing excessive harshness could alienate voters opposed to slavery or sympathetic to those caught up in the aborted insurrection. Pennsylvania posed a particular problem in this respect. A hotbed of radical republicanism and a center for America's growing abolition movement, it would hold its state legislative election in four weeks—with fifteen electoral votes hanging in the balance. Rumors had already placed one of Gabriel's alleged French coconspirators in Philadelphia.

By mid-September, the Federalist press began capitalizing on the episode by presenting it as a natural consequence of republicanism run riot. "The sound of French Liberty and Equality in the ears of these Blacks led them to this desperate measure," one widely reprinted article charged. "Behold America the French doctrine of Insurrection!" another exclaimed. Some articles criticized Republican printers for filling the heads of slaves with notions of freedom. "The slave holders in our county no longer permit the *Aurora* and other *Jacobin* papers to come into their homes as they are convinced the late insurrection is to be attributable entirely to this source," a correspondent supposedly from Virginia wrote in a letter appearing in Federalist papers across the country.

Many articles blamed Jefferson's egalitarian rhetoric for the slaves' actions. "Truly Mr. J.," read a typical charge, "should the business end in massacre, you and your disciples are the men who are the cause of it, and for every outrage and murder the Negroes may commit, you stand accountable." After leveling similar accusations against Virginia Republicans generally, a Pennsylvania newspaper urged state voters "to tread down Jacobin philosophy and fractious reformation; to support by constant precept and example the dominion of religion, order, and law; and to cling solely to the Federal[ist] government as the only rock of their stability." Radical Federalist printer William Cobbett commented, "The late revolt . . . amongst the Negroes of Virginia . . . will make Jefferson and his party very cautious how they do any act which may stir the sleeping embers of that alarming fire which, were it once rekindled, would probably make all the southern states what Hispaniola now is."

The Federalist press also indicted slaveholding Virginia Republicans for hypocrisy in their handling of the affair and suggested that the conspirators died for Jefferson's sins. "He who effects to be a Democrat and is at the same time an owner of slaves, is a devil incarnate," declared one Federalist writer. "Democracy therefore in Virginia is like virtue in hell." One Federalist newspaper depicted the conspiracy as "shallow" and easily suppressed, which carried the implication that Virginia Republicans overreacted in their response to it. Several articles reminded readers of Jefferson's earlier praise for "the boisterous sea of liberty" and, in light of the threatened slave revolt, contrasted that image with the Federalist promise of ordered freedom. "If anything will correct and bring to repentance old hardened sinners in Jacobinism, it must be an *insurrection of their slaves*," the *Boston Gazette* observed. "One old experienced statesman like John Adams, who honestly tells men how wicked they are and that nothing will keep them in good order but the powerful restraints of a strong government, is worth all the speculative philosophers from Thomas Jefferson down."

Potentially the most explosive evidence to emerge from the conspiracy trials in Virginia involved the testimony of multiple witnesses that two white Frenchmen had helped Gabriel. In their confessions, some of the conspirators named at least one of these alleged collaborators and suggested that both played major roles in the effort. Federalist newspapers latched on to this testimony and published it along with accusations that the revolutionary rhetoric of domestic Republicans inspired the slaves to revolt. Anything linking French Jacobins to domestic instability helped to justify the Federalists' Alien Act and counter Republican criticisms of it.

Republicans tried to deflect these charges by denying them. The *Aurora* dismissed published reports that radical Republicans had instigated the Virginia slave conspiracy as "wholly false" and suggested that Federalist policies—such as conducting trade talks with Toussaint Louverture, the Black ruler of Saint-Domingue—contributed more to the unrest than anything Republicans said or did. "While our administration was encouraging . . . revolt and trading with Toussaint in the West Indies, what could be expected from the unfortunate Blacks and slaves in our states from the example?" the newspaper asked.

Notwithstanding undisputed trial testimony to the contrary, Republicans maintained that Gabriel and his fellow slaves acted without outside assistance. According to the *Aurora*, "There was not so much as the slightest foundation for suspecting any Republican American or any Frenchman" played a role in the affair. Republican newspapers around the country reprinted this denial and made it their own. When pressed on the issue shortly before the fall election, Monroe asserted, "According to our present information, the conspiracy was quite a domestic one, conceived and carried to the stage at which it was discovered by some bold adventurers among the slaves." As if for emphasis, he added, "If white men were engaged in it, it is a fact of which we have no proof." Based on his study of the episode, however, historian Douglas Egerton concluded that Monroe probably had received at least some evidence of white participation, but suppressed or destroyed it. Virginia officials neither pursued the accusations of involvement by Frenchmen nor indicted any white people in the case.

By all accounts, Federalists believed what their papers said about Republican complicity in the conspiracy. They made similar comments in private. "I doubt not that the eternal clamor about liberty in Virginia . . . has matured the event which has happened," a leading Federalist diplomat wrote about the affair in a letter to the President's son, John Quincy Adams. "In Virginia, they are beginning to feel the happy effects of liberty and equality," another prominent Federalist added. "The reports from that quarter say it was planned by Frenchmen, and that all the whites, save the French, were to have been sacrificed."

By early fall, Jefferson and Monroe viewed virtually everything—even a desperate slave conspiracy and its violent suppression—in political terms. On September 20, Jefferson gave a cautious reply to Monroe's question about when to stop the hangings. Jefferson always hedged on the issue of slavery: so much so, that one of his best biographers, Joseph Ellis, called him the American sphinx. He owned slaves all his adult life and treated them like property. In his draft for the Declaration of Independence, however, Jefferson listed the institution of slavery as one of the usurpations by the British monarch that justified the American Revolution. A decade later, in *Notes on the State of Virginia*, Jefferson wrote of his hope, "under the auspices of heaven, for a total emancipation [of the slaves] with the consent of the masters." By 1800, whispered rumors circulated that the widowed master of Monticello had sexual relations with his female slaves. Slavery, and the treatment of convicted slave conspirators during a political season, presented Jefferson with hard issues.

"Where to stay the hand of the executioner is an important question," Jefferson wrote to Monroe. Virginians would differ in their answers, Jefferson observed, but the political ramifications reached beyond Virginia. "The other states and the world at large will forever condemn us if we indulge in a principle of revenge or go one step beyond absolute necessity," he wrote. "They cannot lose sight of the rights of the two parties and the object of the unsuccessful one. Our situation is indeed a difficult one."

Jefferson suggested exporting the convicted slaves out of the country rather than hanging them. "I hazard these thoughts for your consideration only," the cautious candidate added, "as I should be unwilling to be quoted in the case." After Jefferson's letter reached Monroe, most convicted conspirators received outright pardons on the court's recommendation of mercy or were "reprieved for transportation" to Spanish Louisiana. The political storm passed with minimal impact on the election.

Before the end of the affair, however, Virginians with power demanded at least one more execution. The $300 bounty offered for Gabriel's capture had worked. On September 23 in Norfolk, a slave with no part in the conspiracy betrayed Gabriel's hiding place to the local sheriff, who arrested him and sent him to the state capital for trial. Gabriel reached Richmond in irons on September 27. His brief public trial was held nine days later. Gabriel was the sixth man tried on that day, and the only one sentenced to die without a recommendation of mercy. The trial drew a large crowd.

Gabriel sat silently as three of his former followers placed him at the center of the conspiracy. They gained their lives for their testimony; he lost his. Gabriel spoke only after the court sentenced him to die on the next day. He asked for a delay of three days so that he could hang with six of his coconspirators previously scheduled for execution on October 10. The court granted his last request. In all, Virginia hanged twenty-six slaves for their role in the conspiracy, with Gabriel being the last of them to die in Richmond.

Despite their partisan wrangling over the causes and handling of the Virginia slave conspiracy, during the campaign of 1800, neither Federalists nor Republicans spoke substantively to the underlying issue of slavery. Even though most northern states had abolished slavery by 1800, it remained deeply entrenched in the South. Neither party could hope to win the presidency if it took a strong stand on slavery, so they both equivocated on what was already emerging as the most divisive topic in American politics.

Both parties were deeply split by the issue. Slavery disgusted Adams—he once called it "an evil of colossal magnitude"—yet, he included three slave owners in his five-member cabinet, and his hope for reelection rode on winning electoral votes from three slave states: Maryland, Delaware, and South Carolina. Many Northern High Federalists opposed slavery on moral or religious grounds, yet their faction's favored candidate for President, Charles Cotesworth Pinckney, possessed vast slave plantations and, as a delegate to the Constitutional Convention, led the successful effort to ensure that the Constitution protected the right of states to maintain slavery. If the Constitution "should fail to insure some security to the southern states against an emancipation of slaves," Pinckney told his fellow delegates, he "would be bound by this duty to his state to vote against [it]."

The Republican Party encompassed a similar diversity of views on slavery, from the ardent support for it expressed by many party leaders in the Deep South through Jefferson's tortured acquiescence of the practice to the fevered abolitionism of such prominent Northern Republicans as Albert Gallatin. "Slavery is inconsistent with every principle of humanity, justice, and right," Gallatin had written in a 1793 legislative report, yet he served as Jefferson's point man in Congress during the 1800 election.

In 1800, none of the national candidates questioned the right of states to authorize slavery or proposed that the government do anything to discourage slavery or restrict the slave trade. At most, partisan pundits postured on the edges of these explosive issues. In articles and pamphlets addressed to voters in their region, for example, Northern Republicans frequently reminded voters of Jefferson's expressed hope for gradual emancipation. "The spirit of the master is abating, that of the slave rising from the dust," Jefferson had written in *Notes on the State of Virginia*—part of a passage critical of slavery that Adams once described as "worth diamonds." Southern Federalists used the same passage, which warned of dire consequences if slavery did not end, to turn white voters in the South against Jefferson. In a published campaign address, a Rhode Island Federalist ridiculed the calls for liberty and equality coming from Virginia Republicans. Should New Englanders "take lessons upon those subjects from the state of Virginia . . . where slavery constitutes a part of the policy of the government?" he asked.

A late-September exchange between Philadelphia's two leading partisan newspapers showed just how far rhetoric departed from reality. "The insurrection of the Negroes in the southern states, *which appears to be organized on the true French plan*, must be decisive with every reflecting man in those states of the election of Mr. Adams and Gen. Pinckney," an essay in the Federalist *Gazette of the United States* asserted. Scared for their safety, white Southern voters would now turn to Federalists for security, the essayist suggested. "We augur better things from this unhappy but, thank God, partial revolt," the Republican *Aurora* replied a day later. "We augur from it . . . the election of [Thomas Jefferson], whose whole life has been marked by measures calculated to procure the emancipation of the Blacks." Whether true or not, that was what Pennsylvania Republicans wanted to hear about their candidate. Although such dueling comments probably did not change many minds, they likely spoke to each party's local political base.

Gabriel was hanged smack in the middle of the first round of voting in the fall state elections that would decide the presidency. Those elections spread over two months. In 1800, state legislatures selected the presidential electors in eleven of the sixteen states. By autumn, voters in seven of these eleven states—New Hampshire, Vermont, Massachusetts, Connecticut, New York, Georgia, and Tennessee—had already chosen their legislatures for 1800. Of these, Federalists controlled the four New England state legislatures while Republicans held a majority of the seats in each of the other three. Except for New York, where Burr had orchestrated a narrow Republican victory in the spring, these were all states where one party dominated and presidential politics had played little part in the elections.

The four remaining states where legislatures chose the electors held their elections for local, state, and congressional offices in October—Delaware on the sixth; Pennsylvania, New Jersey, and South Carolina on the fourteenth. These elections would decide how those states voted for President. Presidential politics dominated the campaign discourse in all four places. The five states where voters directly picked electors balloted in November, beginning with Virginia and North Carolina on the third, moving on to Maryland and Kentucky the following week, and concluding with Rhode Island on the nineteenth.

A steady trickle of election returns, and their meaning for the presidential contest, kept the nation on edge for months. Adding to the complexity, Maryland Federalists continued to promise a switch from district elections to legislative appointment if their party won the state elections on October 6. Further, lawmakers in Pennsylvania remained deadlocked on the manner of choosing electors. The October elections in that state could resolve this impasse by giving complete control to the Republicans. They already controlled the State Assembly by a wide margin and they dreamed of wresting control of the State Senate as well. Only one-fourth of the Senate's seats were up for grabs, however, with Republicans holding most of those positions—making a Republican takeover virtually impossible.

Both sides hoped that the October legislative elections would settle the presidential race in their favor. Federalists expected to win the New Jersey and Delaware elections. If they also maintained control of the legislatures in Maryland and South Carolina, and held on to the Pennsylvania Senate as anticipated, then they could count on Adams and Pinckney securing votes from at least a narrow majority of the electors regardless of what happened in the November elections. If some of their elector candidates then won in North Carolina's district elections during November, as they hoped, that would simply pad their victory. In contrast, if Republicans gained the upper hand in Pennsylvania and South Carolina while winning enough seats in the Maryland legislature to block any bill changing the method of choosing electors, then Jefferson and Burr would surely have a majority of their partisans in the Electoral College—with only the size of that majority in doubt. If these three critical states split, however, the presidential contest could go right down to the wire.

Voters went to the polls in Maryland on the same day as Gabriel went on trial in neighboring Virginia. The slave conspiracy and resulting trials attracted widespread attention in Maryland, which (like Virginia) had a plantation economy based on slave labor. As it turned out, however, only one issue mattered in the state elections: the Federalist proposal to have the legislature appoint presidential electors rather than have them selected in district elections.

Prior to the election, the Federalists controlled both houses of the Maryland legislature and held all statewide offices. The governor could have called a special session of the outgoing legislature to change the method for choosing electors. Instead, he allowed voters to have a say in the matter by leaving it to the incoming legislature. "His refusal to call the old Assembly alone saved Jefferson's election here," crowed Maryland Republican John Francis Mercer, a senior Anti-Federalist who had served in the Continental Congress, Constitutional Convention, and Congress. "It was the popular cry that overwhelmed them," a *Federal Gazette* writer concluded of his party's candidates. Republicans captured a majority of seats in the lower house of the Maryland legislature, which guaranteed that voters would choose the state's electors in district elections. Those contests would proceed as scheduled in November.

Earlier in the year, Federalists in New Hampshire and Massachusetts had instigated a switch from popular elections to legislative appointment for electors without causing a backlash. Republican lawmakers had successfully substituted statewide for district elections in Virginia. Legislators in these states freely conceded that they acted for short-term partisan gain. Only in Maryland, however, did anyone give voters a choice, and their reaction caught the Federalists off guard. Having moved to Washington with the nation's government in June, Treasury Secretary Oliver Wolcott watched the battle over the issue unfold up close. In a private letter to Fisher Ames, Wolcott tried to account for the appeal of voting directly for presidential electors, but succeeded mainly in revealing his High Federalist sensibilities. "The right of suffrage is here considered invaluable," he wrote, "because, in addition to its usual attributes, it levels the distinctions of society, gratifies vulgar curiosity, indulges the plebeian taste for slander, and furnishes the means of riotous indulgence without expense." Without a means to gauge public opinion formally, Wolcott could only guess why the voters objected to the legislative appointment of electors—and attributed base motives to them.

Jefferson saw the issue quite differently. "I congratulate you on the triumphs of Republicanism in the city and county of Baltimore," he wrote to Maryland Congressman Samuel Smith after the October election. "The spirit of '76 had never left the people of our country, but artificial panics . . . had put it to sleep for a while. We owe to our political opponents [credit for] exciting it again by their bold strokes." The Federalists had overreached, Jefferson thought, and their support for appointing electors in Maryland simply made matters worse for them. It substantiated the Republican claim that Federalists sought to consolidate power in the hands of an aristocracy.

Maryland Federalists consoled themselves that the October legislative elections turned on a single issue and did not necessarily reflect a shift in voter allegiances toward the Republicans generally. Prior to the

October elections, partisans on both sides predicted that Republican candidates would win in only three of Maryland's ten electoral districts and did not anticipate that even a bruising defeat by Federalists in the legislative elections would impact the subsequent vote for electors. In opposing legislative appointment, Republicans presumably were fighting for those three votes. Following the October elections, Federalists maintained that nothing had changed. "I see no other consequences to this state, or to the union, from this last election, than that Mr. Adams and General Pinckney may lose three votes," a *Federal Gazette* writer reassured his partisan readers in late October.

Maryland Republicans, in contrast, were almost giddy with triumph and began hoping for even greater gains in November. "I have now the pleasure of communicating to you that," Republican portraitist Charles Peale Polk wrote to Madison immediately after the October election, "from the best information that I have received on the subject, Mr. Jefferson will most probably have seven votes from this state." In a letter to Madison posted a week later, Maryland jurist and former Congressman Gabriel Duvall placed this figure at "five, perhaps six votes." With Republican hopes raised, the electioneering continued in Maryland into November. If Republicans could pull off a swing of four more electoral votes from Adams to Jefferson by winning seven of Maryland's ten votes rather than just three, the feat could well prove decisive.

Voters in Delaware cast their ballots on October 6, the same day as voters in Maryland; New Jersey voters went to the polls a week later. In all these mid-Atlantic states, Federalists sought to retain control of the legislature against unusually vigorous Republican attacks. Unlike their counterparts in Maryland, however, Republicans in Delaware and New Jersey lacked the ready-made issue of defending the people's right to vote for electors. The legislature had always chosen electors in these two states and, as much as Republicans might decry the process, changing it never became a major issue. Instead, state legislative contests became referendums on the national presidential candidates.

Paralleling developments in Virginia, New Jersey Republicans resolved to form their state's first statewide network of local party committees. "The plan, if carried into effect generally, will no doubt contribute greatly to the success of the Republican ticket at the ensuing election," party leaders explained early in 1800. "Opposition we may naturally expect from the aristocrats, the Tories, and the lawyers; but to the respectable farmers of New Jersey, to the Whigs of '76, the resolution is respectfully submitted." Though local Republican committees subsequently sprang up across the state, they proved no match for the Federalist establishment that dominated New Jersey. When Republicans in Gloucester passed a series of resolutions critical of the Adams administration, for example, outraged local Federalists denounced these Republican resolutions as aiming "at the total destruction of the constitution of the United States and the administration thereof, under which we have hitherto lived prosperous and happy."

Federalists closely monitored these Republican campaign efforts, but they remained confident of victory in both states. "A considerable diversion in favor of the opposition has lately been made in New Jersey," Hamilton noted during the summer, "but the best and best-informed men there entertain no doubt that all her electors will still be Federal." In Delaware, as the election approached, the state's lone congressman, Federalist James A. Bayard, assured Hamilton, "Delaware is safe." Hamilton was particularly interested in both states because he harbored hopes that, as High Federalist strongholds, their electors would drop votes from Adams so as to slip Pinckney into first place in the final tally. As a coconspirator in this scheme, Bayard added to his comment about Delaware's "safe" Federalist electors: "They may hesitate whether they will give Mr. Adams a vote."

True to the projections, Federalists carried at least two-thirds of the seats up for election in both New Jersey and Delaware. As if to taunt both Jefferson and Hamilton, the proadministration *Gazette of the United States* reported about the New Jersey election, "No doubt is entertained of a good majority in the legislature for the Adams interest." It took only a simple majority in the legislature to appoint all the state's electors. Republicans needed to look elsewhere for the electoral votes required to win the presidency.

One of Delaware's few surviving Republican legislators, Caesar Rodney, reported to Jefferson following the October 6 election, "Altho' our horizon be clouded [in Delaware], the prospect brightens on turning our eyes to Pennsylvania and Maryland. I trust the old maxim, 'Truth is great and will prevail.'" Republicans had prevailed in the Maryland legislative elections by this time, but Pennsylvanians had yet to vote. Of course, the party had done well in Pennsylvania a year earlier, when McKean won the governorship and its candidates captured the State Assembly in what amounted to the opening round of the presidential campaign—but staggered terms for state senators slowed the process of political realignment there. The legislative elections on October 14 offered Republicans their last chance to take over the State Senate in time to appoint electors. Both sides geared up for a fight.

Although the nation's capital had moved to Washington, Philadelphia remained America's political nerve center throughout the campaign. It vied with New York as the most populous city in the country, and as its hub for trade, commerce, and banking. Most critically, after serving as the seat of government for ten years, Philadelphia was home to the nation's leading partisan newspapers at a time when such papers provided much of the institutional structure for party politics in America. Indeed, a symbiotic relationship linked presses and parties in 1800: Partisan reporting attracted readers and forged party identity.

The number of newspapers shot up in advance of the 1800 election as public interest in the campaign increased readership, wealthy party leaders subsidized printers, and partisans supplied copy for publication. "The engine is the press," Jefferson wrote to Madison in 1799 about the Republican campaign. "Every man must lay his purse and his pen under contribution." As the party out of power, Republicans needed a friendly press to communicate their message to voters.

William Duane's Philadelphia *Aurora* led the Republican pack in

1800. Its crosstown rival, *Gazette of the United States*, countered for the Federalists. Often without attribution, articles lifted directly from these sources reappeared in partisan publications across the country, spreading like ripples on a pond first to newspapers in nearby communities, then to ones in more distant towns, and finally surfacing in the most remote papers. It typically took two or more weeks for an *Aurora* or a *Gazette* article to reappear across the Appalachian Mountains in Kentucky, for example. Other presses also fed original material into the partisan web. As a result, national political news carried the partisan slant given to it from its source of origin, which was often Philadelphia. "On every important subject, the sentiment to be inculcated among the Democrats has been first put into the *Aurora*. This was the heart, the seat of life. From thence the blood has flowed to the extremities," the Federalist *Connecticut Courant* noted in August 1800. "It is even astonishing to remark with how much punctuality and rapidity *the same opinion* has been circulated and repeated." Fisher Ames blamed the spread of Republicanism on "the unceasing use of this engine"; Jefferson credited the *Aurora* with "arrest[ing] the rapid march of our government toward monarchy."

With a split electorate and Congress sitting in Philadelphia for the previous decade, by 1800, Pennsylvania had more decidedly partisan newspapers than any other state. They helped to politicize the population, and their printers wanted nothing more than to stir up passionate partisan interest in the October state elections. Veteran observers knew that those elections would probably not alter the division of power in the Pennsylvania legislature: Republicans enjoyed unassailable dominance in the State Assembly while, because of holdovers, only a clean sweep by Republicans in every contest could dislodge Federalists from their grip on the State Senate. Nevertheless, the approaching contests unleashed a torrent of political activities and partisan newspaper articles. Newspapers on both sides hyped the elections by suggesting that the contest for President would turn on the outcome of the state's senate races.

Discussion during the campaign centered on the continuing legislative deadlock over the manner of choosing electors. Republicans initially had demanded a statewide vote for electors in Pennsylvania because they thought it would favor Jefferson, but now, due to the lack of time for an election, they wanted the legislature to appoint a slate of electors that would somehow reflect their party's greater numbers in the State Assembly and its control of the governorship. Federalists originally had held out for district balloting for electors, which they thought would help Adams, and now sought to use their control of the State Senate either to block Pennsylvania from voting at all or to gain an equal share of its electors.

Pennsylvania Republicans stressed the importance of winning every senate seat up for election in 1800. "Our annual election is now at hand," the *Aurora* declared. "It is, fellow citizens, within the compass of a probability . . . that upon the vote of a single member of the Senate of this state may rest the decision of the mighty contest [for President] which is now agitating the mind of every American citizen." Republicans did their best to mobilize their voters across the state with rallies, pamphlets, and speeches. "It is intended by them to use every effort to obtain favorable changes in the senators to be chosen at the next election," the *Gazette of the United States* warned its Federalist readers. "We beg leave to put you on your guard and earnestly to exhort you to leave nothing undone to secure a favorable return of senators."

When Election Day finally came, both sides pleaded for their supporters to vote. "CITIZENS OF PHILADELPHIA, TAKE YOUR CHOICE," the *Aurora* proclaimed on October 14. "FEDERALISTS TO YOUR POSTS," the *Gazette* countered. "This day decides whether Virtue, Liberty and Independence shall prevail or whether Jacobinic tyranny shall lord o'er COLUMBIA. As you love your country, fly to your polls."

Toward the end of the campaign, electioneering turned sharply negative. Assailing Jefferson, the *Gazette of the United States* asserted, "In a few days, the question will be seriously and strenuously made whether the experiment of a federal republic under religious, moral, and steadfast politicians tracing the high road to order, dignity, glory and independence is still to be essayed; or whether we be willing to submit to the Gallic domination of an acknowledged Deist." Pressing its point, the article added about Jefferson, "Men know his contempt of Christianity, his Parisian policies, his visionary projects, his timidity, his inconsistencies." Republicans, in contrast, warned of tyranny and worse under Adams. "The friends of *peace will vote for Jefferson*; the friends of war will vote for *Adams* or for *Pinckney*," the *Aurora* declared. It reprinted personal letters supplied by Pennsylvania Republican Tench Coxe suggesting that Adams wanted a monarchy and Pinckney supported Britain. Rumors circulated that Adams had once sent Pinckney to England for four mistresses—two for each man—leading Adams to joke, "If this be true, General Pinckney has kept all for himself and cheated me out of my two."

For Republicans, the Pennsylvania election results turned out better than they had expected but not as good as they had hoped. In Pittsburgh, for example, where Federalists had won in 1799, the *Herald of Liberty* reported, "Republicans will carry every candidate from the Coroner to the Congressman. Never was there such a change known." A similar shift occurred in the east-central counties where Fries's Rebellion occurred. Overall, Republicans won 10 of 13 congressional races, 55 of the 78 seats in the State Assembly, and all but 1 of the 7 Senate contests. That still left Federalists in control of the State Senate by a single seat, however. "The elections in that state have been greatly in favor of the Republicans," Jefferson wrote to Charles Pinckney in early November, but "the Federalists carried their [State Senate] member in Lancaster." Either both sides would have to compromise or Pennsylvania would not vote for President. While the situation in Pennsylvania was a simple stalemate, in South Carolina, multiple factors—some personal and some partisan—clouded the prospects.

Voters in South Carolina cast ballots on the same day as Pennsylvanians but under different conditions. Where Pennsylvania lacked an established method of choosing electors, South Carolina law clearly prescribed that the entire legislature, sitting as one body, choose each of their state's eight electors by majority vote of all the members. This left ample room for logrolling, vote trading, and backroom deals among the members. Legislators could choose all eight electors from one party, pick some from each, or name independent electors, as happened in 1796, when South Carolina had cast its votes for Jefferson and Thomas Pinckney. While in Pennsylvania partisan politics had developed to the point where candidates ran exclusively on party tickets, colonial-style patrician politics still survived in South Carolina. Candidates there identified themselves more with elite patrons and wealthy families than with political parties. The Pinckney family—rent between parties—carried the most weight. First cousins Charles Cotesworth Pinckney and Charles Pinckney, ages fifty-four and forty-two respectively, were, by 1800, bitter rivals battling over their state's eight electoral votes.

General Pinckney (as virtually everyone called Charles Cotesworth) was a conservative patriot in the mold of Washington and Hamilton. He had led South Carolina into rebellion against Britain and subsequently served his state and nation in various posts even as he rebuilt his considerable estate after suffering wartime losses. Stout and broad shouldered with a round face and Roman nose, Pinckney had a practical intelligence and a determined nature. He fought the Revolution to preserve what he, as a South Carolina patrician, viewed as the traditional rights of Englishmen, which for him included the God-given right to enslave Africans—a right that prewar legal developments in Britain appeared to threaten. He never saw much wisdom in extending those rights further, certainly not to slaves. In addition to serving as Southern commander for the Additional Army in 1800, General Pinckney was a state legislator and, if reelected, would participate in selecting South Carolina's electors. He felt confident that these electors would vote for him.

Charles Pinckney (called "Blackguard Charlie" by local Federalists) held a lower military rank during the Revolution than his cousin but rose higher in the echelons of South Carolina politics. He served three terms as governor during the 1790s and, by 1800, was a U.S. senator.

Idealized nineteenth-century group portrait of John Adams, Gouverneur Morris, Alexander Hamilton, and Thomas Jefferson as leaders of the Revolutionary Era Continental Congress. Although all four patriot leaders served in the Continental Congress, they did not do so at the same time.

New York Governor John Jay, a Revolutionary Era leader and Federalist supporter of John Adams.

Benjamin Franklin in frontier fur hat such as he wore while serving as American minister to France.

D

John Adams as President, circa 1798.

E

Abigail Adams as First Lady, circa 1800.

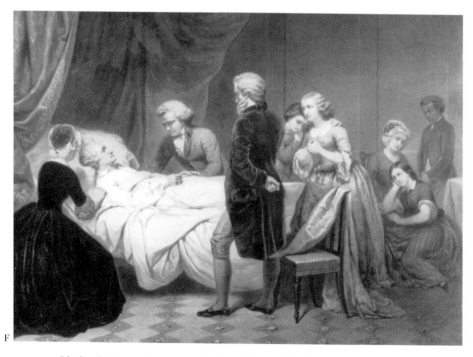

F

Idealized nineteenth-century painting of George Washington on his deathbed
attended by his doctors, friends, and grieving wife.

G

Republican Party founder and leader
James Madison.

H

Virginia Governor and Jefferson ally
James Monroe.

I

1793 cartoon showing Thomas Jefferson leading a riotous Anti-Federalist meeting under the creed, "The People are All and we are the People." The devil appears in the lower left corner stating, "What a pleasure it is to see ones work thrive so well." (Courtesy of The Library Company of Philadelphia)

Pennsylvania Governor and Republican
leader Thomas McKean.

ELECTION.

TO THE ELECTORS OF PENNSYLVANIA,

Beware.—The partizans of ross have secretly projected a plan, on which their last hopes are fixed:—a short space of time before the election, they intend circulating a report in the counties more remote to the city, that Mr. M'Kean is dead of the yellow fever; and prompt the republicans to take up Ger. Muhlenburg, and by such a division secure the election of Ross.—It is hoped the republicans will be aware of this deception. Our pretended Feds often hang themselves with their own halters.

Take Your Choice.

Thomas M'Kean,	Or, James Ross.
1. A devout Christian	1. An avowed Deist
2. A steady Patriot of 1776	2. A trimming Politician of 1794.
3. A true American	3. A British Partizan
4. A Republican	4. A Monarchist
5. A lover of Peace	5. An advocate for War.
6. An experienced Magistrate	6. A litigious Attorney
7. An asserter of the Laws	7. A fomenter of the Western Insurrection
8. An admirer of the militia	8. A friend to standing armies
9. An enemy to oppressive taxation	9. A promoter of the Stamp act, Excise laws, and Land Tax
10. A supporter of the trial by Jury and the freedom of the Press	10. A patron of the Alien and Sedition Bills
11. An honest man	11. A Land Jobber
12. A friend to the poor.	12. An Usurer

Take Notice!

Who are the Friends of Thomas M'Kean, and who are the Friends of James Ross.

1. Old Whigs	1. Old Tories
2. Staunch Republicans	2. Inveterate aristocrats
3. Independent Americans.	3. Office-holders or Office-hunters

Take Care!

Thomas M'Kean's election is sure, and — *James Ross's election will be sure.*

1. If all true Republicans turn out and vote	1. If the Republicans keep at home
2. If the Republicans are firm on the ground of Election	2. If the Republicans are negligent or timid on the ground of Election
3. If there is no foul play in the Election	3. If Election frauds are not detected and prevented.

Take Advice!

1. *LOOK WELL TO YOUR TICKETS:* 3. *LOOK WELL TO YOUR TALLIES:*
2. *LOOK WELL TO YOUR BOXES:* 4. *LOOK WELL TO YOUR RETURNS.*

Now or Never.

Finally, as an Epitome of the Whole.

M'KEAN.	ROSS.
Have the friends of Thomas M'Kean ever associated with any such or with any others, that could in any manner be designated or known, as enemies of Liberty and of the People.	Do not the friends of James Ross associate with British emissaries British pensioners British merchants Old tories Refugees, Traitors Aristocrats Monarchists.
Have not the friends of Thomas M'Kean uniformly opposed all the measures, and all other measures which, could have a tendency to establish a Standing army in time of Peace; to increase Public Salaries and Public Debt.; to create heavy and oppressive Taxes; to prevent Foreigners from emigrating to our country; to violate the Constitution by a Sedition Law, intended to prevent complaint against the injurious and daring violations of the Rights and Liberties of the People, and the constitution of the United States; measures which the friends of M'Kean for ever deprecate.	Do not the friends of James Ross, and James Ross himself, VOTE for Standing armies Loans at Eight Per Centum per Ann. Interest. High Public Salaries Increase of Public Debt Heavy Taxes Excises, Imposts, House Tax, Poll tax Window tax, hearth tax Plough Tax Cattle and horse tax Land tax Alien Bills and Sedition or Gag Bills To Cram every thing down your throats.

Republican broadside for Pennsylvania's
gubernatorial election, October 1799.

Longtime New York Republican leader
George Clinton.

M

Federalist Party founder and leader
Alexander Hamilton, circa 1800.

N

Aaron Burr as a young senator,
circa 1792.

O

General Charles Cotesworth Pinckney,
circa 1800, when he was chosen by the
Federalist congressional caucus to run with
John Adams as their party's candidates for
President and Vice President.

P

American diplomat and 1796 Federalist vice
presidential candidate Thomas Pinckney in
his Revolutionary War uniform.

Q

Napoleon Bonaparte shown after assuming
power as First Consul of France in 1800.

R

Secretary of State and High Federalist leader
Timothy Pickering.

S

Pastoral view of Washington as the nation's new capital in 1801.

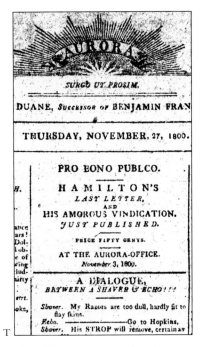

Republican newspaper advertisement for Alexander Hamilton's 1800 letter criticizing John Adams, offered with Hamilton's 1797 confession of adultery.

	Adams.	Pinckney.	Jefferson.	Burr.	Scattering.
N. Hampfhire	6	6	0	0	0
Maffachufetts	16	16	0	0	0
Connecticut	9	9	0	0	0
Vermont	4	4	0	0	0
Rhode-Ifland	4	3	1	0	0
New-York	0	0	12	12	0
New-Jerfey	7	5	2	0	0
Pennfylvania	5	5	10	10	0
Delaware	3	3	0	0	0
Maryland	7	7	3	2	1
Virginia	0	0	21	15	6
N. Carolina	5	3	7	7	2
S. Carolina	8	8	0	0	0
Georgia	2	2	2	2	0
Tenneffee	1	0	3	3	1
Kentucky	1	0	3	3	1
	78	71	60	56	11

The following table exhibits the votes as moft probably they will be given by the Electors :

There are two hundred and feventy fix votes to be counted :—

Adams	78
Pinckney	71
Jefferfon	60
Burr	56
Scattering	11

276

But if South-Carolina fhall vote for Pinckney, and neither for Adams nor Jefferfon, then the votes will be :

For Pinckney	71
Adams	70
Jefferfon	60
Burr	56
Scattaring	19

276

And in cafe Pennfylvania fhall be unanimous in favour of Jefferfon, and give no vote either for Adams or Pinckney, then no perfon will have a majority of votes— They will ftand thus :

Pinckney	66
Jefferfon	65
Adams	65
Burr	61
Scattering	19

276

Projection of the electoral vote from Philadelphia's Federalist *Gazette of the United States* on November 1, 1800. Similar projections appeared in Federalist newspapers throughout the campaign, often depicting a three-way contest between Adams, Pinckney, and Jefferson, with one of the two Federalist candidates winning the presidency. (© *American Antiquarian Society*)

	Jefferfon.	Adams.
Georgia,	4	0
Tenneffee,	3	0
Kentucky,	4	0
South-Carolina,	8	0
North-Carolina,	9	3
Virginia,	21	0
Maryland,	6	4
Delaware,	0	3
Pennfylvania,	—	—
New-Jerfey,	—	—
New-York,	12	0
Connecticut,	0	9
Rhode-Ifland,	0	4
Maffachufetts,	0	16
Vermont,	0	4
New-Hampfhire,	0	6
	67	49

But fhould Pennfylvania and New-Jerfey chofe electors, 22 votes muft be added to Jefferfon, when they will ftand thus,

| | 89 | 49 |

Projection of the electoral vote from Charleston's Republican *City Gazette* on October 30, 1800. Similar projections ran in Republican newspapers throughout the campaign, typically depicting the race for President as between Jefferson and Adams, with Jefferson winning by large margin.

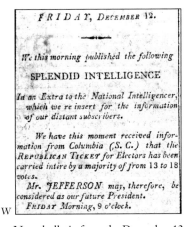

News bulletin from the December 12, 1800, edition of Washington's Republican *National Intelligencer* reporting the electoral vote from South Carolina. (© *American Antiquarian Society*)

X

United States Capitol in 1801, when the House of Representatives met there to elect the President.

Y

Thomas Jefferson, shown with a bust of Franklin,
scientific instruments, and the Declaration of
Independence, circa 1801.

Handsome, vain, openly ambitious, and something of a rake after his wife died in 1794, Pinckney was a political visionary who played a leading role in crafting the U.S. Constitution at the Philadelphia Convention. He jumped to the Republican Party from the Federalist faction during the mid-1790s in reaction to Jay's Treaty with Britain. Becoming a vocal critic of the Adams administration, he worked tirelessly for Jefferson's election in 1800. Under the pseudonym "A Republican," Pinckney penned twenty-four newspaper essays supporting the election of Jefferson over either Adams or his own cousin. Federalists resorted to charging Pinckney with disloyalty to his family, dereliction of his Senate duties, and self-interest in seeking an ambassadorship under Jefferson. Nothing silenced him.

Presidential politics loomed large in South Carolina's state legislative races, which upset some voters unaccustomed to partisan campaigning. One citizen wrote to a local paper, "We are so beset with and run down by *Federalists, Federal Republicans, and their pamphlets* that I begin to think, for the first time, there is something rotten with the system they attempt to support, or why all this violence and electioneering?" Striking a more hopeful note, another correspondent commented, "The citizens of Charleston, and of the state at large, I am certain, have too much spirit and good sense to permit themselves to be led by the sound of a name—whether that of a *Charles* or a *General.*"

Ultimately, the patrician structure of South Carolina politics withstood the partisan wave sweeping the country in 1800. General Pinckney handily won election to the State Senate from Charleston and carried with him nearly all the Federalist candidates running for legislature from the city. Demonstrating the weak hold of party politics, however, six of the fifteen Federalist candidates in Charleston also ran on the Republican ballot. Further, Republican candidates, or what one newspaper dubbed "Mr. C. P.'s Ticket," did well elsewhere. Statewide, more Republicans won than Federalists, but their party loyalty was untested. The new legislators were committed more to personalities than to parties. Thomas Pinckney advised Federalist Congressman John Rutledge Jr., "You know we can form no certain estimates [of party strength] from the persons returned [to the state legislature] because hitherto the distinctions of political parties has been marked by a very faint line" in South Carolina.

Leaving nothing to chance, after Congress reconvened in November, Charles Pinckney decided to stay in South Carolina to urge party discipline on Republican state legislators rather than assume his U.S. Senate seat in Washington. "I have taken post with some valuable friends at Columbia where our legislature meets and are now in session, and here I mean to remain until the thing is settled," he wrote to Madison in November. "I am the *only member of Congress of either side present* and the Federalists view me with a very jealous eye."

The five state legislative elections held during October had failed to resolve the contest for President. Federalists had won in New Jersey and Delaware, but most observers had assumed all along that the ten electoral votes of those two small states would go to the Federalists. In their larger neighbors to the west, Federalists retained control of the Pennsylvania Senate while Republicans took the Maryland House of Representatives, with Federalists in control of the Senate, leaving the twenty-five electoral votes of those two key states in doubt. South Carolina remained anyone's guess until its legislature actually met.

Going into November with less than five weeks until the Electoral College would meet, all four candidates could count on between forty and fifty votes, with seventy needed to win. During November, direct popular voting for electors in Rhode Island, Maryland, North Carolina, Georgia, and Kentucky could clarify the presidential race somewhat, but it now looked as if Pennsylvania and South Carolina legislators would decide it by their choice of electors. Because of their popularity in South Carolina and the distinct possibility that Pennsylvania would not vote, Jefferson and Pinckney appeared to be the front-runners, but any of the four candidates could still win the presidency. In a tight finish, the options were legion.

CHAPTER NINE

THUNDERSTRUCK

To many observers—those not on the inside of political circles—it seemed to strike abruptly, like a bolt from the sky. Federalist insiders, however, knew that it built gradually, somewhat akin to a smoldering volcano that finally erupts. It represented one more convulsion and further calumny in a campaign that already had too many of the former and too much of the latter. After months of more-discreet scheming, in October, Hamilton broke openly with Adams and, in doing so, exposed the true depth of the division between High Federalists and moderates within the party.

High Federalists never forgave Adams for reaching out to France in peace negotiations. "The rage of the Hamilton faction upon that occasion appeared to me then, and has appeared to me ever since, an absolute delirium," Adams later wrote. He saw himself as simply seeking peace for America through a policy of balanced neutrality with the warring parties in Europe. Unlike some Republicans, Adams did not favor France in the European wars, but, unlike the High Federalists, he deeply distrusted Britain. In his own eyes, he pursued a nationalistic policy that served only American interests. High Federalists, in contrast, viewed Adams's overture to France as weakness, and his subsequent decisions to disband the Additional Army, pardon Fries, and sack Pickering and McHenry only increased their fury.

Hamilton had quietly courted Federalist electoral votes for Pinckney throughout the summer. Despairing for the country's future under either Adams or Jefferson, Hamilton had reportedly commented in June that, "for his part, he did not expect his head to remain four years longer on his shoulders unless it was at the head of a victorious army." Perhaps that explained his interest in the Additional Army. During that same month, Hamilton began soliciting material from his confidants within the administration to use in a public exposé of the President's character and policies. The final impetus may have come when he read Secretary of War James McHenry's account of being fired by Adams, which related a diatribe in which the President called Hamilton an immoral intriguer and foreign bastard. Proud and impulsive, Hamilton decided to publish some sort of "statement" that would explain his opposition to Adams.

Back on July 1, Hamilton had asked Treasury Secretary Oliver Wolcott for help in composing the statement on Adams. "It is essential to inform the most discreet of this description of the facts which denote unfitness in Mr. Adams," Hamilton wrote. "To be able to give it, I must derive aid from you. . . . But you must be exact and much in detail." After initially agreeing to supply inside information on Adams, Wolcott cooled toward Hamilton's idea and delayed sending the material.

Hamilton repeated his request to Wolcott in August and spelled out his plan of distributing a letter denouncing Adams and defending himself. "I have serious thoughts of giving to the public my opinion respecting Mr. Adams, with my reasons in a letter to a friend with my signature," he wrote. Printed copies of this letter would circulate among Federalists. To make the letter not appear overtly political, Hamilton proposed couching it as a defense of his personal honor. "I could predicate it on the fact that I am abused by the friends of Mr. Adams who ascribe my opposition to pique and disappointment [at losing my army command], and would give it the shape of a *defense of myself*," Hamilton explained.

Even as he prepared this missive, Hamilton sent two terse notes to the President—one in August, another in October—accusing Adams of "base, wicked, and cruel calumny" and demanding personal satisfaction, as if by a duel. Shocking as it seemed for a party leader to confront a sitting President in this way, Hamilton had a dueler's temperament. Adams prudently ignored these demands, yet doing so may have provided just the pretext that Hamilton was seeking to publish his denunciation.

By September, Hamilton began sharing his idea of a public exposé of the President's character with a wider group of High Federalists and showing drafts of his proposed letter to some of them. They uniformly cautioned him that readers would dismiss the letter as a personal vendetta precipitated by Adams's decision to disband Hamilton's Additional Army. Unless published anonymously, George Cabot warned Hamilton, the letter "will be converted to a new proof that you are a *dangerous man.*" Fisher Ames advised, "*You* ought not with your name, or if practicable in any way that will be traced to *you*, to execute your purpose of exposing the reasons for a change of the executive." In September, even Wolcott told Hamilton, "Whatever *you* may say or write will, by a class of people, be attributed to personal resentment." There was no need to detail Adams's erratic character in a public letter, Wolcott added, because "the people believe that their president is crazy. This is the honest truth and what more can be said on the subject?" McHenry, whom Adams had fired in May, was somewhat more supportive. Though he cautioned that the letter would "come too late" to impact the election, he nonetheless supplied a good deal of damning inside information about Adams to Hamilton for the project.

Against the advice of his friends, Hamilton persisted as if possessed by private demons. Over the years, the brilliant former cabinet member had grown increasingly unable to judge or control his impulsive behavior. "You see I am in a very belligerent humor," Hamilton wrote to Wolcott regarding this matter. "It is plain that unless we give our reasons [for opposing the President] in some form or other—Mr. Adams's personal friends seconded by the Jacobins will completely *run us down in the public opinion.*" *They* will make *us* look "factious," he later added. "If this can not be counteracted, our characters are the sacrifice. To do it, facts must be stated from some authentic stamp. . . . Anony-

mous publications can now affect nothing." Adams's efforts to rehabil-
itate himself as a moderate were working, Hamilton as much as admitted, and threatened to brand High Federalists as extremists.

High Federalists must boldly make their case against the President,
Hamilton reasoned, or they would lose and their cause would fail. By
such arguments, he ultimately secured Wolcott's assistance in crafting
the letter. "Decorum may not permit going into the newspapers,"
Hamilton conceded to Wolcott, "but the letter may be addressed to so
many respectable men of influence as may give its contents general circulation." If sincere, this concession simply revealed Hamilton's political naïveté. To think that his signed attack on the President could
reach "general circulation" without creating a sensation in the press
reflected either stunning innocence or studied ignorance.

Like his two abusive notes to the President, this was an act of madness. Hamilton biographer Ron Chernow concluded, "In writing an
intemperate indictment of John Adams, Hamilton committed a form
of political suicide that blighted the rest of his career." Much as when
he published a pamphlet admitting to an extramarital affair with Maria
Reynolds, Hamilton once more became his own worst enemy.

Published on October 22, Hamilton's "letter" ran fifty-four printed
pages in pamphlet form and read like one long rant. "Not denying to
Mr. Adams patriotism and integrity," Hamilton began, "I should be
deficient in candor were I to conceal the conviction that . . . there are
great and intrinsic defects in his character which unfit him for the
office of Chief Magistrate." He then scrutinized Adams's record of
public service from the Revolutionary War to 1800 in the harshest
light, purporting to find a pattern of bad judgment and an inability to
persevere "in a systematic plan of conduct." For example, he asserted
that Adams's wartime proposal to enlist troops annually during the
Revolution (rather than for the duration of the conflict) would have
"proved the ruin of our cause" and that John Jay (rather than Adams)
deserved credit for negotiating a favorable peace with Britain. At the

time, even Republicans viewed Adams as a hero of the Revolution and honored his service to the country. Criticizing that service, as Hamilton did, inevitably struck readers as petty.

In his letter, Hamilton passed quickly over the eight-year tenure of Adams as Vice President except to disparage his "extreme egotism" and "vanity without boundaries" in office. "His public conduct in that station was satisfactory to the friends of the government, though they were now and then alarmed by appearances of some eccentric tendencies," Hamilton observed. Claiming to have perceived these tendencies early on, Hamilton acknowledged having worked behind the scenes for the election of Thomas Pinckney over Adams in 1796, but disingenuously denied any personal reasons for doing so. "No," Hamilton protested, "the considerations which had reconciled me to the success of Mr. Pinckney were of a nature exclusively public. They resulted from the disgusting egotism, the distempered jealousy, and the ungovernable indiscretion of Mr. Adams's temper, joined to some doubts of the correctness of his maxims of administration." Hamilton's twin motives of defending himself and denouncing Adams, apparent in this passage, made his letter sound at once defensive and spiteful. His motives worked at cross purposes.

In Hamilton's analysis, Adams's eccentric tendencies grew in magnitude to become fatal defects during his term as President. Characterizing this tenure as "a heterogeneous compound of right and wrong, of wisdom and error," Hamilton launched into a one-sided harangue against all that he viewed as wrong with Adams's presidency. In Hamilton's eyes, of course, Adams's greatest failing as President came in his decision to resume peace negotiations with France "after the mortifying humiliations we had endured" from that country. Adams made this allegedly impulsive decision over the objections of his cabinet and without consulting Federalists in Congress. "Very different from the practice of Adams was that of the modest and sage Washington. He consulted much, pondered much, resolved slowly, resolved surely," Hamilton commented.

Behind the various poor decisions made by Adams lay a petulant disposition that fouled his judgment and spoiled his leadership, Hamilton argued. "It is a fact that he is often liable to paroxysms of anger, which deprive him of self command and produce very outrageous behavior to those who approach him," Hamilton wrote. "Most, if not all, his ministers and several distinguished members of the two houses of Congress have been humiliated by the effects of these gusts of passion." One such irrational outburst led to McHenry's dismissal, he asserted, and others unjustly sullied Hamilton himself. "He has denominated me a man destitute of every moral principle," Hamilton complained, "he has stigmatized me as the leader of a British faction." Hamilton self-righteously denied these charges, commenting about the pro-British one, "Of the purity of my public conduct in this, as in other particulars, I may defy the severest investigation."

After fifty-three pages vilifying the President and scarcely a word about Charles Cotesworth Pinckney, Hamilton concluded his letter with the incongruous recommendation that Federalist electors should vote for Adams and Pinckney. "To refrain from a decided opposition to Mr. Adams's reelection has been reluctantly sanctioned by my judgment, which has been not a little perplexed between the unqualified conviction of his unfitness for the station contemplated and a sense of the great importance of cultivating harmony among the supporters of the government," he wrote. After reviewing a draft of the letter in early October, Wolcott urged Hamilton at least to change the end. Why attack Adams and then endorse him? It made little sense then and has puzzled historians ever since. "The final section of the pamphlet seemed particularly absurd," Chernow noted. "For a man of Hamilton's incomparable talent, the pamphlet was a crazily botched job, an extended tantrum in print."

Hamilton may have wanted the letter to circulate only among discreet Federalists, but Republicans obtained copies of it almost immediately and quickly began reprinting the most scandalous parts in their newspapers. Although both Aaron Burr and Republican organizer John

Beckley received credit for filching the document and passing it on to the *Aurora*, these accounts contain discrepancies. Whoever the source was, on October 21—one day before Hamilton's publisher would apply for a copyright on the letter and three days before he released it—the *Aurora* reported, "Alexander Hamilton has been some time occupied in writing another *vindication* of himself *contra* John Adams. It is already printed in New York, 200 copies only. . . . We expect to be able soon to exhibit the secret *curiosity*." Excerpts began appearing the following day. Describing it as "better that [the letter] should appear *in toto* than by *piece meal*," Hamilton's publisher promptly began selling it to the general public for twenty-five cents a copy. The first printing sold out quickly and more followed. In all, five editions of Hamilton's letter appeared by mid-November, including an unauthorized one published by the *Aurora*. Hamilton actually seemed to welcome all the attention given his letter and even discussed writing a revised, expanded version of it. His friends discouraged the effort, however. Most of them were shocked by the letter and unsure how to deal with it.

"The subject which now occupies the public mind and excites much attention is the letter from General Hamilton," New York High Federalist Robert Troup wrote in early November to the American ambassador in London, Rufus King. "The letter has been read by all parties with prodigious avidity, and the spread of it has been extensive." Others made similar comments about the widespread interest in Hamilton's letter. "Disapprobation of it [is] expressed everywhere," Troup added, "and not a man in our whole circle of friends but condemns it." Anticipating the letter's publication, Troup earlier wrote to King, "I cannot describe to you how broken and scattered your Federal friends are! . . . Shadows, clouds, and darkness rest on our future prospects." Two weeks after the letter's publication, Hamilton boasted to McHenry about the response to it, "The press teems with answers." McHenry replied from Maryland, "Those amongst the Federalists in this state . . . consider the publication of your letter rather calculated to distract than to do good."

As news of Hamilton's letter and its contents spread across the country, it became a factor in the presidential campaign. The public now knew that the once unified Federalists were rent into factions with its best-known leaders locked in mortal combat. People seemed less interested in debating the merits of the letter's charges than in speculating about who came off worse in the episode, Hamilton or Adams. While the contents of the letter gave new currency to old doubts about Adams's leadership, its style, substance, and timing raised even graver misgivings about Hamilton's judgment. There were no winners among Federalists. Republicans were ecstatic.

Assuming a stance that served to refute depictions of his ungovernable temper, the President took the high road by not responding publicly to Hamilton. Of course, Adams vented in private and even composed a detailed, point-by-point refutation of Hamilton's letter, but he did not release any of it for nearly a decade, when he published a defense of his presidency. For the time being, he appeared unruffled. "I regret [the letter] more on account of its author than on my own because I am confident it will do him more harm than me," Adams wrote to one correspondent late in 1800. "The public indignation he has excited is punishment enough." Adams also sent a note to New York Governor John Jay, who always backed the administration, volunteering that, "Among the very few truths in [Hamilton's] pamphlet, there is one that I shall ever acknowledge with pleasure, *viz.* that the principal merit of the negotiations for peace was Mr. Jay's." In a gracious comment that betrayed his own embattled state, Adams added, "I often say that when my confidence in Mr. Jay shall cease, I must give up the cause of confidence and renounce it with all men."

Adams deeply resented the betrayal of private confidences by his advisers reflected in Hamilton's letter. Soon after the letter appeared, but without giving it as a reason, Wolcott submitted his resignation to the President, who accepted it. Adams was finally free of the last Hamiltonian in his cabinet.

Abigail Adams took a similar tack as her husband. "I shall not say anything to you upon political subjects," she wrote to her sister in early November, "no not upon the little General's letter, but reserve it for a future letter when . . . you have more health to laugh at the folly and pity the weakness, vanity, and ambitious view of [this] sparrow." In a subsequent letter, she simply stated that a proper answer to Hamilton's "gross lies" should come from someone who better knew the circumstances.

Adams's supporters rallied to his defense in pamphlets and published letters. Federalist lexicographer Noah Webster took the lead in a widely reprinted open letter to Hamilton. "Admitting all your charges against Mr. Adams, they amount to too small a sum to balance the immense hazard of the game you are playing," Webster wrote of Hamilton's scheme to elect Pinckney. "It avails little that you accuse the President of *vanity* for as to this . . . were it an issue between Mr. Adams and yourself, which has the most, you could not rely on an unanimous verdict in your favor," he charged. "That the President is *unmanageable* is, in a degree true: that is, you and your supporters can not manage him; but this will not pass in this country as a crime. That he is unstable is alleged—pray sir . . . did he waver during the Revolutionary War?"

Occasional ill humor and hasty declarations do not equal lunacy, Webster argued. Adams was neither mad nor mentally unfit for office. Webster admonished Hamilton that, by asserting otherwise about the party's candidate for President on the eve of a critical election, "Your conduct on this occasion will be deemed little short of insanity." Given the risk that the letter would either divide the Federalist Party or destroy it, Webster asked, "Will not Federal men, as well as anti-Federal, believe that your ambition, pride, and overbearing temper have destined you to be the evil genius of this country?"

Although High Federalists tended to believe and agree with the substance of Hamilton's letter, many of them objected to its style and timing. "I am *bound* to tell you that you are accused by respectable men of egoism and some very worthy and sensible men say you have exhibited the same *vanity* in your [letter] which you charge as a dangerous quality and great weakness in Mr. Adams," George Cabot admonished Hamilton. Supreme Court Justice Bushrod Washington, the first President's nephew, wrote from South Carolina, "We are all thunderstruck here by General Hamilton's pamphlet." He warned of a backlash against Pinckney by pro-Adams electors. "This letter," Hamilton's longtime friend and ally Robert Troup observed from New York in December, "continues to be disapproved of here. I have not yet met with a dissenting voice." A few High Federalists privately commended Hamilton for speaking the truth about Adams, but even their letters to Hamilton contained reports of criticisms by other party members. Hamilton never regained standing within the party. Moderates now resented him for betraying Adams on the eve of the election, while High Federalists questioned his discretion. Still, by articulating the conservative case against Adams, the letter stoked the opposition of High Federalists to the President.

Writing to the American ambassador in London about Hamilton's letter, Troup added, "Our enemies are universally in triumph." After months of growing uncertainty, Republicans again felt optimistic about the outcome of the election. Madison's cousin, the president of William and Mary College, wrote excitedly to Jefferson on November 1, "Hamilton's attack upon Mr. Adams is perfect confirmation of all that *that* arch and clever fellow Duane has been so long hinting at or rather affirming [in the *Aurora*]. It will be a thunderbolt to both." The Republican *Centinel of Freedom* wryly noted that the severity of Hamilton's attack on the President "would have subjected a [Republican] to federal prosecution, condemnation, fine, and imprisonment" under the Sedition Act. Word of the letter reached Monroe before a copy of it, but he promptly wrote to Madison, "From what I have heard of the work, it will do their whole party more harm than good. I am told that it unmasks the views of that party too much not to injure it."

Despite its concluding call for electors to vote for Adams and Pinckney, virtually everyone assumed that the real purpose of Hamilton's letter was to boost Pinckney at Adams's expense in the forthcoming Electoral College balloting. Of course, Federalist electors need not vote for both Adams and Pinckney: They could vote for either, neither, or both. As was now widely recognized, Hamilton hoped that enough of them would vote for Pinckney and someone on neither ticket so that Pinckney would finish first overall.

Many people further assumed that Hamilton favored the relatively obscure Pinckney for President because he could control him and that he was willing to manipulate the Electoral College system to put his puppet on the throne. Although some High Federalists preferred Pinckney to Adams for President, most Federalist electors undoubtedly intended for Adams to remain President and Pinckney to become Vice President. This placed Pinckney in an awkward position if he appeared to endorse Hamilton's scheme. Federalist electors favoring Adams for President could retaliate by withholding votes from Pinckney, as they had done to Thomas Pinckney in 1796.

Fear that the letter could cost him votes from pro-Adams electors led Pinckney to reaffirm his commitment to run with Adams as a team. On various occasions, he effectively promised not to seek support from electors independently. It became for him a public pledge and Pinckney was, above all, a man of honor. Even if he wanted to win the presidency over Adams, Pinckney now could not show it or he would likely lose; yet, to win, Pinckney needed independent votes, especially from South Carolina. Hamilton's letter effectively restricted his ability to solicit them. In this sense, the letter backfired badly on Hamilton.

By dividing the party, Hamilton's letter also complicated Federalist efforts in the five states where voters directly chose presidential electors: Virginia, North Carolina, Kentucky, Maryland, and Rhode Island. Voters in these states were preparing to cast their ballots just as news broke of Hamilton's letter.

"An eventful period is approaching," one newspaper warned voters on the eve of the November elections. "All the evil spirits which distract and mislead a people have long been and now are actively and indefatigably employed in the United States. It behooves you, therefore, as you value your country's happiness and continued prosperity, to inquire with earnestness into the probable effect of measures recommended." This newspaper supported Adams and Pinckney, but a similar note of urgency also sounded in the Republican press. In the minds of many, the people remained a wild card in presidential politics: That was why lawmakers in most states did not authorize them to vote for electors.

The voting began on the first Monday of November with both a statewide election in Virginia and district elections in North Carolina. This was Jefferson country. Any chance for the Federalists to win electoral votes in Virginia had ended in January, when Governor Monroe and Republicans in the legislature changed the method of choosing electors to a single, statewide general election in which all the candidates ran. Even though Federalist candidates did well in some pockets of Virginia, the overall state vote went heavily Republican. "The elections have exceeded our hopes," Madison wrote from his central Virginia home on November 10. "In this county, out of more than 350 votes, seven only were in the wrong ticket." Republican elector candidates triumphed by a three-to-one margin statewide, giving "the Jefferson ticket" (as Madison called it) all of Virginia's twenty-one electoral votes—the biggest prize in the nation.

In North Carolina, which Charles Pinckney and others had hoped to secure for Jefferson by a switch to a statewide general-ticket method of choosing electors, Federalists actually increased their number of electors from the single one elected in 1796. The state retained its electoral-district method of picking electors, and Federalists prevailed in four out of the state's twelve electoral districts. Some of these elections were extremely close, but the total did not greatly exceed expectations. These were Federalist districts in a Republican state: The party's congressional candidates won in them, too. Perhaps helping the Federalists, news of Hamilton's attack on Adams did not reach North Carolina until after the vote.

Elections in Kentucky and Maryland followed a week later. Both states chose electors in district elections. The method did not matter in Kentucky because the state was uniformly Republican. One of two new states carved out of the trans-Appalachian West during the 1790s, in 1798, its Republican-dominated legislature passed resolutions, anonymously drafted by Jefferson, denouncing the Alien and Sedition Acts as unconstitutional and declaring them void in Kentucky. A frontier people, Kentuckians had little affection for the elite Easterners who dominated the Federalist Party and were certain to cast their four electoral votes for Jefferson regardless of how they selected them. Parties did not formally nominate candidates for elector in Kentucky; individuals simply offered themselves for the post. In some Kentucky districts, both elector candidates pledged themselves to vote Republican, giving voters no real choice.

Whereas political parties took little part in the campaigns for electors from Kentucky, the November district elections in Maryland played out virtually as a continuation of the overtly partisan October elections for the state's legislature. With its rigid political hierarchy dating from its founding as a proprietary colony owned by one of Britain's richest feudal lords, Maryland once appeared to offer the brightest prospect for Federalists in the South. Seven of its ten electors had voted for Adams in 1796, and six of those had cast their other votes for Thomas Pinckney. In 1800, Federalists had expected to do at least as well in Maryland as before, and hoped to do even better if they changed the rules for selecting electors. Those expectations changed, however, when the Federalists' eleventh-hour proposal to have the legislature choose the state's electors backfired and Republicans captured the state's House of Representatives in the October elections.

The rules did not change: Maryland voters would still choose their state's electors in district elections on November 10. Suddenly, however, Republicans began talking about their candidates winning in most of Maryland's electoral districts. The Federalist proposal to have legislators appoint electors had refocused the legislative races on presidential politics and, when the proposal failed, the underlying debate continued through the November elections. As during the legislative campaigns, the contests for electors pitted Federalists, who typically hailed Adams's steady patriotism and denounced Jefferson's alleged atheism, against Republicans, who contrasted Jefferson's love of liberty with Adams's monarchical predilections and policies.

Then something new intervened that might have improved Adams's prospects. On November 7, three days before the scheduled vote in Maryland, word reached Baltimore that Adams's bold gamble for peace had succeeded. The first accounts came from month-old European newspapers carried to the United States aboard the ship *America*. They contained few specifics. The text of the actual agreement, known as the Convention of 1800 or Treaty of Mortefontaine, did not arrive until December. After months of pessimistic reports predicting the imminent suspension of peace talks, the unexpected good news spread rapidly. Under the agreement, naval hostilities between the two countries would cease. The path to peace had opened when American negotiators dropped their demands for indemnities from France for losses to American shipping and the formal termination of the old Franco-American Alliance. Ever since revolutionaries had removed the King from the helm of the French government, Federalists had wanted out of America's supposedly perpetual alliance with France. The parties agreed to reserve these emotional issues for future discussion.

The peace treaty surprised and delighted Adams. Fearing that the negotiation would fail, he had considered asking Congress, when it reconvened in mid-November, for a general declaration of war against France to supplement the limited authorization of naval engagements approved in 1798. "If war in any degree is to be continued, it is a serious question whether it will not be better to take off all the restrictions and limitations," Adams wrote to Secretary of State John Marshall in September. "We shall be tortured with a perpetual conflict of parties . . . until we have either peace or war."

Apparently fearing that Adams might call for war in his opening address to Congress, Jefferson had already decided to delay his arrival in Washington until after the President's speech. As Vice President, he should have presided over the address, but Jefferson did not want to confront Adams publicly on policy matters—particularly the issue of war or peace—until the election was over. Writing from Washington in late November, Abigail Adams joked about the situation in the context of Jefferson's noted taste for luxuries. "'Tis said [Thomas Jefferson] is on his way, but travels with so many delicacies in his rear that he cannot get on fast lest some of them should suffer," she wrote to her daughter, Nabby.

With informal word of a peace agreement but without the actual text of it, Adams could not fully capitalize on having achieved an honorable peace. He passed over the issue quickly in his address to Congress on November 22 by stating simply that Napoleon had received the American negotiators "with the respect due their character." Restoring American neutrality and trading rights at a time of continuing war in Europe stood as the crowning achievement of Adams's presidency, but it came too late to affect the election significantly. Most states had already chosen either their electors or the legislators who would pick them.

Maryland, however, had still to vote. Even there, though, the news made little difference. The deposed war minister, James McHenry of Baltimore, who had supplied Hamilton with confidential information about Adams for his damning letter, now nursed a private grudge against the President. That he and his High Federalist faction controlled the party machinery in Maryland did not bode well for Adams, and news of the tentative peace agreement only fed the animosity. Like McHenry, many of Maryland's leading Federalists would sooner fight France than negotiate with its hated leaders. Further, even if the style and timing of Hamilton's letter offended Federalists generally, many High Federalists found its arguments against Adams compelling. After thanking Hamilton for exposing the President's "unfitness" for office, for example, Charles Carroll of Carrollton, Maryland's oldest surviving signer of the Declaration of Independence, sat out the election. "I fear our Constitution would be more injured by [Adams's] unruly passions, antipathies, and jealousy than by the whimsies of Jefferson," Carroll concluded.

Hamilton's letter presumably contributed to a general torpor within Federalist ranks in the state. "Tomorrow, the electors of this state are to be chosen by the people," McHenry wrote to Wolcott from Baltimore on November 9. "Here, we shall make little or no exertion for the Federal[ist] candidate, not from any indifference to the good old cause, but from . . . an opinion pretty generally imbibed of the utter unfitness of one of the Federal[ist] candidates to fill the office of President." McHenry then added about Adams, "Whether he is sportful, playful, witty, kind, cold, drunk, sober, angry, easy, stiff, jealous, careless, cautious, confident, close, open, it is almost always in the *wrong place* or to the *wrong persons*. For such a chief . . . who can contend?" Reports of peace with France did not placate McHenry. "What kind of convention have our beleaguered ambassadors made with Bonaparte? And what points have they left undecided?" he asked Wolcott.

If, as High Federalists seemed to wish, the Maryland elections served as a referendum on Adams's presidency, then the verdict was mixed. Federalists rebounded from their party's staggering setback in the October legislative elections, but only to parity with the Republicans. In the November elections, each party won in five of the state's ten electoral districts. Maryland voters could have all but determined the presidential contest by giving the lion's share of their electors to one party, but instead the split decision in the elections simply kept the race too close to call.

With only three undecided states remaining—Rhode Island, Pennsylvania, and South Carolina—any one of the four candidates could still win the presidency outright by gaining sufficient votes from these remaining electors. In a late November letter to his son-in-law, Jefferson projected the electoral-vote tally so far: "Setting aside Pennsylvania, Rhode Island, and South Carolina, the Federal scale will have from the other states 53 votes and the Republican 58." This tally was off by one due to incomplete returns from North Carolina. When the final results reached him from North Carolina, Jefferson revised his running tally to stand at 57 to 54 in favor of the Republicans.

If every state named all its electors in 1800, then a candidate for President needed votes from at least 70 of them to win outright. With each elector casting 2 votes, of course, two candidates could potentially receive 70 or more votes. In that event, the candidate with the highest total would win, or, if two tied at top, then Congress would choose between them. Already confident of getting at least 57 votes when the Electoral College met on December 3, Jefferson knew that votes from Pennsylvania's 15 electors could put him over the top. If Pennsylvania did not participate, which remained a distinct possibility, then candidates would need votes from only 62 electors for a majority. South Carolina's 8 electors could supply them for Jefferson. Rhode Island carried less significance at this point because its 4 electors could not tip the contest decisively for any candidate. At most, they could help candidates build their totals.

Of the three remaining undecided states, Rhode Island acted first. It was scheduled to choose its four electors in a statewide general election on November 19. Adams, as a fellow New Englander, was popular with state voters but Republicans nourished hopes of securing at least some of the state's electoral votes. A hotbed of antifederalism in the 1780s and early 1790s, Rhode Island remained hostile territory for High Federalists. The state's independent-minded governor, Arthur Fenner, promised to split his two votes between Adams and Jefferson if he became an elector. Republicans hoped that other Rhode Island electors might follow his lead.

Declaring that "the efforts of both parties will be greater than at any election since independence," one local Republican forecast that Rhode Island's four electors would give "four [votes] for Jefferson, two for Burr, and two for Adams." This highly optimistic projection presumed that two electors would vote for the Republican ticket and two would split their votes between Jefferson and Adams. Jefferson never counted on receiving votes from any New England state, but his supporters had high hopes for Rhode Island. Fearing the worst, one local Federalist pleaded with voters, "How disgraceful will it be to the *sober, steady,* and *consistent* character of *New England* if one of her states should totally depart from that character and range herself under the standard of *Virginia*. . . . Let us remember that we are not voting for a single representative in the Assembly or in Congress, but that the vote of a single [elector] may now decide *who shall administer the executive government of the United States.*"

As it turned out, the Federalist slate led by former Governor William Greene prevailed by a narrow margin in the statewide election. This gave the Federalists 4 additional electors. If all the electors chosen so far duly voted for both candidates of their respective parties, Adams and Pinckney would each receive 58 votes, while Jefferson and Burr would each get 57 votes. Of course, one or more electors might drop a vote from one of their party's candidates, but the running tally highlighted a new and disturbing threat to Jefferson.

Only two states remained to choose electors—Pennsylvania and South Carolina—and the Federalists had pulled ahead. If, as Jefferson feared, Pennsylvania did not vote, then Pinckney could finish ahead of him. That would happen if the South Carolina legislature, against the Republicans' efforts, again chose electors committed to split their votes between the Southern candidates, giving one each to Jefferson and Pinckney, as they had done between Jefferson and Thomas Pinckney in 1796. The final total would then be 66 for Pinckney, 65 for Jefferson, 58 for Adams, and 57 for Burr, with 62 needed for a majority. Jefferson would come in second again, and Adams would be out.

Always pessimistic about his own prospects, Jefferson now saw this outcome as likely. "Putting Pennsylvania, South Carolina, and *Pinckney* out of view, the votes will stand 57 for Jefferson and 58 for Adams, so that South Carolina will decide between these two. As to Pinckney, it is impossible to foresee how the juggle will work," Jefferson wrote confidentially to his son-in-law. "If the Federal[ist] electors of the other states go through with the caucus compact [to vote equally for Pinckney], there is little doubt that South Carolina will make him the president." Jefferson suspected that South Carolina's electors would each cast one vote for him and one vote for their home-state candidate. He now thought that his best hope lay in either the Pennsylvania legislature agreeing on a majority of Republican electors or some pro-Adams electors dropping votes from Pinckney.

Jefferson was hardly alone in musing about these options. In this letter to his son-in-law, written from Washington before word reached there about the outcome in either of the remaining undecided states, Jefferson noted that the election "is the only thing of which anything is said here." The closeness of the race and significance of the choice turned all eyes toward Pennsylvania and South Carolina. Their legislatures had until December 3 to choose electors or relinquish the right to vote. By law, all electors must cast their votes on that first Wednesday of December.

Following the October elections in Pennsylvania, Republican Governor Thomas McKean called a special session of the new legislature to meet in the state capital of Lancaster beginning on November 5. He hoped that somehow this session would lead to the appointment of Republican electors, but he had no clear plan how to achieve that goal. At least some Federalist state senators would need to cooperate for McKean to get his way because his party, despite its sizable majority in the State Assembly, did not control the Senate. Both houses would have to approve any law relating to the selection of electors. With the importance of the state's electoral votes now more readily apparent than ever, both sides dug in for a fight. As if to signal their resolve, Federalists named as State Senate president the brother-in-law of U.S. Senator James Ross, McKean's embittered opponent from 1799. "This I think is a bad symptom," one Republican wrote to Jefferson.

The special session got under way in Lancaster on November 8, with the governor welcoming newly elected lawmakers to the state capital. "The situation of our country is critical," he declared. "It has . . . fallen to the lot of Pennsylvania *not merely to determine an important election*, but to extinguish, by magnanimous example, those feuds and jealousies which have disturbed the order of society and which have threatened to eclipse the glory of the Revolution." Failing to cast electoral votes would disgrace the state and endanger the union, McKean asserted. Although not enough time remained to schedule and hold popular elections before the December 3 deadline for naming electors, the legislature could still appoint them. Lawmakers had twenty-four days to reach agreement.

Petitions flooded into the legislature and letters filled local newspapers urging legislators to reach some solution. Each side accused the other of partisanship while claiming to stand for principle. Attention focused on the State Senate, where holdover Federalists appeared to block the current popular will. "Could the monarchists in the senate of Pennsylvania proceed in robbing this state of her suffrage in the election of President, they would cover themselves with eternal reproach," the *Aurora* proclaimed. Not so, the Federalist *Philadelphia Gazette* countered. "A gracious Providence condescends to watch over the [affairs of the] United States," it advised senators, "and in none, perhaps, has this Divine interposition been more obvious than in the noble stand which is ordained you should make against the inroads of disorganization."

Pennsylvania Republicans argued that the Senate should submit to voters' wishes as reflected in recent elections, in which their candidates had won most of the seats in the State Assembly. "Their doctrine is not less laughable than absurd," the *Philadelphia Gazette* replied, "for they think the majority of the senate ought to yield their opinions and principles to the minority because, both houses taken collectively, there would be a great majority of Jeffersonians. This logic won't do." Rumors of bribes, threats, and violence circulated widely. Protesters purportedly burned an effigy of Federalist Senate floor leader Francis Gurney.

On November 8, Republicans in the State Assembly introduced and promptly passed a bill authorizing legislators to choose presidential electors by a majority vote of the combined membership of the Senate and Assembly, with each member casting one vote. Legislatures in other states typically used this method to choose electors. Pennsylvania Republicans pushed it now because it would give them a two-to-one advantage in voting and certainly would lead to the selection of fifteen Republican electors. Senate Federalists amended the bill to provide instead for the Republican-led Assembly to choose eight electors, who presumably would all be Republicans, and the Federalist-controlled Senate to choose seven electors, who just as surely would all be Federalists. Senate Federalists conceded one elector to the Republicans in return for Assembly Republicans accepting a split that would keep Federalists in contention nationwide. South Carolina would then decide the presidential election, and Federalists expected that state to support its native-son candidate, Charles Cotesworth Pinckney.

After making this opening offer, Federalists refused to give any more ground. "*Francis Gurney's* system of *bargaining* for electors resembles in some respects the plan of a noted Algerian renegade," the *Aurora* complained, "who finding provisions short, and fearing he might be the first victim, conspired with seven of his crew to murder their fellows, and then with the seven others, to murder them, by which means he got rid of both." When neither side backed down, a new impasse ensued.

In subsequent talks, Senate Federalists had the advantage of knowing that, if negotiations failed and Pennsylvania did not vote, the net effect would be much the same as under their plan. They had offered a reasonable compromise and would simply wait for the Republicans to accept it. Although Republicans could not know the precise count from other states, they realized that, from their perspective, even a one-vote advantage in Pennsylvania would help, given how tight the race had become. It might even prove crucial if South Carolina electors ended up voting equally for Jefferson and Pinckney.

Over the next two weeks, Republicans made a series of counteroffers calculated to secure more electors for their side. First they proposed selecting ten Republican and five Federalist electors; then nine and six. Various accounts suggested that Republicans promised favors and threatened reprisals to secure the two votes they needed from Federalists in the Senate, but to no avail. In a remarkable show of party unity, no Federalist broke ranks.

As the December 3 deadline approached, Pennsylvania Republicans finally acceded to the Federalists' conditions, apparently on the advice of party leaders in Congress. "The leading Jacobins at Washington had expresses constantly passing from thence to Lancaster previous to the decision for electors," the *Gazette of the United States* reported, "and when they found that threats, flattery, and corruption had no effect on the *Senate of Pennsylvania*, they advised the lower house to close with the proposition of the Senate." For the Republicans, a net gain of one elector was better than nothing even if it was less than they thought they deserved.

Once party leaders agreed to terms, the legislative process—stalled for weeks by negotiations—unfolded rapidly. On December 1, the State Senate nominated 8 Federalist candidates for elector and the State Assembly nominated 8 Republicans. On December 2, the entire legislature voted on these 16 candidates, with the top 15 of them elected: 8 Republicans and 7 Federalists. Adding these electors to those already designated by other states gave each party a total of 65 electors, with South Carolina still to choose its 8 electors and 70 needed for a majority. Commenting on the strategy of the Federalists in anticipation of the results in South Carolina, the *Aurora* reported the essential news that Pennsylvania "will have eight votes for Jefferson and seven for Pinckney, for with all their professions Adams will be left in the lurch." This comment presumed that South Carolina would split its electoral votes between Jefferson and Pinckney—opening the prospect for a tie between them, and shutting out Adams entirely. The 7 votes cast by Pennsylvania electors for Adams and the 8 votes they cast for Burr then would not matter. With the outcome now hinging on South Carolina, the 1800 election would come down to the question of modern party allegiance versus traditional state and sectional loyalty.

Even as Pennsylvania legislators resolved their deadlock, lawmakers in Columbia, South Carolina, struggled to choose the eight electors who would cast the state's sixteen electoral votes. Because of the distance between the two states, neither group knew what the other had done until two weeks after the fact. Each had to act on the assumption that its votes would decide the presidency. South Carolina legislators also had to factor in Pinckney's prospects of winning the presidency.

Although, remarkably, Adams held out hope of victory to the end, South Carolina electors had never been kind to him. In 1789, when Adams first became Vice President, they had voted for Washington and native son John Rutledge. In 1796, when Adams became President, they voted for Jefferson and native son Thomas Pinckney. Only in 1792, when Adams's sole opponent for Vice President was George Clinton—another Yankee—had any South Carolina electors voted for him. In 1800, Adams realized that the odds stood against his garnering votes from South Carolina.

After the October legislative elections, Jefferson held the clear advantage over Adams in South Carolina. Although party lines had not yet fully formed there, Republicans outnumbered Federalists in the state legislature following the elections, and most nonaligned members preferred Jefferson to Adams. Many of these independents, who held the balance of power in the legislature, surely liked Pinckney better than Adams too. For some of them, state and regional ties probably made the difference. For others, Hamilton's letter, coupled with Tench Coxe's release of Adams's 1792 letter criticizing the Pinckney brothers, may have hardened opposition to Adams. The Pinckneys were patriotic heroes in South Carolina. Calling them pro-British, as Adams had done in his letter, must have struck South Carolinians as highly offensive if not downright ludicrous.

If Republicans and independents had joined forces, they could have quickly secured the selection of electors who would all support Jefferson and Pinckney. Outside South Carolina, many Federalists fully expected this outcome. "At the time we agreed on Mr. Pinckney as a candidate," U.S. House Speaker Theodore Sedgwick noted prior to the October elections, "we had every assurance which could be given by the members from South Carolina that, whatever might be the character of their electors, such was the popularity of General Pinckney that all the votes of that state would be given to him—if federal[ist], of course for Adams and Pinckney; if anti-federal[ist], for Pinckney and Jefferson." Leading Federalists had failed to anticipate, however, the strength of the Republican vote in the October elections or the determination of Republicans to impose party discipline. They also did not foresee Pinckney's refusal to solicit votes independent of Adams. Particularly after the publication of Hamilton's letter, it had become a matter of honor for him not to do so.

The South Carolina legislature convened on November 24 for its regular autumn session, leaving it only eight days to choose the state's presidential electors. Unlike in Pennsylvania, where lawmakers met in special session and publicly debated the process of choosing electors; in South Carolina, the process was set by statute. Negotiations over who would serve as electors took place mostly in private as legislators attended to other matters in public sessions. Members of the state's House of Representatives and Senate—151 persons in all—would vote for electors jointly, each casting one vote for eight different candidates. Each party offered eight candidates, for a total of sixteen. The eight candidates receiving the most votes from the assembled legislators would serve as the state's electors.

Battle lines formed quickly. United States Senator Charles Pinckney led the Republican forces in open opposition to his cousin, the Federalist candidate, who attended as a state senator but tried to remain above the fray. In a November 22 letter to Jefferson, after acknowledging that "my situation is delicate in being obligated to oppose my own kinsman (who does not now on that account speak to me)," Charles Pinckney vowed to remain in the state capital and lobby for the party ticket until the legislature voted. Republican lawmakers caucused privately at the outset—nearly seventy strong by some counts—and pledged themselves to vote for electors committed to support Jefferson and Burr. To bolster their position further, Republicans challenged the credentials of eight Federalist representatives from

Charleston, claiming election fraud and (at Charles Pinckney's suggestion) asking for their immediate suspension from office. This might have given the Republicans a working majority, but their petition died without a vote.

Twice during the ensuing week, delegations representing nonaligned legislators reportedly asked General Pinckney if he would endorse the selection of electors committed to support him and Jefferson. To win, their candidates would need votes from Federalist legislators that only the general could command. Standing by his pledge to run with Adams, he refused to endorse any candidate who did not support the entire Federalist ticket. Although Charles Pinckney later disputed it, these independents, combined with Federalists, might have succeeded in electing a compromise slate of electors committed to the two Southern candidates. "In this dilemma, the Federalists had a very serious discussion of the proper measures to be pursued," one of them later wrote. "If we would give up on Mr. Adams, and consent to vote for electors who would vote for Mr. Jefferson and [Gen.] Pinckney, we could easily secure the election of Gen. Pinckney. . . . After mature deliberation, we resolved to venture all on the election of Mr. Adams and Gen. Pinckney, doubtful as it was." By most accounts, Republicans held only a plurality of seats in the South Carolina legislature and, if given the option, even some of them might have voted for candidates pledged to vote for Jefferson and General Pinckney. If all the Federalists had done so too, those candidates could have won.

General Pinckney recognized the implications of the Federalists' decision to stick with Adams. "Contrary to my former advices to you and all my expectation," he wrote to Secretary of State John Marshall on November 29, "I am sorry to inform you that the anti-federalists will have a *small* majority in our legislature, tho' sufficiently strong to carry their ticket for electors, which every man is pledged to support Jefferson and Burr. So far therefore as it rests on South Carolina, the election is settled."

Still the legislature hesitated to act, perhaps because some members hoped for a compromise. One Republican argued his party's case to wavering legislators in the press. "Gen. Pinckney is well known to you all; highly amiable in private life; and deservedly estimated as a man of true honor and integrity," he wrote. "But do not suffer yourselves to be deceived. If you do vote for Mr. Jefferson and General Pinckney together, let it be with your eyes open to the consequences. General Pinckney is no longer run as Vice President; it is the avowed object of the Federal Party to make him President; and, as proof of this, I refer you to Gen. Hamilton's letter. . . . By voting in the contemplated manner, you secure the success of the Federal candidate."

As the days wore on, South Carolina newspapers published every bit of news from the Pennsylvania legislature as it arrived, but because of the communications lag, legislators ultimately had to vote without knowing those results. They waited until the last possible moment. Then, shortly after noon on December 2, they chose from among candidates on two partisan slates. Each slate had eight names—one all Republicans and another all Federalists. Although not every legislator voted strictly along party lines, each Republican candidate received more votes than any Federalist candidate.

The electors met at the state capitol in Columbia on December 3. "The constitution and laws . . . as they relate to the election of a president and vice president of the United States were read," an observer noted, "after which the electors proceeded to ballot; and upon counting the votes, it appeared that Thomas Jefferson of Virginia had eight votes; that Aaron Burr of New York had also eight votes; and that no other person was mentioned on the ballots of the said electors." Anxious about security, the electors then signed and sealed three certified copies of the results, sent one to Washington by personal messenger, mailed one to Washington, and deposited one with the state's federal district court judge.

Pinckney had failed to carry a single electoral vote in his home state and received only nine votes from Southern electors—the same number as Adams. Years in opposition had forged the Republicans into a united party, especially in the South. Voting on the same day, one Rhode Island elector dropped his vote for Pinckney so that Adams would outpoll his running mate. Because of this, even with all of South Carolina's electoral votes, Pinckney would have finished behind Jefferson, though ahead of Adams and Burr. By carrying four electoral districts in North Carolina as compared to only one in 1796, Adams had actually done slightly better in the South than four years earlier—but not well enough to overcome his loss of New York's twelve electors.

Jefferson learned of the South Carolina vote in a letter from Republican printer Peter Freneau, who covered the event for his Charleston newspaper. The letter, dated December 2, identified the electors chosen by the South Carolina legislature and their party affiliation. They would not actually cast their ballots until December 3, of course, so the letter could only predict how they would vote. In fact, it incorrectly forecast that one of them would drop a vote for Burr to ensure Jefferson's victory. Reports suggested that Republican electors in other states might do the same on Election Day.

Jefferson received Freneau's letter on December 12 and immediately shared the news with his family. "I believe we may consider the election as decided," he wrote from Washington. "The votes will stand probably T. J. 73, Burr about 70, Mr. Adams 65, Pinckney probably lower than that. It is fortunate that some difference will be made between the two highest candidates, because it is said the Feds here held a caucus and came to the resolution that in the event of their being equal, they would prevent an election . . . by dividing the House of Representatives." At least at this point, Jefferson assumed that one or more electors on each side would drop votes from their party's second candidate. He also realized, however, that the Federalists in Congress were prepared to exploit the situation should the two Republican candidates end in a tie for first.

The concluding commentary about the Federalist caucus betrayed Jefferson's one lingering concern about the election. He knew there were seventy-three Republican electors and only sixty-five Federalist electors. He counted on all the Republican electors voting for him. Republicans had become so unified in their opposition to Federalists, however, that every Republican might also vote for Burr out of fear that otherwise Adams or Pinckney might slip in ahead of Burr in the final tally, just as Jefferson had slipped in ahead of Thomas Pinckney in 1796 and become Vice President. If both Republican candidates received seventy-three electoral votes, however, neither of them would win outright and, under the Constitution, Congress would choose between them for the presidency. With the Federalists holding the balance of power in Congress, this was a sobering prospect.

CHAPTER TEN

THE TIE

" SPLENDID INTELLIGENCE," read the headline in Washington's new Republican newspaper, *The National Intelligencer*, on December 12. "We have this moment received information from Columbia (S.C.) that the Republican ticket for electors has been carried entire. . . . Mr. Jefferson may, therefore, be considered as our future President," the article proclaimed. It went on to report without further comment that Jefferson and Burr would receive all the state's electoral votes. By this time, politicians in the nation's capital also knew of the results in Pennsylvania and enough of the other states to establish that a majority of the nation's electors would be Republican. This momentous news gradually spread across the land with the fastest riders, coaches, and ships.

In 1800, electors from all sixteen states met in their respective states and cast their votes on December 3—the date prescribed by law. Although, under the Constitution, Congress (or, more precisely, the president of the Senate with Congress present) would not open and count the ballots until February 11, 1801, word of how the electors voted trickled out steadily from the various state capitals. Although unofficial until counted, the votes were not secret. Electors could, and did, tell people how they voted. Newspapers reported it. With electors free to vote as they pleased and the contest very close in 1800, no one could know the final outcome for certain until reports of all the states reached them—which inevitably took weeks. Lacking a central news source, Americans anxiously awaited word of the precise electoral-vote count from each state. Rhode Islanders would not hear how Georgia's electors voted for over a month, for example, and reports from Kentucky and Tennessee could take almost as long to reach some East Coast communities. Keeping track of the various accounts and drawing up tallies kept the candidates and newspaper printers occupied throughout December.

As news spread out from South Carolina of the Republican victory there, it intersected with reports on how electors voted in other states. The issue of *The National Intelligencer* that proclaimed the sweep by Jefferson and Burr in South Carolina also reported news from the West that the Republican ticket had carried all the electoral votes of Kentucky and Tennessee. Word soon came from the North that, contrary to the assurances of Burr and some other Northeastern Republicans, Jefferson had not received any electoral votes in New England or New Jersey. Georgia electors, it turned out, had voted solidly for the Republican ticket, dashing Jefferson's hope that perhaps one of them would withhold a vote from Burr, as some rumors suggested. Republican leaders had thought that one or more electors in Rhode Island, Vermont, New Jersey, Georgia, Kentucky, or Tennessee would vote for Jefferson but not Burr. No one, however, either confirmed the arrangement or directed any particular elector to drop a vote from Burr so that Jefferson could prevail. Jefferson himself and his two closest political allies, Madison and Monroe, had held back from making such arrangements due to their commitments made to Burr. The failure of any other party leaders to attend to the issue was a remarkable oversight in an otherwise well-managed campaign.

By the third week of December, a consistent pattern of highly disciplined party-line voting had become clear. Republican electors had voted with such unity that, it now became apparent, Jefferson and Burr would likely end up in a dead heat with seventy-three electoral votes each. The best estimates had them finishing eight votes ahead of Adams and nine in front of Pinckney.

This development, even though he had foreseen it as a possibility, shocked and deeply troubled Jefferson. Already on December 15, when he still expected to finish alone on top, Jefferson had written to Burr about the coordination of voting by Republican electors. "It was badly managed not to have arranged with certainty what seems to have been left to hazard," Jefferson observed. "I never once asked whether arrangements had been made . . . [for] dropping votes intentionally . . . nor did I doubt till lately that such had been made." Burr did not respond to Jefferson on this point but he must have anticipated the possibility of a tie. He had pressed for votes from every Republican elector from the outset.

By the third week of December, Jefferson knew the final tally. "There will be an absolute parity between the two Republican candidates," he wrote to Madison from Washington on December 19. "This has produced great dismay and gloom on the Republican gentlemen here, and equal exultation in the Federalists." Adams, Hamilton, and the other Federalists had also assumed that the Republicans would manage the electoral vote better. With a tie between Jefferson and Burr now apparently the result, though, the final session of the Sixth Congress, which began on November 17 with a light agenda, was suddenly shaping up as historic. Its members, which included many lame-duck Federalists, would choose the next President.

By nature, Jefferson was pessimistic about his political prospects and saw dark conspiracies against him. In this case, he only slightly exaggerated the situation. Under the Constitution, in the case of a tie between two candidates for President, each with votes from more than half of the electors, the House of Representatives chooses between the two top finishers. Rather than participate as individuals, however, members from each state voted as a unit, with each state having one vote. The state's vote would go to whichever candidate a majority of congressmen from that state supported. If they split evenly, the state would abstain.

With sixteen states, an absolute majority of nine votes was required for victory regardless of how many states actually voted. Jefferson keenly calculated and recalculated his chances. From the outset, he felt confident that he would receive votes from all eight state delegations with a majority of Republican members. This included the five-man New Jersey contingent, in which the crossover of a nonaligned member had created a three-to-two Republican tilt, and the two-member Georgia delegation, over which the recent death of a Federalist member had left its lone Republican in charge. After all, Jefferson reasoned, Republicans uniformly considered him as their party's candidate for President and the electors and people had voted with that understanding. All Republican congressmen should support him.

The Federalists, in contrast, held a majority of the House seats of seven states. In one of these, Maryland, a Federalist congressman, George Dent, announced that he would vote for Jefferson, just as most of the voters in his district had done, which split the state's delegation four to four. The Vermont delegation was also split evenly, with one member from each party. Other than Maryland, the Federalist-dominated states would likely vote for Burr. Partisanship had by now become so fierce that they would choose to give the presidency to the wildly ambitious but unprincipled opponent who had beaten them in New York rather than give their votes to Jefferson, the acknowledged Republican leader. With their delegations divided, Vermont and Maryland would probably abstain. The House would deadlock, with eight states voting for Jefferson, six for Burr, and two not voting. In utter frustration, Jefferson wrote to Monroe on December 20 about the tie with Burr, "The Feds in the legislature have expressed dispositions to make all they can of the embarrassment so that after the most energetic efforts, crowned with success, we remain in the hands of our enemies by want of foresight in the original arrangement."

With only their six states, of course, Federalists could never win a House vote for President. They might, however, still benefit from their power to block Jefferson's election. In several private, late-December letters to Republican collaborators, Jefferson outlined two schemes that Federalists might use to extend their rule.

By deadlocking the House, Jefferson noted, Federalists could allow the presidency to devolve to the president pro tempore of the Senate. Under the Constitution, if the top two posts become vacant, this officer acts as U.S. President. The presidential and vice presidential terms would end on March 3, 1801, and, if Congress had not chosen between Jefferson and Burr by that date, the Senate president pro tempore might claim power. The Senate did not have a president pro tempore, however. Under the reasoning that the Senate did not need a president pro tempore if the Vice President was sitting as its president (or presiding officer), the rules authorized the Senate to choose a president pro tempore only in the Vice President's absence. As long as he remained Vice President, Jefferson could stop the Federalist-led Senate from electing a president pro tempore simply by attending every session in his constitutional role as president of the Senate, which he vowed to do. This left open the question of what might happen if the Senate remained in session after Jefferson's term ended on March 3. Senators, or at least those senators whose terms had not also expired on March 3, might then try to elect a president pro tempore, who might move to claim the powers of the United States presidency.

Further, the Constitution clearly authorized Congress to enact legislation designating which officer would lead the nation in the absence of both a President and Vice President. Congress could pass a law providing, for example, that some specific cabinet member or judicial officer would assume power in such a crisis. Jefferson realized that this offered a second means for the Federalists to cling to power after March 3. In particular, he worried that they would use their power in Congress to designate as the next in line for presidential succession either the Secretary of State—then Virginia Federalist John Marshall—or the Chief Justice—probably Federalist senior statesman John Jay, whom Jefferson presumed would soon fill that then-vacant post.

To Republicans, either approach would constitute a naked usurpation of power, but they feared the worst from their opponents. Federalist leaders in Congress did in fact consider both options, as well as the extraconstitutional alternative of calling a new national election. The

Federalist press openly defended all three approaches for retaining power even as Republican newspapers railed against them. In one widely reprinted response, *The National Intelligencer* argued that if March 3 came and went without the election of a President, rather than the president pro tempore taking power, the Articles of Confederation "will be revived by the termination of the . . . federal Constitution." Although of doubtful authority, this response raised the stakes for the Federalists, whose very existence as a party was identified with the effort to ratify and defend the Constitution. "Some, tho' Federalists, will prefer yielding to the wishes of the people rather than have no government," Jefferson explained in a letter to his daughter, Martha.

A more likely scenario than any of these approaches had Burr conspiring with the Federalists and a handful of Republican congressmen to win the election in the House. Republicans held only a slender advantage in several of the congressional delegations that they controlled. In Vermont, New Jersey, Maryland, Georgia, and Tennessee, even a single Republican defection could turn the state's vote against Jefferson. Two defections could swing Burr's home state of New York. If every Federalist congressman voted for him, Burr would need only three or four strategically placed Republican votes to carry nine states. Never short on self-confidence, Burr reportedly believed that, if he sought out their support, he could muster enough votes from Republican congressmen to win the presidency. To Jefferson, however, he professed his loyalty. "My personal friends," he assured Jefferson in a December 23 letter written before Burr knew the final electoral-vote count, "are perfectly informed of my wishes on the subject and can never think of diverting a single vote from you." Thereafter, Burr became so equivocal in his comments that no one could be sure of his intentions.

Representative Samuel Smith of Maryland contacted Burr repeatedly on behalf of Republicans in Congress to gain his promise not to stand in Jefferson's way but received back mixed messages. After pledging unwavering support for Jefferson in a December 16 letter to Smith that the congressman released to the press, Burr drew back. In a December 29 letter to Smith, Burr refused to say whether he would decline the presidency if chosen by the House. At an early-January meeting between the two men in Philadelphia, Burr left Smith with the distinct impression that if elected President, he would serve. "Keep the game perfectly in your hand," Federalist Congressman Robert Goodloe Harper advised Burr in a December 24 letter, and Burr did just that. He remained in intermittent contact with House members throughout the process but he never went to Washington. Apparently Burr decided not to solicit votes but to accept those that came his way, which was how the Federalist press reported it at the time.

The Republican press betrayed little of the concern about Burr now growing among Republican leaders in Congress. "A drowning man will grasp at a straw," the Republican *Herald of Liberty* commented in early January on the Federalists' effort to elect Burr, but "it will not save him." It mattered less "whether Thomas Jefferson or Aaron Burr should be President as that a period should be put to the excesses and enormities of the Federal[ist] faction by electing a Republican to the presidential chair," the writer concluded. After assuring its readers in mid-January that "Mr. Burr would certainly make an excellent President," *The National Intelligencer* simply added "that no man will doubt, and Mr. Burr himself will, with an honorable candor, admit that the people, their legislatures, and the electors intended Mr. Jefferson to be President and Mr. Burr to be Vice President." After boosting the party ticket for months, Republican printers could hardly turn against one of their two candidates.

Although perhaps grasping at straws, Federalists did cite various rationales for backing Burr over Jefferson. "The considerations concluding to this point are of a negative nature principally, and drawn from the greater unfitness of Jefferson," House Speaker Theodore Sedgwick wrote to his son on January 11 about Burr. "He is not an enthusiastic theorist. He is not under the direction of Virginian Jacobins. He is not a *declared* infidel." Perhaps most important of all, Sedgwick added, "He would not be able to administer the government without the aid of the Federalists and this aid he cannot obtain unless his administration is Federal[ist]." Republicans in Congress would surely abandon Burr if he took the presidency over Jefferson, the wily House Speaker reasoned, and so he must work with the Federalists to enact his proposals or even to confirm his appointments. "There are many reasons why Col. Burr is preferable to Mr. Jefferson," the Federalist *Albany Centinel* explained in early January. "His father was a very pious and worthy clergyman, he is not beloved by [Republicans], but above all, those who know him best have the fullest belief that he will set up a rigid government."

Virtually all Federalists in Congress viewed Burr as grasping, selfish, and unprincipled. "A profligate without character and without property—a bankrupt in both," Sedgwick called him at the time. These very traits made him all the more likely, though, to cooperate with them in maintaining a strong national government, Federalists believed. "By persons friendly to Mr. Burr, it is distinctly stated that he is willing to consider the Federalists as his friends and to accept the office of President as their gift," Delaware Representative James A. Bayard asserted on the basis of some contacts apparently not authorized by Burr. "He must lean on those who bring him to the chair, or he must fall to never rise again," Virginia Congressman Henry Lee added. In short, by electing him President, Federalists hoped to turn Burr into their creature. "I believe," Maryland Representative William Hindman noted, "that he would support the Federal[ist] cause as the Jeffersonians would become his bitter implacable enemies."

On the positive side, Federalists also viewed Burr as more vigorous and pragmatic than Jefferson, whom they scorned as a cowardly, misguided visionary. Hindman wrote of Burr, "He is a soldier and a man of energy and decision." "To courage he joins generosity," New York Senator Gouverneur Morris added. "If Mr. Burr succeeds, we may flatter ourselves that he will not suffer the executive power to be frittered into insignificance," James McHenry stated. "Either will be bad," Connecticut Senator Uriah Tracy conceded, but "I am . . . in favor of Burr principally because I think a paralytic complaint is most to be shunned by a popular government." Federalists also anticipated that Burr, as a New York commercial lawyer, would support Federalist business interests more than Jefferson, a Virginia agrarian. "His very selfishness," Sedgwick wryly noted about Burr and the business interests, "will afford some security that he will not only patronize their support but their invigoration."

"It is fashionable with Feds to declare in favor of Mr. Burr," one of them informed America's ambassador to Britain in a late-December letter. Another soon wrote to McHenry, "The Federalists, almost with one mind from every quarter of the union, say elect Burr." The partisan *Philadelphia Gazette* expressed the thoughts of many embittered Federalists. "If Mr. Burr should indeed be elevated to the executive," it exclaimed, "in what a deplorable situation will the Jeffersonian party be! Quite thrown off the hinges of hope! Gone the sweet expectancy of office!" By some manner of twisted reasoning, by the beginning of 1801, Burr had become the Federalists' white knight. No solid evidence exists that he ever promised anything in exchange for their support. Faced with the prospect of losing power for the first time, they simply gave it to him on faith.

As Republicans and Federalists scrambled for position in the new political order, Adams held himself above the fray. With three months left in his presidency, he had suffered a double shock on December 3. On the same day as a majority of electors voted for Republican candidates over Federalist ones, Adams learned that his thirty-year-old son, Charles, had died from the effects of alcoholism. Only a year earlier, Adams first learned that Charles, his most sensitive and troubled child, had abandoned his wife and young children, turned to drink, and become bankrupt. Adams summarily renounced his wayward son and never spoke to him again. Nevertheless, Charles's death grieved Adams greatly. Then news came of his electoral defeat. "My little bark has been overset in a squall of thunder and lightning and hail attended by the strong smell of sulfur," he wrote to his youngest son, Thomas, on

December 17. "The melancholy decease of your brother is an affliction of a more serious nature to this family than any other. Oh! that I had died for him if that would have relieved him from his faults as well as his disease." The President signed his letter, "I am, my dear son, your affectionate father."

Many Federalists blamed Adams for the party's losses. By "sending the last mission to France," McHenry observed in words that gave voice to the party line, "Mr. Adams had taken . . . a course which has lost to him the presidency and led to his utter debasement." Pickering soon added, "The President, I am told, is in a state of deep dejection. His feelings are not to be envied. To *his* UNADVISED (to use a mild term) *measures* are traced the evils with which the whole of our country is now perplexed and depressed." The truth is, though, that although he lost the election, Adams did better than his party as a whole. Outside New York, he received more electoral votes in 1800 than in 1796, when he won. The Republicans' narrow victory in the New York City elections had indeed turned the tide. Even without New York, Adams lost only because of the inflated number of electors accorded to southern states due to their nonvoting slave property. The bizarre constitutional compromise that treated each slave as three-fifths of a person for purposes of apportioning U.S. House seats and electoral votes effectively gave free citizens in slave states added political clout. If only free citizens had counted in allocating electoral votes, Adams would have won by two votes. Meanwhile, Federalists lost control of Congress for the first time in the nation's history, dropping more than ten seats in the Senate and more than twice that number in the House. Amid a Republican surge, Adams did remarkably well.

Near the end of December, Adams wrote to a cousin in Massachusetts, "I shall be in Quincy as early in the spring as the roads and the weather will permit. The only question remaining for me is, what shall I do with myself? Something I must do or ennui will rain upon me in buckets." At age sixty-five and after more than twenty-five years of continuous public service dating back to the First Continental Congress, Adams suggested that he might resume farming or practicing law.

In grief and disappointment, Adams took no part in the final phase of the presidential election. Although he favored Jefferson over Burr, Adams left the decision wholly to Congress. On the final day of December, though, he vented his feelings about Burr and the partisanship that would lift him to national office. "How mighty a power is the spirit of party! How decisive and unanimous it is! Seventy-three for Mr. Jefferson and seventy-three for Mr. Burr," Adams wrote to a friend about Burr. "All the old patriots, all the splendid talents, the long experience, both of Federalists and Anti-Federalists, must be subject to the humiliation of seeing this dexterous gentleman rise, like a balloon filled with inflammable air, over their heads. . . . What an encouragement to party intrigue and corruption!"

In contrast, stating that she had "turned and turned and overturned in my mind the merits and demerits of the two candidates," Abigail Adams remained undecided. "Long acquaintance, private friendship and the full belief that the private character of one is much purer than the other, inclines me to" Jefferson, she explained to her sister. "Yet . . . I am sometimes inclined to believe that the more bold, daring and decisive character would succeed in supporting the government for a longer time." That meant Burr. The First Lady then added a question of great moment to her. Would God protect America if Americans knowingly chose as President a heretic like Jefferson, "who makes no pretension to the belief of an all wise and supreme governor of the world ordering or directing or overruling the events that take place in it?" she asked about Jefferson. They had come so far, these former friends, from those convivial days in Paris. Still, on a similar score, she worried about Burr too. "Yet [Burr], if he is more of a [Christian] believer," she wrote, "has more to answer for because he has grossly offended against those doctrines by his practice." For many pious Federalists, it was a devil's choice.

In the waning days of his administration, Adams concentrated on securing Senate approval of the peace convention with France and attending to the various measures passed by the outgoing Federalist Congress, many of them highly partisan. One final opportunity to shape future events had arisen when Chief Justice Oliver Ellsworth resigned office unexpectedly. Adams offered the post first to John Jay, but Jay declined for health reasons. He then tapped his loyal Secretary of State, John Marshall, for the position. It was a brilliant choice for the Federalists. As the Republicans consolidated their hold on the elected branches of government, Marshall almost single-handedly extended his party's influence in national affairs for another thirty-five years. By enunciating the principle of judicial review over statutes and executive decisions in *Marbury v. Madison*, for example, Marshall helped to secure power in the courts to restrain the sort of extraconstitutional assaults on property that Federalists feared most from Republicans.

Only one prominent Federalist leader actively tried to stop his party's mad rush to embrace Burr. Having battled him over the years in New York with mixed results, the prospect of Burr becoming President horrified Alexander Hamilton. "There is no circumstance which has occurred in the course of our political affairs that has given me so much pain as the idea that Mr. Burr might be elevated to the presidency by the means of the Federalists," he wrote to Oliver Wolcott in December. "Let it not be imagined that Burr can be won to the Federal[ist] view. . . . His ambition will not be content with those objects which virtuous men of either party will allot to it, and his situation and his habits will oblige him to have recourse to corrupt expedients." At least Jefferson "has pretensions to character," Hamilton explained. "As to *Burr*, there is nothing in his favor." After having his attack on Adams criticized as personal, Hamilton now stressed that he got along "well" with Burr. "If there be a man in the world I ought to hate, it is Jefferson," he wrote, "but the public good must be paramount to every private consideration."

In late December, Hamilton launched an extraordinary letter-writing campaign to alert Federalists in Congress to the danger. In these letters, he portrayed Burr as a cunning, diabolical intriguer willing to say or do anything to gain political power and private wealth.

"Burr loves nothing but himself; thinks of nothing but his own aggrandizement; and will be content with nothing short of permanent power in his own hands," Hamilton admonished Congressman Harrison Gray Otis of Massachusetts. In several letters, he compared Burr to the Roman conspirator Catiline and warned that, if elected, Burr would start a foreign war to consolidate his power. "No mortal can tell what his political principles are," Hamilton cautioned South Carolina's John Rutledge. "If he has any theory, 'tis that of simple *despotism*." To the House Speaker, he pleaded, "I beg you, as you love your country, your friends and yourself, to reconsider dispassionately the opinion you have expressed in favor of Burr."

All these congressmen wrote back to Hamilton expressing their determination to back Burr. In the wake of the devastating defeat of his hand-picked candidates by Burr's slate in New York's state elections, Hamilton again sounded vindictive. He had cried wolf once too often and had lost credibility within his own party.

Hamilton held out, though, one key source of hope. In his letter-writing campaign, he worked especially hard to change the mind of thirty-three-year-old James Bayard. As Delaware's lone House member, Bayard held an entire state's presidential vote, one of sixteen, in his hands. However he voted, Delaware voted. Bayard was a loyal Federalist but not an embittered partisan. With Jefferson by all accounts only one state shy of having a majority in the House, everyone knew that he could win with Bayard's vote, but virtually no one expected that he could get it.

In three letters written over the course of eight weeks, Hamilton reasoned with the young congressman. His December 27 letter concluded with the warning, "Mr. Burr [is] the most unfit man in the U.S. for the office of president. Disgrace abroad, ruin at home are the probable fruits of his elevation." Bayard replied politely but firmly. Although not bound to follow his Federalist colleagues, given his pivotal position, "I ought certainly to be impressed with the most undoubting conviction before I separated myself from them," he wrote. "I have not the least doubt of their agreeing to support Burr."

Even as Hamilton worked furiously behind the scenes to derail the Federalist effort to elect Burr, he was not willing to concede the presidency to Jefferson without getting something in return for Federalist votes in Congress. In fact, just as soon as an electoral-vote tie had started to look likely, he had begun urging Federalists in Congress to wring concessions from Jefferson in exchange for their votes. Specifically, Hamilton wanted a pledge that Jefferson would not repudiate the national debt, ally the country with France, disband the Navy, or dismiss Federalists from government jobs. Federalists could trust the Virginian to honor his commitments, Hamilton assured them. The same promises from Burr would mean nothing, he warned, because no one could trust him to keep his word. "While making it, he will laugh in his sleeve at the credulity of those with whom he makes it," Hamilton wrote in a letter to Bayard, "and the first moment it suits his views to break it, he will do so."

In dealing with Burr, Hamilton suggested that the Federalists should "throw out a lure for him, in order to tempt him to start for the plate and thus lay the foundation of dissension between the two chiefs." The power-hungry Burr would show his true face in response to an offer of votes from Federalists, Hamilton believed, and Jefferson would never again trust him. The ensuing dissension between the new President and Vice President might divide the opposition, he hoped. As much as Hamilton might favor Jefferson, he could not refrain from partisan scheming.

A new century formally began on January 1, 1801, but the partisan positions taken in December did not change. Congress returned from its Christmas recess deeply divided. Every Republican in the House agreed to support Jefferson; all but four of the Federalists favored Burr. Except for Maryland's Dent, however, these dissenters came from Republican-dominated states where their votes for Jefferson would not matter. The projected vote remained eight to six with two states tied. Jefferson hoped that once news of the extent of his party's gains in the fall elections reached Philadelphia, including confirmation that Republicans would take control of Congress, the Federalists might bow to the apparent popular will. Instead, the news only made them less willing to compromise during the two months remaining until the current presidential and congressional terms ended on March 3. The Federalists seemed more determined than ever to wield power while they had it and hope that, by securing Burr's election, they could retain it in some fashion.

With time running out, Federalists in Congress set out to accomplish as many partisan objectives as possible prior to relinquishing power on March 3. Although the Senate and House of Representatives had convened in late November, members waited on the election results before concluding any major business. Many of them arrived late for the session or went home early for Christmas. By the first of January, however, Federalists knew that they had lost the presidency and probably the Congress. This gave them a new sense of urgency. "They are about to experience a heavy gale of adverse wind," Gouverneur Morris said of his colleagues. "Can they be blamed for casting many anchors to hold their ship through the storm?"

Their main anchor was the Judiciary Act of 1801, which the Federalist Congress passed as one of its last acts in February. The new law expanded federal-court jurisdiction and created an intermediate level of independent appellate courts. It also increased the number of federal judicial districts. Boasting that "we shall profit of our short lived majority," Representative John Rutledge noted that the measure "will greatly extend the judiciary power and, of course, greatly widen the basis of government." Federalists always viewed the national judiciary as a means to reach into the states with their centralizing, probusiness policies, which made creating more courts and packing them with like-minded judges all the more important to them. Morris deftly described the proposed Judiciary Act as "giving additional fiber to the roots of government." Senator James Gunn of Georgia more crudely spoke of it "extending the influence of *our* judiciary," and warned that "if neglected by the Federalists, the ground will be occupied by the enemy at the very next session of Congress." Writing to Madison about the bill, Jefferson noted, "I dread this above all the measures meditated because [judicial] appointments [are] . . . difficult to undo." Adams reportedly worked late into the night of his final day in office signing commissions for these appointees, leading Republicans to scorn them as "midnight judges."

Most other partisan bills fell short of passage during the brief session. One would have funded the construction of roads to unify the nation and carry its commerce. Depicting the measure as "the richest provision for jobs to favorites that has ever yet been proposed," Jefferson privately objected that "the mines of Peru could not supply the monies which would be wasted on this object." Federalists also proposed erecting a 150-foot-tall pyramid in the nation's capital to entomb Washington's remains in pharaonic splendor. The leveling spirit of republican populism doomed the project, however. Only a memorial obelisk later arose. Most radical of all, House Federalists moved to extend the Sedition Act beyond its scheduled expiration. Stating that he "saw nothing in the law . . . which an honest man should fear," House committee chair Jonas Platt proposed the extension in mid-January, and (over Republican jeers) the House initially agreed. Renowned historian Samuel Eliot Morison described this effort as "the most striking instance of the unteachableness of Federalism."

Adams did manage to secure Senate ratification of his peace convention with France, but only after High Federalists defeated it once and then puckishly struck out the virtually meaningless provision relating to indemnities and the Franco-American Alliance. The initial defeat at the hands of his own party infuriated him. Nothing mattered more to Adams than this treaty, not even the election of his successor. "He is extremely irritated in consequence of the treaty not being accepted," Bayard observed in late January, "and would be apt to insult the person who should mention the subject to him." His dry wit restored, Adams later characterized peace with France as "the most splendid diamond in my crown or, if any one thinks this expression too monarchical, . . . the most brilliant feather in my cap."

*   *   *

Conditions in the nation's new capital aggravated the partisan divisions that beset Congress. In cosmopolitan Philadelphia, lawmakers met in the historic old State House and enjoyed the distractions of the nation's largest and most cultivated city. In frontier Washington, politics consumed them. There was little else to do. "A few, indeed, drink, and some gamble, but the majority drink naught but politics," House Republican leader Albert Gallatin wrote in mid-January about his colleagues, "and by not mixing with men of different or more moderate sentiments, they inflame one another. On that account, principally, I see some danger in the fate of the [presidential] election which I had not before contemplated."

With few private homes to rent in town, most Senators and Representatives crowded into eight modest boardinghouses near the Capitol. "I arrived here last evening after a very tedious and fatiguing ride," Bayard wrote to his family from Washington on January 3. "I have no lodgings yet and am in no manner arranged. The city I have seen only from the windows of the Capitol. The prospect furnishes a view of a few scattered houses and a great deal of dreary, rough country." He soon found accommodations with fellow Federalists in Stelle's Hotel.

Joint living arrangements became common during the first session in Washington, but rarely crossed party lines. Gallatin, who also arrived in January, shared a double room at Conrad and McMunn's Apartments. This boardinghouse became the Republican command post, with Jefferson occupying its only private suite. Gallatin likened dining at its common table to eating at "a refectory of monks": One topic predominated and everyone thought alike. "You may suppose that being all thrown together in a few boarding houses, without hardly any other society than ourselves, we are not likely to be either very moderate politicians or to think of anything but politics," he confessed to his wife, who remained behind in Pennsylvania.

According to various accounts of the local social scene, Philadelphia's grand balls had given way to Washington's low saloons. Certainly fewer congressional wives accompanied their husbands to Washington than to Philadelphia. "There is a great want of society, especially female," one member complained. "There is nobody to visit nor means of visiting. As soon as night comes, the tables for cards are introduced." Federalists and Republicans had mixed freely in Philadelphia society. In Washington, however, they rarely met except in partisan combat. The urbane Massachusetts Federalist Harrison Gray Otis, who once delighted in Philadelphia's bipartisan social circle, wrote to his wife in February about leaving a Washington party attended by Republicans. "I have concluded to go to no more balls," he declared, because "I do not enjoy myself with these people."

House members endured the further frustration of having no permanent meeting place. With the roof not yet over its official chambers, the House had to convene in either smaller rooms of the Capitol or a nearby temporary structure called "the Oven." No other options existed. Even the Executive Mansion remained little more than an elegant shell. "Not one room or chamber is finished of the whole," Abigail Adams complained. "It is habitable by fires in every part, thirteen of which we are obliged to keep daily or sleep in wet and damp places." Put to use in much the same condition, both the War Offices and Treasury Building caught fire during those first few months. Some Republicans charged outgoing Federalist officeholders with setting the blazes to destroy evidence of their corrupt dealings. "Party will believe it," Gallatin wrote to his wife on January 29, "but I do not."

With less than two weeks until the critical House vote for President, trust had broken down completely between the parties. Each side attributed only the worst motives to the other. Gallatin's letters suggest only one topic of agreement. "The Federal City," he wrote, "is hated by every member of Congress without exception of persons or parties." By the middle of February, lawmakers were in no mood to compromise, or even to act rationally. The presidency hung in the balance.

Compelled by the Constitution to wait until February 11 to begin voting, Federalists and Republicans in the House spent the first six weeks of the new year posturing and plotting. Faced with a novel political situation and operating under a relatively new constitution that Americans did not yet venerate, anything seemed possible and rumors spread wildly. To a remarkable degree, however, both sides operated within parameters suggested by the Constitution.

Republicans worried primarily that their opponents might make the bold move of enacting legislation to designate some Federalist officeholder as the interim executive pending the election of a President by the House. Such a measure, if signed into law by Adams, could extend the Federalists' hold on power. "Is it possible that Mr. Adams should give his sanction to it," Madison asked Jefferson in early January, "or that he would not hold it his duty or his policy, in case the present House should obstinately refuse to [elect a President], to appoint . . . for the succeeding House to meet and supply the omission?" Republicans would control that next House, but it could not convene until December unless called by the President. Adams could thus use his remaining power to tilt the outcome either way. Madison and Gallatin urged Jefferson to seek Adams's help, but when Jefferson later did so, Adams reportedly rebuffed him.

Instead, the President issued an advance call for a special session of the new Senate on March 4, ostensibly to confirm the next President's appointments. Some Republicans smelled a rat. Knowing that many newly elected Republican senators could not arrive in time for the special session, they feared that the rump Senate would promptly elect a Federalist president pro tempore, who could assume the reins of government if the House failed to act. Already intense, the intrigue increased daily.

Responding to the supposed Federalist scheme, Republicans vowed to resist all efforts to install an interim executive. Madison called them "substantial violations of the will of the people, of the scope of the Constitution, and of the public order and interest." Gallatin agreed. "Whether the assumption be made by law or without it, the act of the person designated by the law or of the President *pro temp.* assuming the power is clearly unconstitutional," he advised House Republicans.

"Any assumption on their part is usurpation. Usurpation must be resisted by freemen whenever they have the power of resisting." He called upon individuals and Republican-controlled state governments to refuse to obey "those acts which may flow from the usurper as President." Even Burr agreed on this point, writing to Gallatin on February 12, "In case of usurpation by law, by President of the Senate pro tem., or in any other way, . . . I shall act in defiance of all timid, temporizing projects."

Resistance could become violent, Republicans warned. "It was threatened that if any man should be thus appointed President by law and accept the office, he would instantaneously be put to death," Gallatin later acknowledged. Word spread that Governors McKean and Monroe would dispatch their state militias to suppress any Federalist coup and that the Republican states would join in forming a new government under a revised constitution. Some Federalists spoke of their states responding in kind, raising the specter of disunion or civil war.

According to his own account, Jefferson verbally threatened Adams with "resistance by force and incalculable consequences" if the Federalists tried to install an interim President. "We thought it best to declare openly and firmly, [to] one and all, that the day such an act passed, the middle states would arm and that no such usurpation, even for a single day, should be submitted to," Jefferson explained in a February 15 letter to Monroe. Republicans would reluctantly acquiesce if the House legally elected Burr, Jefferson later informed McKean, "but in the event of an usurpation, I was decidedly with those who were determined not to permit it because that precedent once set, would be artificially reproduced, and end soon in a dictator." The specter of Napoleon's coup and its authoritarian consequences for France still hung heavily on Americans.

Republicans had their own ideas about what should happen if the House did not elect a President, but no consensus plan. "Let the two candidates agree between themselves . . . which of them shall act as President and which as Vice President," McKean suggested in a letter to Jefferson. "Thus the constitutional choice of the people will be substantially carried into effect." In this manner, Burr could have resolved the matter at any point by publicly and unequivocally declaring that he would not accept the presidency over Jefferson—but he never did. Instead, his words and deeds suggested that he would take the post if Congress offered it. Madison proposed that Jefferson and Burr jointly call the new House into special session after March 3. "The prerogative of convening the legislature must reside in one or [the] other of them," he explained to Jefferson, "and if, in reference to the Constitution, the preceding might be not strictly regular, the irregularity will . . . lie in form only rather than substance." The new Republican-controlled House would elect Jefferson, Madison presumed.

If all else failed, Gallatin urged Republicans to go along with the Federalists' proposal of holding new national elections. "Let them order a new election whenever they please," he noted deviously, "they cannot count the votes and complete the election without Congress being convened, and then the next House may act either on the new or on the present election." All these options would result in a Republican President, their proponents insisted. Any of them would suffice. Republicans adamantly objected only to continued Federalist rule.

Perhaps in response to Republican threats, on February 9, the House adopted procedural rules that effectively precluded it from passing a law to designate an interim President. The rules, drafted by a Federalist-dominated committee, gave a literalistic reading to the constitutional provision stating that in the case of a tie between two candidates for President, the House "shall immediately choose by ballot one of them." The key proviso in the new rules stated that if the first ballot did not decide the issue, then "the House shall continue to ballot for a President, without interruption by other business, until it shall appear that a President is duly chosen . . . [and] shall not adjourn until a choice is made." In effect, members would remain in session, conducting no other business, until either they elected a President or their terms expired on March 3, whichever occurred first.

These rules signaled that House Federalists wanted to select the President. If they failed, of course, the Senate could still try to elect a president pro tempore to serve as an interim executive following the end of Jefferson's current term as Vice President, but the House would have no say in it. Voting along party lines, the House also decided to proceed in secret, with only members present. "We are to be shut up for God knows how long, though it cannot be longer than the third of March," Otis wrote to his wife. "Our committee room must be garnished with beefsteaks, and a few Turk[ish] carpets to lie upon would not be amiss."

Both sides went into the House vote on February 11 with high hopes. The Federalists expected all the Republicans to vote for Jefferson on the first ballot, but believed that some would eventually split off if the balloting continued. Burr had friends in Congress, particularly among the Republicans in the closely divided New York and New Jersey delegations. Tennessee's lone representative, a Republican, also seemed open to persuasion, as did Vermont's Republican congressman. To win, Burr needed only one or two of these possible votes in any three of these four delegations.

Rumors swirled of bribes and job offers—but these promises, if made, apparently came from zealous Federalists rather than from Burr himself. Jefferson, in contrast, needed only one more Federalist vote from either Maryland or Vermont, or Bayard's vote from Delaware, to prevail. Republicans believed that he would win on the first ballot. "I hear both parties, and cannot help being amazed by the certainty of success which is declared by each," Gouverneur Morris observed in early February.

A snowstorm enveloped Washington on the morning of Wednesday, February 11, as legislators made their way to the Capitol for the opening and counting of the states' electoral votes. The weather made travel especially difficult for Maryland Representative Joseph H. Nicholson, who suffered from the symptoms of pneumonia. Republicans needed him to stalemate (or perhaps to carry for Jefferson) the vote of his state's divided delegation. Despite a raging fever, bearers (who perhaps included some of his slaves) carried Nicholson two miles on a litter from his residence to the Capitol for the official vote count and ensuing election. "It is a chance that this kills him," Otis wrote to his wife. "I would not thus expose myself for any President on earth." Nicholson's health improved over time, however, and he never missed a vote.

The entire House and Senate crowded into the ornate Senate chambers at noon to observe the vote count. Performing one of his few constitutionally mandated duties as Vice President, Jefferson read aloud the sixteen state ballots and announced the final totals. As everyone anticipated, the two Republican candidates had 73 votes each; Adams had 65; Pinckney 64; and John Jay 1.

When reading the ballots, Jefferson undoubtedly noticed that the one from Georgia lacked the requisite certification and signatures of the electors. He moved on quickly, though, not mentioning the technical deficiency. A partisan dispute over the validity of Georgia's votes for Jefferson and Burr could have disrupted the counting process, but no member raised the issue at the time, even though some apparently knew about it. Without votes from Georgia's four electors, the Federalists could have claimed that no candidate had votes from a majority of the 138 named electors. Under the Constitution, the House could then choose from among the top 5 candidates, which would include Adams, Pinckney, and Jay. Republicans would have countered that Jefferson and Burr still had votes from a majority of the 134 participating electors, and thus remained the only 2 eligible candidates. Raising this issue would further complicate an already complicated matter without fundamentally changing the dynamics: Even with their candidates back in the race, the Federalists would still not have enough votes to elect them. In addition, no one seriously doubted that Georgia's electors meant to vote for Jefferson and Burr.

Congress moved on too. "The votes having been entered on the journals," *The National Intelligencer* reported, "the House returned to its own chamber and, with closed doors, proceeded to the ballot." Jefferson's archfoe, House Speaker Theodore Sedgwick, presided. The voting began promptly at 1:00 PM.

Republican members of Congress felt supremely confident. "On the day on which we began balloting for President, we knew positively that Mr. [George] Baer of Maryland was determined to cast his vote for Jefferson," Gallatin later wrote, "and his vote was sufficient to give us that of Maryland and decide the election. I was certain from personal intercourse with him that Mr. [Lewis] Morris of Vermont would do the same, and thus give us the vote of that state."

In private correspondence prior to the vote, various Republicans boasted that Jefferson would carry both of these states and Delaware to boot. "I was informed as I passed thro' Wilmington that Mr. Bayard, their Representative, was decidedly in favor of your election," one member assured Jefferson. "If so, I think the question is settled. God grant it may be so!" Other Republicans joked about the pressures on Maryland's William Craik. "Mr. C's lady, it is said, will renounce her husband if he does not vote for Mr. J," one informant told Monroe.

Remembering the iron discipline of both parties in the battle over Pennsylvania's presidential electors, however, Jefferson was characteristically circumspect about his prospects. "I am far from confiding that a single state will come over," he wrote to his son-in-law. "Pennsylvania has shown what men are when party takes place of principle." Jefferson was right. Not a single one of the allegedly wavering Federalists voted for him. On the first ballot, Jefferson carried the eight Republican states; Burr took the six Federalist ones; Maryland and Vermont split evenly along party lines and did not vote. Neither candidate received the necessary majority. Bayard later explained, "By the arrangements I made, I became encircled by all the doubtful votes and made myself responsible for the issue." He voted with his party and the Federalist "phalanx" (as one Republican termed it) held.

Following the first vote, some members called for a break before taking a second vote, but the majority voted them down. Convinced that their opponents lacked principle, Federalists believed that some of them would soon switch sides. Persistent rumors spoke of offers made by various Federalists to Republicans in the New York, New Jersey, and Maryland delegations for their votes. The Federalists expected these states to move quickly into Burr's column. "A second ballot will be taken," a leading New York Federalist had predicted in advance, and "in this event, some of the [Republicans] will come over to vote for Burr." Republican congressmen from New York and New Jersey had held a secret caucus a few days earlier, however, and pledged to stick by Jefferson. This too spawned rumors of private deals, with Jefferson and other Republican leaders now the alleged sources of the offers and threats. "The business is now fixed," Representative George Jackson assured Madison following the caucus. Six more votes occurred in rapid succession, but not a single vote shifted.

After the seventh ballot, Congress rested. "We are in conclave and in a snowstorm," Otis wrote home at this point. "We have balloted in the House *seven* times. Thus it stands, for Jefferson 8, for Burr 6, divided 2. We have agreed not to adjourn, but we have suspended balloting for *one* hour to eat a mouthful. Perhaps we shall continue here a week."

Members cast twenty more ballots on that first day and night, voting typically at one-hour intervals until eight o'clock Thursday morning. Nothing changed. They voted again at noon on Thursday, but reached the same result. Exhausted, the members agreed to recess until 11:00 AM on Friday, February 13. "What the Feds, especially those of Maryland, mean, I cannot tell," Republican Representative John Dawson wrote to Madison during the recess. "*We* are resolv'd never to yield, and sooner hazard everything than to prevent the voice and wishes of the people being carried into effect. I have not closed my eyes for 36 hours."

Petitions circulated in some Maryland communities urging their Federalist representatives to end the stalemate by voting for Jefferson. Some area residents feared that if Congress failed to elect a President, the national government would collapse and the capital might move. Hecklers reportedly jeered Federalists as they left the Capitol. Maryland's leading Federalist newspapers urged members to stand firm, however. "*Unworthy* will he be, and consecrated his name to infamy, who . . . has hitherto strenuously opposed the exaltation of Mr. Jefferson to the presidential chair, shall now meanly and inconsistently lend his aid to promote it," the local *Washington Federalist* proclaimed.

The recess did not resolve the impasse. "All stand firm," Federalist Representative William Cooper (the father of writer James Fenimore Cooper) reported following the vote on Friday. "Had Burr done any thing for himself, he would long ere have been President." Again the House recessed, this time until noon on Saturday. By then, Governor Monroe had become so alarmed by the situation and frustrated at the lack of news that he directed Virginia militia riders to organize a relay to carry confidential reports between the Republicans in Washington and Richmond. "We request information of the actual state and probable results, as on your answer we shall decide whether it will be proper to convene the [state] assembly," he wrote to Virginia's two U.S. senators. "We trust that none of the Republican states will give ground." After voting four times on Saturday, the House broke for the Christian Sabbath. Four days and thirty-three ballots had not altered a single state's vote. On Sunday, in a letter to his daughter Maria, Jefferson complained of the "cabal, intrigue, and hatred" of Washington. "The scene passing here makes me pant to be away from it," he wrote. "I feel no impulse from personal ambition to the office now proposed to me, but on account of yourself and your sister, and those dear to you. I feel a sincere wish indeed to see our government brought back to its republican principles . . . [so] that when I retire, it may be under full security that we are to continue free and happy."

The continuing stalemate convinced Bayard that Burr could not win. From the outset, the Delaware congressman had resolved to cast his state's vote for Jefferson rather than let the election fail and risk disunion. "Representing the smallest state," he explained to Adams on February 19, "I was compelled by the obligation of a sacred duty, so to act, and not to hazard the Constitution upon which the political existence of the state depends." Representatives Baer and Craik of Maryland and Morris of Vermont agreed to follow Bayard's lead. They would give House Federalists ample time to rally support for Burr—indeed, by some accounts, Bayard even tried to solicit Republican votes for Burr—but if that failed, they would swing the contest to Jefferson. Burr probably knew better than to promote his own candidacy. He needed at least three Republican votes to win, and any deals that he made for them surely would become public, with dire consequences for all those involved. The party and the people wanted Jefferson.

Exactly what followed Bayard's decision to abandon Burr became the subject of impassioned arguments (and even lawsuits) as long as any of the participants lived and remains obscured by their conflicting accounts. "In determining to recede from the opposition to Mr. Jefferson, it occurred to us that probably instead of being obligated to surrender at discretion, we might obtain terms of capitulation," Bayard later testified. He added that Baer, Craik, and Morris "authorized me to declare their concurrence with me upon the best terms that could be procured."

According to Jefferson, during the impasse in Congress, various Federalists offered him the presidency in return for his promise to honor government debts, maintain the Navy, and retain current non-policymaking officials. When approached by the Federalists, Jefferson assured Monroe at the time, "I have declared to them unequivocally that I would not receive the government on capitulation." Bayard instead raised those same issues through a Republican intermediary, Congressman Samuel Smith, and specifically named two port collectors whom he wanted retained. Although Jefferson vehemently denied making any deals for the presidency, Smith later admitted raising the issues obliquely with him and reporting Jefferson's favorable response to Bayard. "I have taken good care of you," Bayard soon wrote to one of the named officers. "You are safe." Both officials kept their jobs for as long as they wanted them.

At a closed party caucus during the weekend recess, Bayard told House Federalists that he intended to abandon Burr. "The clamor was prodigious. The reproaches vehement," he wrote to a cousin. "We broke up in confusion." According to some accounts, party leaders asked for added time to see if Burr would offer concessions that could gain him votes. They expected letters from him soon. Accordingly, Bayard voted the party line once more on Monday, and the tally remained constant. Although Burr's letters are lost, apparently they arrived that day. In them, Burr "explicitly resigns his pretensions" to the presidency, House Speaker Sedgwick reported sourly, which may have simply meant that Burr refused to offer any concessions. "The gig is therefore up," the Speaker concluded. "Burr has acted a miserable paltry part. The election was in his power," Bayard informed Delaware's governor on Monday. As for House Federalists, he added, "We meet again tonight merely to agree upon the mode of surrendering." The thirty-fifth and final ballot for President would occur at noon on Tuesday, February 17.

Ultimately, no Federalists switched sides to vote for Jefferson. In an apparent display of party solidarity and continued opposition to Jefferson, Federalist congressmen from Connecticut, Massachusetts, New Hampshire, and Rhode Island stuck with Burr; the rest simply abstained. This gave the votes of Maryland and Vermont to Jefferson. He carried the election by a margin of ten votes to four, with Delaware and South Carolina not voting.

Participants viewed the House election through partisan lenses that polarized their sight. "Thus has ended the most wicked and absurd attempt ever tried by the Federalists," Gallatin wrote after the final vote. "They had but one proper mode to pursue, and that was for the whole party to come over; instead of which they contrived merely to suffer Mr. Jefferson to be chosen without a single man of theirs voting for him."

Federalists saw it differently. Congressman John Cotton Smith, an outspoken Christian and a future Connecticut governor, closed his account of the House battle by observing, "Thus ended the electoral drama, with a catastrophe sufficiently bitter in its effects on the vital interests of the country . . . [to have] fully justified the vote we gave." Following the final ballot, the detached New York Federalist, Gouverneur Morris, cautioned a senior Republican official, "This farce of life contains nothing which should put us out of humor." Few took Morris's worldly advice. Preparing to leave Congress at the session's end, one the staunchest holdouts for Burr, Harrison Gray Otis, wrote to his wife, "Yes my beloved angel, with you, I shall retire from this scene of anxiety . . . and remain a silent spectator of the follies and confusion, of the strife and licentiousness incident to all popular government, and to ours in the most eminent degree." In the next session, a Republican would represent his Boston congressional district in the heart of Federalist New England.

Sixteen months after Pennsylvania voters cast the first ballots in the contest and only two weeks before the scheduled presidential inauguration, the election of 1800 finally ended. Abigail Adams learned the final outcome as she passed through Philadelphia on her way home to Massachusetts. "I have heard some of the Democratic rejoicing such as ringing bells and firing cannon," she wrote to her husband. "What an inconsistency, said a lady to me today, the bells of Christ Church ringing peals of rejoicing for an infidel president!"

As the news reached them, Republicans across the nation celebrated with parades, banquets, bonfires, and making loud noises. "The question which has so long held the Union in doubtful suspense was yesterday decided by the election of the honorable Thomas Jefferson as President," a Baltimore newspaper reported on February 18. "The news was immediately announced to the city by a discharge of 16 cannon from the Observatory."

From start to finish, conflicting hopes for liberty and fears of disorder spurred Americans to an unprecedented level of partisan activity. "I was willing to take Burr," Bayard wrote on the eve of Jefferson's inauguration, "but I was enabled soon to discover that he was determined not to shackle himself with Federal[ist] principles." Forced to take a Republican, Bayard accepted the Virginian, but he still did not vote for him. The manner by which Federalists conceded the election by not voting outraged Jefferson. "We consider this therefore as a declaration of war on the part of this band," he wrote to Madison after the final House ballot.

Partisanship prevailed to the bitter end and showed no signs of abating. Over the campaign's extended course, George Washington's vision of elite, consensus leadership had died, and a popular, two-party republic, conceived in the crucible of the Adams presidency, was born.

INAUGURATION DAY, MARCH 4, 1801

*J*OHN ADAMS left the Executive Mansion about three hours before sunrise on Wednesday, March 4, to catch the 4:00 AM public stage for Baltimore on the first leg of his journey back to Massachusetts. His term as President had ended at midnight, and he wasted no time in leaving the cavernous, unfinished mansion, later known as the White House, that had served as his home for scarcely four months. On his first full day in the building, when he still hoped for an extended stay, Adams had prayed, "May none but honest and wise men ever rule under this roof." Now he left it to his successor beset by grave doubts about the honesty and wisdom of the policies that Republicans would bring with them into power. Other departing Federalists, including former House Speaker Theodore Sedgwick, rode in the same public coach—all choosing to leave town before Jefferson's inauguration at noon. They traveled by the light of a nearly full moon for two hours before the first streaks of dawn brightened the morning sky. Defeat embittered and embarrassed Adams for years to come.

Thomas Jefferson surely rose before the sun that day too; he always did. He still roomed in a small suite at Conrad and McMunn's boardinghouse near the Capitol, and would stay there for two more weeks as work progressed on the Executive Mansion. After other boarders got up and dressed, Jefferson ate breakfast with them at the common table and reportedly declined their invitation to sit at its head. Escorted by soldiers of the Virginia militia and flanked by various members of Congress and other dignitaries, Jefferson then walked to the Senate chamber for his inauguration. His predecessors had ridden in a coach with liveried attendants on such occasions. Jefferson wore a plain suit and, unlike Washington and Adams at their inaugurals, he neither powdered his hair nor carried a sword. He wanted to set a democratic tone for his administration, and continued doing so by curtailing official levees, accepting a handshake rather than a bow, and otherwise introducing an informal style to state functions. A better writer than speaker, Jefferson sent his messages to Congress rather than deliver them to assembled lawmakers. Before taking the oath of office, however, in a shy, small voice all but lost in the ornate, crowded Senate chamber, Jefferson gave the greatest speech of his political career. He beautifully crafted it to claim the middle ground after the bitter, divisive campaign. Newspapers carried it to the nation.

"During the contest of opinion through which we have passed, the animation of discussion and of exertions has sometimes worn an aspect which might impose on strangers unused to think freely," Jefferson began. "But this being now decided by the voice of the people . . . let us restore to social intercourse that harmony and affection without which liberty, and even life itself, are but dreary things." Among the causes of these differences, he stressed the divided opinion "as to measures of safety" against the widening European war. "Every difference of opinion is not a difference of principle," Jefferson cautioned in a statement calculated to reach out to moderates. "We are all Republicans: We are all Federalists. If there be any among us who would wish to dissolve this Union, or to challenge its republican form, let them stand undisturbed as monuments of the safety with which error of opinion may be tolerated where reason is left free." He then restated his political principles in centrist terms: neutrality abroad, the freedom of religion and the press at home, full payment of the national debt, and equal justice with impartial juries. No Federalist could have expected more from a Republican; many expected much less from Jefferson. In an apparent answer to those who questioned his belief in God, he closed with prayer: "May that Infinite Power which rules the destinies of the universe lead our councils to what is best, and give them a favorable issue for your peace and prosperity."

Expanding on his speech in letters to party leaders and senior statesmen, Jefferson expressed a determination to promote republicanism by weaning rank-in-file Federalists from their High Federalist leaders. "I am in hopes my inaugural address will . . . present the leading objects to be conciliation and adherence to sound principle," Jefferson wrote to Monroe. "This I know is impracticable with the leaders of the late faction, whom I abandon as incurables . . . but with the main body of the Federalists, I believe it very practicable." To his new Attorney General, Levi Lincoln, Jefferson added, "The consolidation of our fellow citizens in general is the great object we ought to keep in view" by reaching out to those whom he called "the federal sect of republicans." At the same time, he added, "We must strip of all the means of influence the Essex Junto and their associate monocrats in every part of the Union." Hamilton remained a particular worry. In a conciliatory letter to Washington's former War Secretary, Henry Knox, Jefferson warned, "I know indeed there are monarchists among us." To the senior Revolutionary Era leader John Dickinson, Jefferson noted, "I consider the pure Federalist as a republican who would prefer a somewhat stronger executive; and the Republican as one more willing to trust the legislature." Both, he noted, "should see and fear the monarchist as their common enemy."

In the flush of victory, Jefferson depicted the prior administration as a passing aberration in America's democratic tradition caused by fear and religious obscurantism. "The frenzy . . . wrought partly by ill conduct in France, partly by artifices practiced on [our citizens], is almost extinct," he wrote on March 18 to Thomas Paine in Paris—and invited the aging revolutionary to return home. "What an effort . . . of bigotry in politics and religion have we gone through!" Jefferson added to the noted chemist and liberal theologian Joseph Priestley. "The barbarians really flattered themselves they should be able to bring back the times of Vandalism when ignorance put everything into the hands of power and priestcraft. All advances in science were proscribed as innovations."

Jefferson saw his victory as a turning point. "We may now say that the U.S. from New York southwardly are as unanimous in the principles of '76 as they were in '76," he reported to Elbridge Gerry of Massachusetts. "Your part of the union, tho' as absolutely republican as ours, had drunk deeper of the delusion and is therefore slower in recovering from it. The aegis of government and the temples of religion and justice have all been prostituted there to toll us back to the times when we burnt witches. But your people will rise again." Indeed, he assured Samuel Adams on March 29, "The storm is over, and we are in port." Years later, Jefferson characterized the election of 1800 as "a revolution in the principles of our government."

Federalism retrenched and, concentrated in the Northeast, its leaders fought on as an opposition force. "Party is an association of honest men for honest purposes and, when the state falls into bad hands, is the only efficient defense; a champion who never flinches, a watchman who never sleeps," Fisher Ames wrote on March 19. "An active spirit must be roused in every town to check the incessant proselytizing arts of the Jacobins," he declared on behalf of his partisans. "We must speak in the name and with the voice of the good and the wise, the lovers of liberty and the owners of property." With his relationship to Republicans strained by the prolonged House election for President and no chance of them nominating him for a second term as Vice President, Burr flirted with joining the Federalists. Hamilton resisted Burr's efforts to gain party support for an 1804 gubernatorial campaign in New York, which led to a series of escalating exchanges between the two men, culminating on July 11 in the duel that ended Hamilton's life and Burr's political career.

Although rivals in Virginia politics, Chief Justice John Marshall represented a type of Federalist that Jefferson did not automatically dismiss as monarchical. He asked him to administer the oath of office, and Marshall agreed. "Today the new political year commences," the

Chief Justice wrote to Charles Cotesworth Pinckney on the morning of March 4. "The [Republicans] are divided into speculative theorists and absolute terrorists: With the latter I am not disposed to class Mr. Jefferson." Later that day, Marshall added a postscript about Jefferson's speech. "It is in the general well judged and conciliatory," he wrote, "in direct terms giving the lie to the violent party declamation which has elected him." Pinckney, however, was not persuaded—and stood as the Federalist candidate for President against Jefferson in 1804. He carried only two small states, Delaware and Connecticut, and two districts in Maryland. The strategy of winning over the center through moderate policies and republican rhetoric succeeded brilliantly for Jefferson, just as it would for Madison and Monroe: three successive, two-term Presidents from Virginia. By the 1804 election, the Twelfth Amendment would, however, enshrine partisan politics in the U.S. Constitution by requiring electors to vote separately for President and Vice President rather than the two best candidates. For good or ill, the likes of an Adams and a Jefferson would never again serve together in those offices.

It took a few more years before John Adams yielded to the new order. "The Federalists, by their intolerance, have gone far toward justifying, or at least excusing, Jefferson for his; and for the future, it seems to be established as a principle that our government is forever to be not a national but a party government," Adams wrote in confidence during the heated 1808 presidential campaign, which pitted Madison against Pinckney. "While it lasts all we can hope is that, in the game at leap frog, once in eight or twelve years the party of the OUTS will leap over the head and shoulders of the INS; for, I own to you, I have so little confidence in the wisdom, prudence, or virtue of either party that I should be nearly as willing that one should be absolute and unchecked as the other."

By the 1812 election, after his son, John Quincy, converted to the Republicans and became ambassador to Russia on his way to the presidency, the elder Adams and Jefferson reconciled. Beginning that year, the two former Presidents began an intense and intimate correspondence that continued for the rest of their lives. They bantered over politics, religion, books, farming, family, and their deteriorating health in a remarkable series of letters spanning fourteen years. Early in the exchange, Adams wrote to Jefferson, "You and I ought not to die before we have explained ourselves to each other"—and to posterity, he could have added, because both men knew that future generations would read these letters.

The two old friends and former rivals outlived most of the founding generation of Revolutionary leaders, and all but one other signer of the Declaration of Independence, Charles Carroll of Carrollton. On the fiftieth anniversary of its signing, July 4, 1826, and twenty-five years after Jefferson became President, both men succumbed to their accumulated infirmities. Adams was then age ninety; Jefferson was eighty-three. Both were surrounded by family. Adams was up the day before and had smoked a final cigar; Jefferson was bedridden by then and heavily medicated. They lived to see that jubilee of liberty, and when it came, Adams observed, "It is a great day. It is a *good* day." Near the end, Jefferson could barely speak and was rarely conscious. He knew the day had come, however. About half past six o'clock in the evening, after whispering in a weakening voice, "Thomas Jefferson survives," John Adams took his last breath. Jefferson had died approximately five hours earlier. The entire nation mourned their passing.

NOTES

LIST OF ABBREVIATIONS

Annals of Congress—*The Debates and Proceedings in the Congress of the United States*, 42 vols. (Washington: Gales & Seaton, 1834–56).

AFC—L. H. Butterfield, Wendell D. Garrett, and Marjorie E. Sprague, eds., *Adams Family Correspondence* (Cambridge: Belknap Press, 1963–93).

AFP—*Adams Family Papers*, Massachusetts Historical Society, Boston, 1954–59 (microfilm edition).

AJL—Lester J. Cappon, ed., *The Adams-Jefferson Letters: The Complete Correspondence Between Thomas Jefferson and Abigail and John Adams*, 2 vols. (Chapel Hill: University of North Carolina Press, 1961).

Complete Jefferson—Saul K. Padover, ed., *The Complete Jefferson*, 2 vols. (New York: Duell, Sloan, & Pearce, 1943; rpt. Irvine: Reprint Services Corp., 1991).

CJJ—Henry P. Johnston, ed., *The Correspondence and Public Papers of John Jay*, 4 vols. (New York: G. P. Putnam, 1890–93; rpt. New York: Bert Franklin, 1970).

DAJA—L. H. Butterfield, Leonard C. Faber, and Wendell D. Garrett, eds., *Diary and Autobiography of John Adams*, 4 vols. (Cambridge: Belknap Press, 1961).

DGW—Donald Jackson and Dorothy Twohig, eds., *The Diaries of George Washington*, 6 vols. (Charlottesville: University Press of Virginia, 1976–79).

DLGM—Anne Cary Morris, ed., *The Diary and Letters of Gouverneur Morris*, 2 vols. (New York: Charles Scribner's Sons, 1888).

EAI—*Early American Imprints, Series 1: Evans, 1639–1800*, Archive of Americana, Readex (online database).

FLJT—Edwin Morris Betts and James A. Bear, eds., *The Family Letters of Thomas Jefferson* (Columbia: University of Missouri Press, 1966).

Gibbs Memoirs—George Gibbs, ed., *Memoirs of the Administrations of Washington and John Adams Edited from the Papers of Oliver Wolcott, Secretary of the Treasury*, 2 vols. (New York: Private Printing, 1846; rpt. New York: Burt Franklin, 1971).

LAG—Henry Adams, *The Life of Albert Gallatin* (Philadelphia: J. B. Lippincott & Co., 1880).

LCJM—Bernard C. Steiner, ed., *The Life and Correspondence of James McHenry, Secretary of War Under Washington and Adams* (Cleveland: Burrows Brothers Co., 1907).

LCRK—Charles R. King, ed., *The Life and Correspondence of Rufus King*, 6 vols. (New York: Putnam, 1894–1900).

LGM—Jared Sparks, *The Life of Gouverneur Morris*, 3 vols. (Boston: Gray & Bowen, 1832).

LLGC—Henry Cabot Lodge, ed., *Life and Letters of George Cabot* (Boston: Little, Brown, & Co., 1877; rpt. New York: Da Capo Press, 1974).

LLHGO—Samuel Eliot Morrison, *The Life and Letters of Harrison Gray Otis, Federalist, 1765–1848* (Boston: Houghton Mifflin, 1913).

LMA—Charles Francis Adams, ed., *Letters of Mrs. Adams, the Wife of John Adams*, 2nd ed., 2 vols. (Boston: C. C. Little and J. Brown, 1840).

MAB—Matthew L. Davis, ed., *Memoirs of Aaron Burr*, 2 vols. (New York: Harper & Brothers, 1837).

NLAA—Stewart Mitchell, ed., *New Letters of Abigail Adams* (Boston: Houghton Mifflin, 1947).

PAG—*The Papers of Albert Gallatin*, Scholarly Resources, Wilmington, Delaware, 1985 (microfilm edition).

PAH—Harold C. Syrett and Jacob E. Cooke, eds., *Papers of Alexander Hamilton*, 27 vols. (New York: Columbia University Press, 1961–87).

PCAB—Mary-Jo Kline, ed., *Political Correspondence and Public Papers of Aaron Burr*, 2 vols. (Princeton: Princeton University Press, 1983).

PGW—Dorothy Twohig et al., eds., *The Papers of George Washington: Retirement Series*, 4 vols. (Charlottesville: University Press of Virginia, 1998–99).

PJA—Robert J. Taylor, et al., eds., *Papers of John Adams*, 8 vols. (Cambridge: Belknap Press, 1977–89).

PJM—William T. Hutchinson et al., eds., *Papers [of James Madison]*, 17 vols. (Chicago: University of Chicago Press; Charlottesville: University Press of Virginia, 1962–1991).

PJMar—Herbert A. Johnson, ed., *The Papers of John Marshall*, 12 vols. (Chapel Hill: University of North Carolina Press, 1974–2006).

PP—Frederick S. Allis, Jr., ed., *The Timothy Pickering Papers*, Massachusetts Historical Society, Boston, 1966 (microfilm edition).

PTJ—Julian P. Boyd et al., eds., *The Papers of Thomas Jefferson*, 32 vols. (Princeton: Princeton University Press, 1950–2006).

Spur of Fame—John A. Schutz and Douglass Adair, eds., *The Spur of Fame: Dialogues of John Adams and Benjamin Rush, 1805–1813* (San Marino: Huntington Library, 1966).

WAG—Henry Adams, ed., *The Writings of Albert Gallatin*, 3 vols. (Philadelphia: J. B. Lippincott & Co., 1879).

WAH—Henry Cabot Lodge, ed., *The Works of Alexander Hamilton*, 9 vols. (New York: G. P. Putnam's Sons, 1885–86).

WFA—W. B. Allen, ed., *Works of Fisher Ames*, 2 vols. (Indianapolis: Liberty Classics, 1983).

WGW—John C. Fitzpatrick, ed., *The Writings of George Washington*, 39 vols. (Washington: Government Printing Office, 1931–44).

WJA—Charles Francis Adams, ed., *The Works of John Adams*, 10 vols. (Boston: Little, Brown and Company, 1850–56).

WJM—Stanislaus Murray Hamilton, ed., *The Writings of James Monroe*, 7 vols. (New York: G. P. Putnam's Sons, 1898–1903).

WTJ (Ford)—Paul Leicester Ford, ed., *The Works of Thomas Jefferson*, 12 vols. (New York: G. P. Putnam's Sons, 1904–05).

WTJ (Lipscomb & Bergh)—A. A. Lipscomb and A. E. Bergh, eds., *The Writings of Thomas Jefferson*, 20 vols. (Washington: Thomas Jefferson Memorial Association of the United States, 1900–04).

INTRODUCTION: INDEPENDENCE DAY, JULY 4, 1776

PAGE

2 "My good man": Abigail Adams to Mary Smith Cranch, Oct. 6, 1766, *AFC*, 1:56.

2 "He should be painted": John Adams to William Tutor, Mar. 29, 1817, *WJA*, 10:245.

2 "a morose philosopher": John Adams to Mercy Otis Warren, Nov. 25, 1775, *PJA*, 3:318.

2 "Vanity": John Adams, May 3, 1756, *DAJA*, 1:25.

2 "There must be" and "we must, indeed": John Hancock and Benjamin Franklin, in Jarad Sparks, *Works of Benjamin Franklin*, 1 (Boston: Gray, 1840), p. 408 (apparent source for these quotes).

3 "I shall have": Benjamin Harrison, in Benjamin Rush to John Adams, July 20, 1811, ed. L. H. Butterfield, *Letters of Benjamin Rush*, 2 (Princeton: Princeton University Press, 1951), p. 1090 (Rush's firsthand recollection of Harrison's quip).

CHAPTER ONE: FROM FRIENDS TO RIVALS

PAGE

6 "Qu'il etoit charmant" and following: John Adams, Apr. 29, 1778, *DAJA*, 4:81.

6 "The attention of the court": John Adams, Feb. 9, 1779, *DAJA*, 2:347.

7 "It was a settled point": John Adams, Feb. 11, 1779, *DAJA*, 2:352.

7 "The life of Mr. Franklin" and following: John Adams, May 26, 1778, *DAJA*, 4:118–19.

8 "Always an honest man": Benjamin Franklin to Robert R. Livingston, July 22, 1783, *Benjamin Franklin: Writings* (New York: Library of America, 1987), p. 1065.

8 "the sufficiency": Thomas Jefferson to Citizens of Albemarle County, Virginia, Feb. 12, 1790, *PTJ*, 16:179.

8 "appointment gives": John Adams to James Warren, Aug. 27, 1784, *PTJ*, 7:382.

8 "Jefferson is an excellent" and following: John Adams to Elbridge Gerry, Dec. 12, 1784, *PTJ*, 7:382.

8 "My new partner": John Adams to Arthur Lee, Jan. 31, 1785; *PTJ*, 7:382.

9 "appeared to me": John Adams to Thomas Jefferson, Jan. 22, 1825, *AJL*, 2:606–07.

9 "the only person": Abigail Adams to Thomas Jefferson, June 6, 1785, *PTJ*, 8:178.

9 "The departure": Thomas Jefferson to John Adams, May 25, 1785, *PTJ*, 8:164.

10 "I do love this people": Thomas Jefferson to Abigail Adams, June 21, 1785, *PTJ*, 8:239.

10 "He is so amiable": Thomas Jefferson to James Madison, Jan. 30, 1787, *PTJ*, 11:95

10 "I am with an affection": John Adams to Thomas Jefferson, Jan. 2, 1789, *PTJ*, 14:411.

11 "Reputation ought to be": John Adams, Mar. 14, 1759, *DAJA*, 1:78.

11 "I am not ashamed": John Adams to Jonathan Sewall, Feb. 1760, *PJA*, 1:42.

11 "could tear himself": John Page, in Dumas Malone, *Jefferson: The Virginian* (Boston: Little Brown, 1948), p. 58.

12 "be admired": Thomas Jefferson to John Page, Dec. 25, 1762, *PTJ*, 1:5.

12 "advantage" and following: Thomas Jefferson, "Education for a Lawyer," c. 1767, *Complete Jefferson*, 2:1043–46.

12 "Determine never": Thomas Jefferson to Martha Jefferson, May 5, 1787, *PTJ*, 11:349.

12 Thinking back: John Adams to Thomas Jefferson, Nov. 15, 1817, *AJL*, 2:403; Thomas Jefferson to John Adams, Oct. 18, 1813, *AJL*, 2:389.

12 "When heaven designs" and following: John Adams to Jonathan Sewall, Feb. 1760, *PJA*, 1:41.

13 "How shall I gain": John Adams, Mar. 14, 1759, *DAJA*, 1:78.

13 "fabricated by the British": John Adams, Dec. 18, 1765, *DAJA*, 1:263.

13 "will neither lead": John Adams, Jan. 30, 1767, *DAJA*, 1:337.

13 "desultory life": John Adams, Jan. 30, 1768, *DAJA*, 1:238.

13 "dull": John Adams to Abigail Adams, June 30, 1774, *AFC*, 1:115.

13 "tedious": John Adams to Abigail Adams, June 23, 1874, *AFC*, 1:109.

13 "irksome": John Adams to Abigail Adams, June 29, 1769, *AFC*, 1:66; John Adams to Abigail Adams, July 9, 1774, *AFC*, 1:134.

13 "mere jargon": Thomas Jefferson to John Page, Dec. 25, 1762, *PTJ*, 1:5.

14 "so prompt, frank": John Adams to Timothy Pickering, Oct. 6, 1822, *WJA*, 2:514.

14 "We hold these truths": Thomas Jefferson, "Original Rough Draft," *PTJ*, 1:243.

17 "You are afraid": John Adams to Thomas Jefferson, Dec. 6, 1787, *AJL*, 1:213.

18 "No man on earth": Thomas Jefferson to John Adams, May 10, 1789, *PTJ*, 15:116.

18 "the best in the world": Alexander Hamilton, in Edward J. Larson and Michael P. Winship, *The Constitutional Convention: A Narrative History from the Notes of James Madison* (New York: Modern Library, 2005), p. 49 (from Madison's notes).

19 "Those who labor": Thomas Jefferson, *Notes on the State of Virginia* (1781–85), in *Complete Jefferson*, 2:678.

19 "The will of the majority": Thomas Jefferson to Citizens of Albemarle County, Virginia, Feb. 12, 1790, *PTJ*, 16:179.

19 "The voice of the people": Alexander Hamilton, in Larson and Winship, *Constitutional Convention*, p. 50 (from Yates's notes).

19 "the avarice": John Adams to Thomas Jefferson, Nov. 15, 1813, *AJL*, 2:398.

20 "balanced": E.g., John Adams praised the "balanced" British Constitution in John Adams, *Discourses on Davila* (New York: Da Capo, 1973 facs. rpt.), p. 248.

20 "I like a little": Thomas Jefferson to Abigail Adams, Feb. 22, 1787, *PTJ*, 11:174.

21 "Ignorant, restless": Abigail Adams to Thomas Jefferson, Jan. 29, 1787, *PTJ*, 11:86.

21 "the absence of want": Thomas Jefferson, *The Anas*, in *WTJ* (Lipscomb and Bergh), 1:280.

21 "Republican": E.g., James Madison, "The Union: Who Are Its Real Friends?" Mar. 31, 1792, *PJM*, 14:275.

22 "regal" and following: John Adams, quoted in James H. Huston, "John Adams' Title Campaign," *New England Review*, 41 (1968), p. 34.

22 "the most superlatively": Thomas Jefferson to James Madison, July 29, 1789, *PTJ*, 15:315.

22 "I hope the terms": Thomas Jefferson to William Carmichael, Aug. 9, 1789, *PTJ*, 15:336–37.

22 "almost all the nations" and following: [John Adams], "Discourses on Davila," *Gazette of the United States*, Apr. 27, 1791, p. 1.

22 "Mr. Adams had": Thomas Jefferson, *The Anas*, in *WTJ* (Lipscomb and Bergh), 1:279–80.

22 "heretic": Thomas Jefferson to James Madison, May 9, 1791, *PTJ*, 20:293 (reporting what he told Adams).

23 "that something is": Thomas Jefferson to Jonathan B. Smith, Apr. 26, 1791, *PTJ*, 20:290.

23 "I had in my view": Thomas Jefferson to George Washington, May 8, 1791, *PTJ*, 20:291–92.

23 "That you and I": Thomas Jefferson to John Adams, July 17, 1791, *PTJ*, 20:302.

23   "The friendship": John Adams to Thomas Jefferson, July 29, 1791, *PTJ*, 20:307.

24   "The revolution of France": Thomas Jefferson to James Madison, May 11, 1789, *PTJ*, 15:121.

25   "They took all the arms" and following: Thomas Jefferson to John Jay, July 19, 1789, *PTJ*, 15:288 and 290.

25   "This scene is too interesting": Thomas Jefferson to James Madison, July 22, 1789, *PTJ*, 15:301.

26   "The liberty of the whole earth": Thomas Jefferson to William Short, Jan. 3, 1793, *PTJ*, 25:14.

26   "France standing on": William Wordsworth, *The Prelude*, lns. 341–42 (impression of France in 1790, following Louis XVI's initial concessions to the National Assembly).

26   "It has served": Alexander Hamilton, "Fragment on the French Revolution," *WAH*, 7:376.

27   "I'll tell you what": John Adams, quoted in Thomas Jefferson, *The Anas*, Dec. 26, 1797, *WTJ* (Lipscomb & Bergh), 1:417.

27   "Our news from France": Thomas Jefferson to Thomas Mann Randolph, Jan. 7, 1793, *PTJ*, 25:30.

28   "None can deny": Alexander Hamilton, "Americanus No. 1," Jan. 31, 1794, *PAH*, 15:670–71.

29   "Jefferson thinks": John Adams, in Merrill D. Peterson, *Thomas Jefferson and the New Nation* (New York: Oxford University Press, 1970), p. 516.

29   "It seems the mode": John Adams to Abigail Adams, Jan. 14, 1797, *AFP*, reel 383.

30   competition: Jonathan Dayton to Oliver Wolcott, Sept. 15, 1796, *Gibbs Memoirs*, 1:383–84 (referring to the emerging contest for President as a "competition").

30   "the most insignificant": John Adams to Abigail Adams, Dec. 19, 1793, *WJA*, 1:460.

30   "I am heir apparent": John Adams to Abigail Adams, Jan. 20, 1796, *AFP*, reel 381.

30   "Prince of Wales": John Adams to Henry Knox, Mar. 30, 1797, *WJA*, 8:536.

32   "My letters inform": Thomas Jefferson to James Madison, Jan. 22, 1797, *PTJ*, 29:271.

32   "where our road": Thomas Jefferson, *The Anas*, Mar. 2, 1797, *WTJ* (Lipscomb and Bergh), 1:415.

34   "delighted": Alexander Hamilton to Timothy Pickering, Mar. 27, 1798, *PAH*, 21:379.

34   "insane": Thomas Jefferson to James Madison, Mar. 21, 1798, *PTJ*, 30:189.

35   "were war measures": John Adams, "Correspondence Originally Published in the *Boston Patriot*," (1809), *WJA*, 9:29.

CHAPTER TWO: CROSSING THE BAR

PAGE

37 "I have been occupied": George Washington to William Vans Murray, Dec. 3, 1797, *WGW,* 36:88.

38 "I was the *first*": George Washington to Burgess Ball, Sept. 22, 1799, *PGW,* R-4:318.

38 "good health": George Washington to Jonathan Trumbull Jr., July 21, 1799, *PGW,* R-4:202.

39 "From the moment": Thomas Jefferson, *The Anas, WTJ* (Lipscomb and Bergh), 1:282–83.

39 "An Anglican": Thomas Jefferson to Philip Mazzei, Apr. 24, 1796, *PTJ,* 29:82.

43 "the next election": Jonathan Trumbull Jr. to George Washington, June 22, 1799, *PGW,* R-4:144.

43 "My fears": Jonathan Trumbull Jr. to George Washington, Aug. 10, 1799, *PGW,* R-4:236.

43 "The leading federal": Gouverneur Morris to George Washington, Dec. 9, 1799, *PGW,* R-4:452.

44 "About one o'clock": George Washington, Dec. 12, 1799, *DGW,* 6:378.

44 "He had taken cold": Tobias Lear, "Narrative Accounts of the Death of George Washington," Dec. 14–15, 1799, *PGW,* R-4:543.

44 "In this sense": George Washington, "Farewell Address," Sept. 19, 1796, *WGW,* 35:222 and 225.

45 "Against us are": Thomas Jefferson to Philip Mazzei, Apr. 24, 1796, *PTJ,* 29:82.

45 "At that time": George Washington to Jonathan Trumbull Jr., July 21, 1799, *PGW,* R-4:202.

45 "hanging upon": George Washington to Jonathan Trumbull Jr., Aug. 30, 1799, *PGW,* R-4:275.

46 "Virginia's misfortune": *Virginia Federalist,* Dec. 7, 1799, p. 2.

46 "He appeared" and ensuing quotes about Washington's death: Tobias Lear, "Narrative Accounts of the Death of George Washington: Diary Account," Dec. 14–15, 1799, *PGW,* R-4:543–49.

48 "His last scene": Tobias Lear to John Adams, Dec. 16, 1799, *WGW,* 14:260.

48 "Every paper": *Columbian Centinel,* Dec. 28, 1799, p. 2.

49 "I feel myself alone": John Adams to Gentlemen of the Senate, Dec. 3, 1799, *WGW,* 14:264.

50 "First in war" and ensuing quotes from Lee's eulogy: Henry Lee, *Funeral Oration on the Death of General Washington* (Boston: Nancrede, 1800), pp. 3 and 14–15.

50 "Civil liberty": John Jay, "Charge to the Grand Juries," Apr. 4, 1790, *CJJ,* 3:395.

51   "the Jacobins": Theophilus Parsons to John Jay, May 5, 1800, *CJJ*, 4:269–70.

51   "The Federalists": Fisher Ames to Oliver Wolcott, Aug. 3, 1800, in Richard Hildreth, *History of the United States of America*, rev. ed., vol. 5 (New York: Harper, 1879), p. 376.

52   "faction" and ensuing quotes from Morris's eulogy: Gouverneur Morris, *An Oration upon the Death of General Washington* (New York: Furman, 1800), pp. 16, 18, and 20.

52   "When the people": Gouverneur Morris to Roger Griswold, Nov. 3, 1803, in David Hackett Fischer, *Revolution in American Conservatism* (New York: Harper & Row, 1965), pp. 25–26.

52   "The whole United States" and ensuing quote from Rush: George W. Corner, ed., *The Autobiography of Benjamin Rush* (Princeton: Princeton University Press, 1948), p. 249.

52   "Many will join": Elaine Forman Crane, ed., *The Diary of Elizabeth Drinker* (Boston: Northeastern University Press, 1991), p. 1248 (entry for Dec. 25, 1799).

53   "There is no": John Adams to James McHenry, Oct. 22, 1798, *AFP*, reel 119.

53   "resistance": Alexander Hamilton to Theodore Sedgwick, Feb. 2, 1799, *PAH*, 22:453.

53   "take possession": Alexander Hamilton to Harrison Gray Otis, Jan. 26, 1799, *PAH*, 22:441.

53   "This man is stark mad": John Adams to Harrison Gray Otis, May 9, 1823, *AFP*, reel 124 (recalling an earlier declaration made in response to Adams seeing some letters by Hamilton, which seems to have included ones about Hamilton's plans for the Army).

54   "That army": John Adams to James Lloyd, Feb. 11, 1815, *WJA*, 10:118.

54   "blasphemous panegyrics" and ensuing quotes from Philip Freneau, "Stanzas," in Fred Lewis Pattee, ed., *Poems of Philip Freneau: Poet of the American Revolution*, 3 (Princeton: University Library, 1907), pp. 235 and 237.

55   "said nothing in public": Dumas Malone, *Jefferson and the Ordeal of Liberty* (Boston: Little, Brown & Co., 1962), p. 444.

55   "Had this party magistrate" and ensuing quote from *Gazette of the United States*, Jan. 18, 1800, p. 3.

57   "The effects": *Gazette of the United States*, Mar. 5, 1799, p. 3 (reprint of Federalist broadside).

58   "This state is greatly": Alexander Addison to George Washington, July 6, 1799, *PGW*, R-4:176.

59   "a British partisan": *Aurora*, Oct. 8, 1799, p. 3 (reprint of Republican broadside).

59   "the Federalists": *Aurora*, Sept. 11, 1799, p. 2 (reprint of Republican broadside).

59 "This national infatuation": *Aurora*, Sept. 21, 1799, p. 2.

59 "Mr. McKean": "Address to the Freemen of Pennsylvania," (Germantown: Poulson, 1799), pp. 7, 8, 10, 12, Federalist pamphlet reprinted in *EAI* 1: Evans no. 35081.

59 "happiness and independence": Levi Hollingsworth et al., "Philadelphia," May 27, 1799 (Federalist broadside reprinted in *EAI* 1: Evans no. 48956).

59 "the whole state": *Gazette of the United States*, Mar. 5, 1799, p. 3 (reprint of Federalist broadside).

60 "a devout Christian": *Aurora*, Oct. 8, 1799, p. 3 (reprint of Republican broadside).

60 "The Federal Party": *Aurora*, Oct. 10, 1799, p. 2.

60 "Such a fire": *Gazette of the United States*, Oct. 29, 1799, p. 3.

60 "an event most disgraceful": Theodore Sedgwick to Rufus King, Nov. 15, 1799, *LCRK*, 3:146.

61 "The state of Pennsylvania": Abigail Adams to William Shaw, in Richard N. Rosenfeld, *American Aurora: A Democratic-Republican Returns* (New York: St. Martin's Press, 1997), p. 711.

61 "The election of my Democratic judge": William Cobbett, *Porcupine's Works*, 11 (London: Cobbett & Morgan, 1801), pp. 97 and 107 (bound version of articles from *Porcupine's Gazette*).

61 "the faithful guardian": *Kline's Carlisle Weekly Gazette*, Nov. 6, 1799, p. 2.

61 "May the spirit": *Aurora*, Nov. 12, 1799, p. 2.

61 "Ye true sons": *Aurora*, Nov. 9, 1799, p. 3.

62 "The success of McKean's election": Thomas Jefferson to Charles Pinckney, Oct. 29, 1799, *PTJ*, 31:227.

62 "The success of the Republican interest": Charles Pinckney to James Madison, Sept. 30, 1799, *PJM*, 17:272–73.

63 "All agree": Thomas Jefferson to James Monroe, Jan. 12, 1800, *PTJ*, 31:300.

63 "The present assembly": James Madison to Thomas Jefferson, Jan. 12, 1800, *PJM*, 17:355.

64 "exclude *one third*": *Virginia Federalist*, Mar. 19, 1800, pp. 2–3.

64 "the ancient usages": *Virginia Federalist*, May 28, 1800, p. 3 (reprint of Federalist broadside also in *EAI* 1: Evans nos. 36773 and 36774).

64 "best calculated to preserve": Franklin, *Vindication of the General Ticket Law* (Richmond: Samuel Pleasants, March 1800), p. 7.

65 "guard against *one* antifederal vote": unnamed Federalist member of Congress quoted in Susan Dunn, *Jefferson's Second Revolution: The Election Crisis of 1800 and the Triumph of Republicanism* (Boston: Houghton Mifflin, 2004), p. 186.

66 "republican spirit": Benjamin Rush to Thomas Jefferson, Mar. 12, 1801, L. H. Butterfield, ed., *Letters of Benjamin Rush*, 2 (Princeton: Princeton University Press, 1951), p. 832 (refers to earlier letter from Jefferson).

66 "The death of the General!": Henry Van Schaack to Theodore Sedgwick, Dec. 26, 1799, in Fischer, *Revolution of American Conservatism*, p. 56.

CHAPTER THREE: "ELECTIONEERING HAS ALREADY BEGUN"
PAGE

67 "The French Republic": *Gazette of the United States*, Feb. 7, 1800, p. 2.

67 "That revolution": John Marshall, *The Life of George Washington*, 5 (Philadelphia: Wayne, 1807), p. 389.

68 "The rights of mankind": George Washington to Thomas Jefferson, Jan. 1, 1788, *PTJ*, 12:490.

68 "The [French] nation": Thomas Jefferson to George Washington, Nov. 4, 1788, *PTJ*, 14:330.

68 "the union of principles": George Washington to French Ambassador, Feb. 1793, in Marshall, *Life of Washington*, 5:391.

68 "There seems to be": Marshall, *Life of Washington*, 5:390.

69 "I much fear": Charles Carroll of Carrollton to Alexander Hamilton, Aug. 27, 1800, *PAH*, 25:94.

69 "The friends of order": William Cobbett, *Porcupine's Works*, 12 (London: Cobbett & Morgan, 1801), pp. 114–15.

70 "If our people": Fisher Ames to Oliver Wolcott, Jan. 12, 1800, *WFA*, 2:1349.

70 "must act as his party" and following: Fisher Ames to Oliver Wolcott, June 12, 1800, *WFA*, 2:1360–61.

70 "should prevail" and following: *Boston Gazette*, Apr. 1799, reprint in *WFA*, 1:189–90.

70 "the great arch priest": Theophilus Parsons to John Jay, May 5, 1800, *CJJ*, 4:270.

70 "Whatever his views": Thomas Jefferson to Samuel Adams, Feb. 26, 1800, *PTJ*, 31:395.

71 "Whether the lesson," James Madison to Thomas Jefferson, Feb. 14, 1800, *PJM*, 19:364.

71 "Nothing more solemnly": *Aurora*, Jan. 30, 1800, p. 2.

71 "The enemies of our Constitution": Thomas Jefferson to Thomas Mann Randolph, Feb. 2, 1800, *PTJ*, 31:358.

71 "were endeavoring to": Elbridge Gerry, "Minutes of a Conference with the President," Mar. 26, 1799, quoted in Stanley Elkins and Eric McKitrick, *The Age of Federalism* (New York: Oxford University Press, 1993), p. 617 (quoting Adams).

72 "The people of [France]": Thomas Jefferson to John Breckenridge, Jan. 29, 1800, *PTJ*, 31:344–45.

72 "The late defection": James Madison to Thomas Jefferson, Apr. 4, 1800, *PJM*, 17:377.

72   "had to struggle": *Aurora*, Jan. 29, 1800, p. 2.

72   "Our vessel": Thomas Jefferson to John Breckenridge, Jan. 29, 1800, *PTJ*, 31:345.

73   "a thousand anecdotes": John Adams to James Lloyd, Feb. 11, 1815, *WJA*, 10:118.

73   "to write": U.S. Statutes at Large, 1:596–97.

73   "palpably in the teeth": Thomas Jefferson to James Madison, June 7, 1798, *PTJ*, 30:393.

73   "altogether void": Kentucky Legislature, in *WTJ* (Ford), 8:458–59.

73   "reign of witches": Thomas Jefferson to John Taylor, June 4, 1798, *PTJ*, 30:389.

74   "The most vigorous": Stevens Thomson Mason to James Madison, Apr. 23, 1800, *PJM*, 19:382.

74   "pests of society": Timothy Pickering to P. Johnson, *Albany Centinel*, Sept. 22, 1798, p. 2.

75   "a disbanding": Cobbett, *Porcupine's Works*, 12:45.

76   "devote their valor": *The Bee*, May 8, 1799, p. 2.

76   "publication to be": *Newport Mercury*, May 6, 1800, p. 2.

76   "libel against": John Adams to Thomas Pickering, Aug. 13, 1799, *WJA*, 9:13–14.

77   "in his former": Abigail Adams to Mary Smith Cranch, Nov. 26, 1799, *NLAA*, p. 216.

77   "A more oppressive": Stevens Thomson Mason to James Madison, Apr. 23, 1800, *PJM*, 17:382.

77   "If a man attempts": Samuel Chase, in *Account of the Trial of Thomas Cooper* (Philadelphia: John Bioren, 1800), pp. 42–43.

77   "Chase's repository": *Aurora*, Nov. 5, 1800, p. 4.

77   "Punishment only hardens": *The Bee*, Sept. 3, 1800, p. 4.

77   "the conspicuous victim": *Aurora*, Nov. 5, 1800, p. 2.

78   "I consider these laws": Thomas Jefferson to Stevens Thomson Mason, Oct. 11, 1798, *PTJ*, 30:560.

78   "The report": *Aurora*, Feb. 19, 1800, p. 2.

79   "properly appointed": James Ross, Jan. 23, 1800, *Annals of Congress*, 10:29.

79   "Their being no law": Theodore Sedgwick to Rufus King, May 11, 1800, *LCRK*, 3:237.

79   "If this course": Oliver Wolcott to Fisher Ames, Dec. 29, 1799, *WFA*, 2:1339–40.

80   "This bill was a sweeper": Cobbett, *Porcupine's Works*, 12:41.

80   "In every state": Charles Pinckney, Mar. 28, 1800, *Annals of Congress*, 10:134–35.

81   "obnoxious principles": Stevens Thomson Mason to James Madison, Mar. 7, 1800, *JMP*, 17:371.

81   "deadly blow": John Beckley to Tench Coxe, Jan. 24, 1800, Gerard W. Gawalt, ed., *Justifying Jefferson: The Political Writings of John James Beckley* (Washington: Library of Congress, 1995), p. 164.

81   "The bill brought": *Kline's Carlisle Weekly Gazette*, May 7, 1800, p. 2. See also *Aurora*, May 1, 1800, p. 2.

81   "alarming attempt": *Aurora*, Jan. 27, 1800, p. 2.

81   "Venetian Council": *Aurora*, Feb. 22, 1800, p. 2.

81   "If there was nothing": *Aurora*, Mar. 11, 1800, p. 2.

81   "Is there any thing evil": John Adams to Thomas Pickering, Aug. 1, 1799, *WJA*, 9:5.

82   "The right of self-preservation": Uriah Tracy, Mar. 5, 1800, *Annals of Congress*, 10:87.

82   "Although you": John Dawson to James Madison, Mar. 30, 1800, *PJM*, 17:376.

82   "be sure to reach": *Aurora*, Mar. 28, 1800, p. 3.

82   "Questions of privilege": John Marshall to James Markham Marshall, Apr. 4, 1800, *PJM*, 4:121–22.

83   "that the House": Stevens Thomson Mason to James Madison, Mar. 7, 1800, *PJM*, 17:371.

83   "On this question": Theodore Sedgwick to Rufus King, May 11, 1800, *LCRK*, 3:238.

83   "Let me do what I will": John Marshall to James Markham Marshall, Apr. 4, 1800, *PJMar*, 4:124.

84   "Next week Congress": Abigail Adams to Mary Smith Cranch, Nov. 26, 1799, *NLAA*, p. 217.

84   "In all our measures": Theodore Sedgwick to Rufus King, Dec. 12, 1799, *LCRK*, 3:155.

84   "Our parties in Congress": Fisher Ames to Christopher Gore, Mar. 5, 1800, *WFA*, 2:1355.

84   "Congress will rise": Thomas Jefferson to James Madison, May 12, 1800, *PTJ*, 31:579.

84   "a real feebleness" and following quote: Theodore Sedgwick to Rufus King, May 11, 1800, *LCRK*, 3:237.

85   "This seems to be": Thomas Jefferson to James Madison, Mar. 8, 1800, *PTJ*, 31:408–09.

CHAPTER FOUR: BURR V. HAMILTON

PAGE

88   "I have never known": John Adams to James Lloyd, Feb. 17, 1815, *WJA*, 10:123.

88   "a bastard brat": John Adams to Benjamin Rush, Jan. 25, 1800, *Spur of Fame*, p. 48. Adams used the same phrase in John Adams to Thomas Jefferson, July 12, 1813, *AJL* (Cappon), 2:354.

89   "Colonel Burr": George Washington quoted in John Adams to James Lloyd, Feb. 17, 1815, *WJA*, 10:124.

89   "the most restless": John Adams to James Lloyd, Feb. 17, 1815, *WJA*, 10:124.

89   "It was ever one": Matthew L. Davis, in *MAB*, 2:55–56.

90   "As a public man": Alexander Hamilton to unnamed correspondent, Sept. 26, 1792, *PAH*, 12:480.

91   "I suspect": Gore Vidal, *Burr: A Novel* (New York: Random House, 1973), p. 221.

91   "If the *city* election": Thomas Jefferson to James Madison, Mar. 4, 1800, *PTJ*, 31:409.

91   "We are full": Robert Troup to Rufus King, Mar. 9, 1800, *LCRK*, 3:209.

92   "It is asserted": Charles Carroll of Carrollton to Alexander Hamilton, Apr. 18, 1800, *PAH*, 24:412.

92   "In the new election": Thomas Jefferson to James Monroe, Jan. 12, 1800, *PTJ*, 31:301.

93   "Your fellow citizens": Christopher Gore to Rufus King, Apr. 24, 1800, *LCRK*, 3:228.

93   "the election": *Commercial Advertiser*, Apr. 23, 1800, p. 2.

93   "Citizens choose": *Daily Advertiser*, Apr. 28, 1800, p. 3.

94   "Great God": *Commercial Advertiser*, Apr. 26, 1800, p. 2.

94   "Merchants, your ships": *Daily Advertiser*, Apr. 28, 1800, p. 3.

94   "It is for you": *Daily Advertiser*, Apr. 30, 1800, p. 2.

94   "Those of you": *Daily Advertiser*, Apr. 29, 1800, p. 2.

94   "men of little weight": John Adams to Benjamin Stoddard, Nov. 16, 1811, *AFP*, reel 118. For similar comments, see John Adams to James Lloyd, Feb. 17, 1815, *WJA*, 10:125.

95   "men of no note": Abigail Adams to John Quincy Adams, May 15, 1800, *AFP*, reel 397.

95   "Hamilton, who ruled": James McHenry to John Adams, May 31, 1800, *AFP*, reel 397 (recounting Adams's comments to McHenry).

96   "It is next": Robert Troup to Rufus King, Mar. 9, 1800, *LCRK*, 3:208.

96   "Now I have him": John Adams to James Lloyd, Feb. 17, 1815, *WJA*, 10:125.

96   "If the Federal ticket": *Commercial Advertiser*, Apr. 23, 1800, p. 2.

96   "the standing army": *American Citizen*, Apr. 5, 1800, p. 3.

96   "Peace or war": *American Citizen*, Apr. 9, 1800, p. 3.

96   "The political happiness": *American Citizen*, Apr. 19, 1800, p. 3.

97   "that whoever disapproves": *American Citizen*, Apr. 30, 1800, p. 2.

97   "if you waver": *American Citizen*, Apr. 8, 1800, p. 3.

97   "A little patience": Thomas Jefferson to John Taylor, June 4, 1798, *PTJ*, 308:389.

97   "The Republican spirit": Thomas Jefferson to James Madison, Mar. 25, 1800, *PTJ*, 31:455.

97   "By this time": Thomas Jefferson to Edward Livingston, Apr. 30, 1800, *PTJ*, 31:546–47.

98   "The [Federalist] bank": Matthew L. Davis to Albert Gallatin, Mar. 29, 1800, *PAG*, reel 4.

98   *"Here, when all"*: Pasquin Petronius, *The Echo*, pp. 276–77, quoted in Arthur Irving Bernstein, *The Rise of the Democratic-Republican Party in New York City, 1789–1800*, 1964 Ph.D. Disc., Columbia University, p. 403.

99   "Mr. Burr is arranging": Matthew L. Davis to Albert Gallatin, Mar. 29, 1800, *PAG*, reel 4.

99   "to himself the right": Matthew L. Davis, *MAB*, 2:58.

99   "I believe we shall": Matthew L. Davis to Albert Gallatin, Mar. 29, 1800, *PAG*, reel 4.

99   "They have got names": *Commercial Advertiser*, Apr. 25, 1800, p. 2.

100   "Citizen Clinton": *Daily Advertiser*, Apr. 26, 1800, p. 2.

100   "their sole object": *Commercial Advertiser*, April 25, 1800, p. 2.

100   "If the General": *Daily Advertiser*, Apr. 30, 1800, p. 2.

100   "the veterans": "Recollections of Washington Irving," *Continental Monthly*, 1 (1862), p. 691.

100   "As soon as the room": Mordici Myers, *Reminiscences, 1780 to 1814* (Washington: Crane, 1900), p. 11.

100   "Our organization": Ibid., p. 12.

101   "Never have I observed": Matthew L. Davis to Albert Gallatin, Apr. 15, 1800, *PAG*, reel 4.

101   "pledged himself": Matthew L. Davis to Albert Gallatin, Mar. 29, 1800, *PAG*, reel 4.

101   "Many people wonder": *Daily Advertiser*, Apr. 28, 1800, p. 3.

101   "Every day he is seen": *Commercial Advertiser*, Apr. 25, 1800, quoted in Milton Lomask, *Aaron Burr: The Years from Princeton to the Vice President, 1756–1805* (New York: Farrar, Straus, 1979), p. 244.

102   "Both parties": Elizabeth DeHart Bleecker, *Diary*, p. 115, quoted in Bernstein, *Rise of the Democratic-Republican Party in New York City*, p. 407.

102   "Can it be possible": *American Citizen*, Apr. 30, 1800, p. 2.

102   "the unconciliating conduct": Joseph Hale to Rufus King, May 13, 1800, *LCRK*, 3:240.

102   "They repeatedly addressed": Matthew L. Davis, *MAB*, 2:60.

102   "I have been night": Robert Troup to Peter Van Schaack, May 2, 1800, quoted in Noble E. Cunningham Jr., *The Jeffersonian Republicans: The For-*

mation of Party Organization, 1789–1801 (Chapel Hill: University of North Carolina Press, 1957), p. 183.

103 "carriages, chairs": *New York Gazette*, May 13, 1800, quoted in Lomask, *Aaron Burr*, p. 245. (The Sixth Ward was in what is now the Tribeca neighborhood, and the Seventh Ward comprised parts of what became known as Little Italy and the Lower East Side.)

103 "This morning": *Commercial Advertiser*, May 1, 1800, p. 3.

103 "The purse-proud landlord": *Commercial Advertiser*, Apr. 30, 1800, p. 3.

103 "This day": Matthew L. Davis to Albert Gallatin, May 1, 1800, *PAG*, reel 4.

104 "Republicanism Triumphant": Ibid.

104 "The New York election": Aaron Burr quoted in Lomask, *Aaron Burr*, p. 246.

104 "an earthquake": Edward Livingston to Thomas Jefferson, May 3, 1800, in ed. James A. Padgett, "Letters of Edward Livingston to United States Presidents," *Louisiana Historical Quarterly*, 19 (1976), p. 941.

104 "Dear Sir!": John Dawson to James Madison, May 4, 1800, *PJM*, 17:386.

104 "To Colonel Burr": Matthew L. Davis to Albert Gallatin, May 1, 1800, *PAG*, reel 4.

104 "The management": Matthew L. Davis to Albert Gallatin, May 5, 1800, *PAG*, reel 4.

105 "His generalship": James Nicholson to Albert Gallatin, May 6, 1800, *PAG*, reel 4.

105 "The victory": Aaron Burr to Thomas Jefferson, May 3, 1800, *PCAB*, 1:426.

105 "We have beat": Aaron Burr quoted in Lomask, *Aaron Burr*, p. 246.

105 "But yesterday": Edward Livingston to Thomas Jefferson, May 3, 1800, in ed. Padgett, "Letters of Edward Livingston," p. 940.

105 "The event": Peter Augustus Jay to John Jay, May 3, 1800, *PJJ* (Columbia), no. 6094.

105 "They do not confine": *Commercial Advertiser*, May 5, 1800, p. 2.

106 "These people": Abigail Adams to John Quincy Adams, May 15, 1800, *AFP*, reel 4.

106 "the defection of New York": Abigail Adams to Thomas B. Adams, Nov. 13, 1800, *LMA*, 2:239.

106 "Hamilton has been opposing": James McHenry to John Adams, May 31, 1800, *AFP*, reel 397 (recounting Adams's comments to McHenry).

106 "To reign by fear": *American Citizen*, May 6, 1800, p. 3.

106 "a lesson": Robert R. Livingston to Thomas Jefferson, May 8, 1800, quoted in Bernstein, *Rise of the Democratic-Republican Party in New York City*, p. 415.

107 "a figure of rage": John Dawson to James Monroe, May 4, 1800, quoted in ibid., p. 417.

107 "invest him with the power" and following quotes: *Aurora*, May 7, 1800, p. 2.

107 "infamous lie": New York newspaper quoted in *MAB*, 2:61.

108 "This measure will" and following quotes from Hamilton and Schuyler: Alexander Hamilton to John Jay, May 7, 1800, *CJJ*, 4:271–72; Philip Schuyler to John Jay, *CJJ*, 4:273.

109 "Hamilton's appeal": Ron Chernow, *Alexander Hamilton* (New York: Penguin Press, 2004), p. 609.

109 "Proposing a measure": Alexander Hamilton to John Jay, May 7, 1800, *CJJ*, 4:272n.

109 "several of our friends": Theodore Sedgwick to Rufus King, Dec. 12, 1799, *LCRK*, 3:155.

110 "Pray how": John Dawson to James Madison, Feb. 23, 1800, *PJM*, 17:366.

110 "I have no reason": James Madison to Thomas Jefferson, Mar. 15, 1800, *PJM*, 17:373.

110 "That the election": Franklin, *Vindication of the General Ticket Law* (Richmond: Samuel Pleasants, 1800), p. 22.

110 "I find that": James Madison to Thomas Jefferson, Apr. 20, 1800, *PJM*, 17:381.

110 "The elections so far": James Monroe to Thomas Jefferson, Apr. 26, 1800, *WJM*, 3:175.

110 "The patrons": James Madison to Thomas Jefferson, Apr. 27, 1800, *PJM*, 17:383.

111 "The Feds begin": Thomas Jefferson to James Madison, Mar. 8, 1800, *PTJ*, 31:408.

111 "The results": *Aurora*, May 6, 1800, p. 2

111 "New York, by an effort": Abigail Adams to Mary Smith Cranch, May 5, 1800, *NLAA*, pp. 251–52.

CHAPTER FIVE: CAUCUSES AND CALUMNY

PAGE

113 "Some person": James Monroe to James Madison, Oct. 9, 1792, *Monroe Writings*, 1:243.

114 "the whole body": John Beckley to James Madison, June 20, 1796, *PJM*, 16:371.

115 "has effected all": Matthew L. Davis to Albert Gallatin, May 5, 1800, *PAG*, reel 4.

115 "principally": Matthew L. Davis to Albert Gallatin, Mar. 29, 1800, *PAG*, reel 4.

115 "It is generally": Ibid.

116 "Who is to be": Albert Gallatin to Hannah Gallatin, May 6, 1800, *PAG*, reel 4.

116   "After much conversation" and following: George Clinton to DeWitt Clinton, Dec. 13, 1803, Papers of DeWitt Clinton, reel 1, Columbia University Rare Book and Manuscript Library.

117   "of all the Republicans" and following: James Nicholson to Albert Gallatin, May 7, 1800, *PAG*, reel 4.

117   "Burr says": Hannah Gallatin to Albert Gallatin, May 7, 1800, *PAG*, reel 4.

118   "fractious meeting" and following: *Aurora*, Sept. 22, 1800, p. 2.

118   "We had last night": Albert Gallatin to Hannah Gallatin, May 12, 1800, *PAG*, reel 4.

118   "It is our mutual duty": Thomas Jefferson to Pierce Butler, Aug. 11, 1800, *PTJ*, 32:91.

119   "*Can we, may we*": David Gelston to James Madison, Oct. 8, 1800, *PJM*, 17:418–19.

119   "It would be superfluous": James Madison to James Monroe, Oct. 21, 1800, *PJM*, 17:426.

119   "crooked gun": Thomas Jefferson to William Branch Giles, Apr. 20, 1807, *WTJ* (Ford) 10:387.

120   "singular and mysterious" and following: Fisher Ames to Rufus King, July 15, 1800, *LCRK*, 3:275.

120   "No, no" and following: Various wordings of Pinckney's response appear in Marvin R. Zahniser, *Charles Cotesworth Pinckney: Founding Father* (Chapel Hill: University of North Carolina Press, 1967), p. 170.

121   "To support *Adams*": Alexander Hamilton to Theodore Sedgwick, May 4, 1800, *PAH*, 24:452–53.

122   "It is therefore": Ibid.

122   "hocus-pocus": Thomas Jefferson to Thomas M. Randolph, May 7, 1800, in *PTJ*, 31:562.

122   "It is understood": Fisher Ames to Chauncey Goodrich, June 12, 1800, *Gibbs Memoirs*, 2:367.

122   "We have had": Theodore Sedgwick to Rufus King, May 11, 1800, *LCRK*, 3:238.

122   "Had the foulest": Theodore Sedgwick, in David G. McCollough, *John Adams* (New York: Simon and Schuster, 2001), p. 524.

122   "It is true": Theodore Sedgwick to Rufus King, May 11, 1800, *LCRK*, 3:238.

123   "He says that": Theodore Sedgwick to Alexander Hamilton, May 7, 1800, *PAH*, 24:467.

123   "He is" and following: Alexander Hamilton to Theodore Sedgwick, May 10, 1800, *PAH*, 24:475.

123   "would vote unanimously": George Cabot to Oliver Wolcott, June 14, 1800, *Gibbs Memoirs*, 2:370.

124 "would join in": Fisher Ames to Chauncey Goodrich, June 12, 1800, *WFA*, 2:1356.

124 "much British influence": William Cobbett, *Porcupine's Works*, 12 (London: Cobbett & Morgan, 1801), p. 143 (reprint of Adams's letter).

124 "absolutely out of his": Benjamin Franklin to Robert R. Livingston, July 22, 1783, *Benjamin Franklin: Writings* (New York: Library of America, 1987), p. 1065.

125 "Hamilton had opposed": John Adams to Benjamin Stoddert, Nov. 16, 1811, *AFP*, reel 118.

125 "Mr. Pickering": John Adams to William Cunningham, Oct. 15, 1808, *Correspondence Between the Hon. John Adams and the Late William Cunningham, Esq.* (Boston: True and Greene, 1823), p. 40.

125 "He is a man": John Adams to William Cunningham, Nov. 7, 1808, ibid., p. 50.

125 "Pickering could never": John Adams to Benjamin Stoddert, Nov. 16, 1811, *AFP*, reel 118.

125 "considers Col. Pickering": Oliver Wolcott to Fisher Ames, Dec. 29, 1799, *Gibbs Memoirs*, 2:315.

126 "became indecorous" and following: James McHenry to John McHenry, May 20, 1800, *Gibbs Memoirs*, 2:348.

126 "Hamilton is an intriguer": James McHenry to John Adams, May 31, 1800, *AFP*, reel 397 (in his letter, McHenry used the older word *intriguant* rather than *intriguer*).

126 "At times": James McHenry to John McHenry, May 20, 1800, *Gibbs Memoirs*, 2:347.

126 "Oh mad!": Alexander Hamilton to James McHenry, May 23, 1800, *LCJM*, p. 458.

127 "I do not feel": Timothy Pickering to John Adams, May 12, 1800, *AFP*, reel 397.

127 "one of the most deliberate": John Adams to William Cunningham, Oct. 15, 1808, *Correspondence Between Adams and Cunningham*, p. 39.

127 "all such documents": Alexander Hamilton to Timothy Pickering [May 14, 1800], *PAH*, 24:487.

127 "I intended": Timothy Pickering to Alexander Hamilton, May 15, 1800, *PAH*, 24:490.

128 "This bill": Cobbett, *Porcupine's Works*, 12:44–45.

128 "to Major Generals": John Adams to James McHenry, May 19, 1800, *JAW*, 9:55.

128 "amount to treason": John Adams, "Proclamation," Mar. 12, 1800, reprinted in Francis Wharton, *State Trials of the United States During the Administration of Washington and Adams* (Philadelphia: Carey & Hart, 1851), p. 459.

129 "just" and "the well disposed": Charles Lee, Oliver Wolcott, and Benjamin Stoddert to John Adams, May 20, 1800, *WJA*, 9:59.

129 "The cause of humanity": Ibid., p. 60.

129 "I feel a calm": Timothy Pickering to John Adams, May 10, 1799, *PP*, 37:418.

129 "riot": John Adams to Heads of Department, May 20, 1800, *WJA*, 9:58.

129 "The latter party": *Aurora*, May 16, 1800, p. 2.

130 "The miserable policy": Thomas Pickering to Rufus King, May 7, 1800, *LCRK*, 3:232.

130 "The cause of Federalism": Timothy Pickering to David Humphreys, May 28, 1800, *PP*, 11:166.

130 "It is with grief": Oliver Wolcott to George Cabot, June 16, 1800, *Gibbs Memoirs*, 2:371.

130 "the greatest possible": Oliver Wolcott to James McHenry, July 18, 1800, *Gibbs Memoirs*, 2:381.

131 "An open attack": Fisher Ames to Chauncey Goodrich, June 12, 1800, *WFA*, 2:1357.

131 "nothing further": Richard Stockton to Oliver Wolcott, June 27, 1800, *Gibbs Memoirs*, 2:374.

131 "they are however convinced": Robert G. Harper to Alexander Hamilton, June 5, 1800, *PAH*, 24:569.

131 "If any alteration": Charles Cotesworth Pinckney to James McHenry, June 19, 1800, *LCJM*, p. 460.

132 "Have our party": James McHenry to Oliver Wolcott, July 22, 1800, *LCJM*, p. 462.

132 "I have good reason": Theodore Sedgwick to Alexander Hamilton, May 13, 1800, *PAH*, 24:482.

132 "to form a party": Charles Cotesworth Pinckney to James McHenry, June 1, 1800, *LCJM*, p. 460.

133 "All our friends": Gouverneur Morris to Rufus King, June 4, 1800, *LCRK*, 3:251–52.

134 "Such papers cannot": Thomas Jefferson to James Thomson Callender, Oct. 6, 1799, in Worthington Chauncey Ford, ed., "Thomas Jefferson and James Thomson Callender," *New England Historical and Genealogical Register*, 50 (1896), p. 449.

134 "The reign of Mr. Adams" and following: James Thomson Callender, *The Prospect before Us*, 1 (Richmond: Jones, Pleasants & Lyon, 1800), pp. 30, 73, 156, 167.

134 "all the host": Abigail Adams to Mary Smith Cranch, May 5, 1800, in *NLAA*, p. 251.

134 "Judge Chase": *Aurora*, June 3, 1800, p. 2.

135 "Can any man": "Trial of James Thomson Callender," edited transcript in Wharton, *State Trials*, p. 695.

135   "irregular and inadmissible": Ibid., p. 709.

135   "that the laws": *Albany Register*, June 17, 1800, p. 3 (reprinting article from Richmond *Examiner*, June 6, 1800).

135   "insolent, inconsistent": James Thomson Callender, *The Prospect before Us*, 2, pt. 2 (Richmond: Pace, 1801), pp. 80–81.

135   "The judge spoke": *Albany Register*, June 17, 1800, p. 3 (reprinting article from Richmond *Examiner*, June 6, 1800).

136   "Human nature": Thomas Jefferson to James Monroe, July 15, 1802, reprinted in Wharton, *State Trials*, p. 720.

136   "The Fed[eralist]s have split": Thomas Boylston Adams to Joseph Pitcairn, May 31, 1800, in "Letters of Thomas Boylston Adams to Joseph Pitcairn," *Historical and Philosophical Society of Ohio Quarterly Publication*, 12 (1917), p. 36.

CHAPTER SIX: A NEW KIND OF CAMPAIGN

PAGE

139   "No stranger can": Oliver Wolcott to Mrs. Wolcott, July 4, 1800, *Gibbs Memoirs*, 2:378.

139   "resembling more": *Salem Gazette*, Dec. 5, 1800, p. 3.

139   "*Where tribunes rule*": Thomas Moore, in Constance McLaughlin Green, *Washington: Village and Capital, 1800–1878* (Princeton: Princeton University Press, 1962), p. 39.

140   "Notice.": *Centinel of Liberty*, June 3, 1800, p. 3 (reprint of *Aurora* classified ad).

140   "I cannot but consider" and following: Oliver Wolcott to Mrs. Wolcott, July 4, 1800, *Gibbs Memoirs*, 2:317.

141   "If the twelve years": Abigail Adams to Abigail Adams Smith, Nov. 21, 1800, *LMA*, 2:242.

142   "Is gone—what!": *Aurora*, June 7, 1800, p. 2.

142   "Remarkably cheap": William Shaw to Abigail Adams, June 5, 1800, *AFP*, reel 398.

142   "In re-visiting": *Gazette of the United States*, June 6, 1800, p. 2.

143   "Your presence": *Philadelphia Gazette*, June 6, 1800, p. 3.

143   "was received": *Gazette of the United States*, June 7, 1800, p. 3.

143   "the early" and following: *Maryland Herald*, June 19, 1800, p. 3.

143   "Every inch": William Shaw to Abigail Adams, June 5, 1800, *AFP*, reel 398.

144   "I have seen many cities": John Adams to Abigail Adams, June 13, 1800, *AFP*, reel 398.

144   "There was not": *Aurora*, June 18, 1800, p. 3.

145   "injustice" and following: *Philadelphia Gazette*, June 16, 1800, p. 3.

145 "rousing the spirit": George Cabot to Oliver Wolcott, July 20, 1800, *LLGC*, p. 282.

145 "eminent and long services" and following: *Maryland Herald*, June 26, 1800, p. 2.

146 "The very affectionate": *Gazette of the United States*, June 18, 1800, p. 3.

146 "It appears now certain": *Herald of Liberty* (Washington, Pennsylvania), June 9, 1800, p. 3.

147 "have come to an agreement": *Times* (Alexandria), June 9, 1800, p. 2; and *Federal Gazette* (Baltimore), June 7, 1800, p. 2.

147 "that Mr. Adams": *Maryland Herald*, June 19, 1800, p. 2.

148 "Their silence": *Aurora*, July 4, 1800, p. 3.

148 "in our important": *American Mercury*, July 10, 1800, p. 3.

148 "the prescribed patriots" and following: *Constitutional Telegraphe*, July 16, 1800, p. 3.

148 "High Federalists": George Cabot to Rufus King, July 19, 1800, *LCRK*, 3:278.

149 "The great man" and following: Fisher Ames to Rufus King, July 15, 1800, *LCRK*, 3:276.

149 "Mr. Adams' insufferable madness": Benjamin Goodhue to Oliver Wolcott, July 10, 1800, *Gibbs Memoirs*, 2:379.

149 "No man ever" and following: John Adams, "To the Inhabitants of the County of Edgecombe, North Carolina," Aug. 13, 1800, *WJA*, 9:235.

149 "the most glorious": Fisher Ames to Rufus King, Sept. 24, 1800, *LCRK*, 3:305.

150 "He everywhere denounces": Theodore Sedgwick to Rufus King, Sept. 26, 1800, *LCRK*, 3:308.

150 "is, by prating": Fisher Ames to Oliver Wolcott, Aug. 3, 1800, *Gibbs Memoirs*, 2:396.

150 "Perhaps a party": Ibid.

150 "If under the present administration": Robert Goodloe Harper to Constituents, May 13, 1800, reprinted in *Commercial Advertiser*, May 15, 1800, p. 2.

151 "It really appears": John Jay to Theophilus Parsons, July 1, 1800, *CJJ*, 4:274.

151 "The public feeling": George Cabot to Oliver Wolcott, July 20, 1800, *Gibbs Memoirs*, 2:383.

151 "great pains": George Cabot to Oliver Wolcott, Dec. 16, 1799, *Gibbs Memoirs*, 2:312.

151 "If General Pinckney": Oliver Wolcott to George Cabot, June 18, 1800, *LLGC*, p. 278.

152 "of the second" and following: Alexander Hamilton to Oliver Wolcott, July 1, 1800, *Gibbs Memoirs*, 2:376.

152 "The General": Abigail Adams to Thomas Boylston Adams, July 12, 1800, *AFP*, reel 398.

152   "as complete a politician": Fisher Ames to Rufus King, Sept. 24, 1800, *LCRK*, 3:304.

153   "At no public feast": *Massachusetts Spy*, June 25, 1800, p. 3.

153   "I then asked": Arthur Fenner [to Christopher Champlin], Dec. 14, 1800, *PAH*, 24:596.

153   "I yesterday returned": Alexander Hamilton to Charles Carroll of Carroll-ton, July 1, 1800, *PAH*, 25:1.

154   "Electioneering topics": Joseph Hale to Rufus King, July 9, 1800, *LCRK*, 3:270.

154   "You know he": Fisher Ames to Rufus King, July 15, 1800, *LCRK*, 3:276.

154   "The Alien and Sedition Acts" and following: Thomas Jefferson to Elbridge Gerry, Jan. 26, 1799, *PTJ*, 30:649–50.

155   "I have a letter": Thomas Jefferson to James Madison, Sept. 17, 1800, *PTJ*, 32:146.

157   "Our country is too large": Thomas Jefferson to Gideon Granger, Aug. 13, 1800, *PTJ*, 32:96.

158   "Politics are such a torment": Thomas Jefferson to Martha Jefferson Randolph, Feb. 11, 1800, *FLTJ*, p. 184.

158   "whereby you would": James Monroe to Thomas Jefferson, May 25, 1800, *WJM*, 3:179–80.

158   "Rally round": Thomas Jefferson to Gideon Granger, Aug. 13, 1800, *PTJ*, 32:97.

159   "is intriguing": Alexander Hamilton to James A. Bayard, Aug. 6, 1800, *PAH*, 25:58.

159   "He will have": Aaron Burr to James Madison, Oct. 9, 1800, *PJM*, 17:420–21.

159   "the logic of it": Milton Lomask, *Aaron Burr: The Years from Princeton to Vice President, 1756–1805* (New York: Farrar, Straus, Giroux, 1979), p. 260.

160   "great and imposing": "An Address to the Voters for Electors," in *Virginia Federalist*, May 28, 1800, p. 3 (reprint of circular).

161   "There is indeed": "To the Citizens of Virginia," July 7, 1800, in *Virginia Argus*, Sept. 12, 1800, p. 1 (reprint of circular).

161   "I cannot but augur": Philip N. Nicholas to Thomas Jefferson, Feb. 2, 1800, in Noble E. Cunningham Jr., *The Jeffersonian Republicans: The Formation of Political Organization, 1789–1801* (Chapel Hill: University of North Carolina Press, 1957), p. 152.

161   "fools in earnest": Fisher Ames to Oliver Wolcott, Jan. 12, 1800, *WFA*, 2:1347–48.

161   "The spirit of faction": Alexander Hamilton to Rufus King, Jan. 5, 1800, *PAH*, 24:168.

161   "to receive all": Proceedings of a Meeting, Jan. 23, 1800, in ed. H. W. Flournoy, *Calendar of Virginia State Papers*, 9 (Richmond: [State Printing], 1890), p. 76.

161 "We have begun": Philip N. Nicholas to Thomas Jefferson, Feb. 2, 1800, in Cunningham, *Jeffersonian Republicans*, p. 153.

161 "Let the contest be": "To the Citizens," p. 1.

162 "they are deceived": James Monroe to James Madison, May 15, 1800, *PJM*, 17:388.

162 "so industriously": James Madison to James Monroe, May 23, 1800, *PJM*, 17:390.

162 "and give no pretext": James Monroe to Thomas Jefferson, May 25, 1800, *WJM*, 3:180.

163 "force a resistance": Thomas Jefferson to Charles Pinckney, Oct. 29, 1799, *PTJ*, 31:226.

CHAPTER SEVEN: FOR GOD AND PARTY

PAGE

167 "no man shall": William Waller Hening, ed., *The Statutes at Large: Being a Collection of all the Law of Virginia*, 12 (Richmond: Pleasants, 1823), pp. 84–86 (emphasis added). Jefferson's draft containing these same words is in Thomas Jefferson, *Writings* (New York: Library of America, 1984), pp. 346–47.

168 "*And the sixth angel*" and following quotes from Dwight: Timothy Dwight, "The Duty of Americans at the Present Crisis Illustrated in a Discourse Preached on the Fourth of July, 1798" (New Haven: Green, 1798), pp. 5, 10, 12, 18, 20, 23, and 28.

169 "Pope of Connecticut": E.g., *American Citizen and General Advertiser*, Aug. 26, 1800, p. 3.

169 "Dr. Dwight": George Cabot to Alexander Hamilton, Oct. 11, 1800, *PAH*, 25:149.

170 "His overheated imagination": *The Bee*, July 19, 1799, p. 2.

171 "My answer was": Thomas Jefferson to John Adams, Jan. 11, 1817, *WTJ* (Lipscomb and Bergh), 15:100.

171 "I am a Christian": Thomas Jefferson to Benjamin Rush, Apr. 21, 1803, *WTJ* (Lipscomb and Bergh), 10:380.

171 "The legitimate powers": Jefferson, *Writings*, p. 285 (*Notes on the State of Virginia*, Query 27).

171 "Ponder well" and following quotes from Mason: John Mitchell Mason, "Voice of Warning to Christians on the Ensuing Election of A President of the United States" (New York: Hopkins, 1800), pp. 19–20 and 32.

172 "Let my neighbor" and following quotes from Linn: William Linn, "Serious Considerations on the Election of a President" (New York: Furman, 1800), pp. 19, 20, and 28.

172 "at an age": Jefferson, *Writings*, p. 273 (*Notes on the State of Virginia*, Query 25).

172   "It is good": E.g., Mason, "Voice of Warning," pp. 21–22.

173   "If Jefferson is": A Christian Federalist, "A Short Address to the Voters of Delaware" (Dover: Black, 1800), p. 3.

173   "THE GRAND QUESTION": E.g., *Gazette of the United States*, Sept. 13, 1800, p. 3.

173   "lying pamphlets" and "absolute falsehoods": Thomas Jefferson to Benjamin Rush, Sept. 23, 1800, *PTJ*, 32:168.

173   "As to the calumny": Thomas Jefferson to James Monroe, May 26, 1800, *PTJ*, 31:590.

173   "I have a view" and following: Thomas Jefferson to Benjamin Rush, Sept. 23, 1800, *WTJ* (Ford), 9:148. In the original, Jefferson used the Latin phrase from Horace, "genus irritabile vatum," which, in context, I have translated "irritable race of critics"—though perhaps Jefferson had Dwight in mind and did mean "poets."

174   "an adorer of our God": John James Beckley, "Address to the People of the United States with an Epitome and Vindication of the Public Life and Character of Thomas Jefferson" (Philadelphia: Carey, 1800), p. 32.

174   "a real Christian" and following quotes from Clinton [DeWitt Clinton]: "A Vindication of Thomas Jefferson Against the Charges Contained in a Pamphlet Entitled 'Serious Considerations' etc." (New York: Denniston, 1800), pp. 6 and 33.

174   "It will, I trust": John Beckley to James Monroe, Aug. 26, 1800, in Noble E. Cunningham Jr., *The Jeffersonian Republicans: The Formation of Party Organization, 1789–1801* (Chapel Hill: University of North Carolina Press, 1957), p. 198.

174   "sound practical": Tench Coxe, et al., "To the Republican Citizens of the State of Pennsylvania" (Lancaster: Dickson, 1800), p. 14.

174   "does not think": Joseph Bloomfield, "To the People of New-Jersey," p. 1, in *EAI*, Evans no. 38656.

174   "The fact is": *Independent Chronicle*, July 17–21, 1800, p. 2.

175   "Mr. Jefferson stands": *Independent Chronicle*, June 26–30, 1800, p. 2.

175   "I have always": [Clinton], "Vindication of Jefferson," p. 33.

175   "the first of men": Timothy Dwight, "The Triumph of Infidelity Rightly Attended" (1788), complete text in Early America's Digital Archive at http://narcissus.umd.edu/eada. For an example of the political use of this poem by Republicans, see Marcus Brutus, "Serious Facts Opposed to 'Serious Consideration'" (n.c: n.p., 1800), p. 10.

175   "Now I don't know": *Centinel of Freedom*, Nov. 4, 1800, p. 1.

175   "Your President": Mason, "Voice of Warning," p. 30.

176   "Mr. Adams *may*": *Carolina Gazette*, Oct. 23, 1800, p. 1.

176   "No people differ more": *National Intelligencer*, Nov. 10, 1800, p. 2.

176   "an established church": *Aurora*, Oct. 14, 1800, p. 2.

176 "indignation at the charge": Fisher Ames to Rufus King, Sept. 24, 1800, *LCRK*, 3:304.

177 "done more to shuffle": John Adams to John Trumbull, Sept. 10, 1800, *WJA*, 9:83.

177 "The secret whisper": John Adams to Benjamin Rush, June 12, 1812, *Spur of Fame*, p. 224.

178 "The foundation" and following quotes from Bishop: Abraham Bishop, "An Oration on the Extent and Power of Political Delusion" (Philadelphia: Carey, 1800), pp. iii, 15, and 26.

178 "Do you ask": Jonathan Russell, "To the Freemen of Rhode Island" (Providence: n.p., 1800), pp. 2–3.

178 "and an enslaved": Brutus, "Serious Facts," p. 4.

178 "Federalism a mask": *Aurora*, Oct. 14, 1800, p. 2.

178 "I believe in Alexander Hamilton": *Centinel of Freedom*, Dec. 9, 1800, p. 2 (reprint from *Hartford Mercury*).

179 "Mr. Adams, it is said": *Constitutional Telegraphe*, June 25, 1800, p. 1.

179 "the two Mr. Pinckneys": *Constitutional Telegraphe*, Oct. 18, 1800, p. 1 (reprint of Adams's letter).

180 "must have been founded": *Constitutional Telegraphe*, Oct. 18, 1800, p. 1 (reprint of Pinckney's letter).

180 "proof, strong proof": *Constitutional Telegraphe*, Oct. 18, 1800, p. 1 (reprint of Adams's letter).

180 "Our country is prosperous": *Federal Gazette*, Aug. 11, 1800, p. 2.

180 "This is the 12th year": Christian Federalist, "Short Address," p. 5.

180 "They are composed": *Connecticut Courant*, Nov. 24, 1800, p. 2.

180 "chimney-sweeper politicians": *Gazette of the United States*, quoted in Susan Dunn, *Jefferson's Second Revolution: The Election Crisis of 1800 and the Triumph of Republicanism* (Boston: Houghton Mifflin, 2004), p. 150.

180 "the very *refuse*": *Gazette of the United States*, Aug. 5, 1800, p. 2.

181 "The lower class": Oliver Wolcott to Fisher Ames, Aug. 10, 1800, *Gibbs Memoirs*, 2:401.

181 "The People": *Philadelphia Gazette*, May 5, 1800, p. 3.

181 "May he not be": Charles Carroll of Carrollton to Alexander Hamilton, Aug. 27, 1800, *PAH*, 25:95.

181 "Science and government": A Layman, "The Claims of Thomas Jefferson to the Presidency Examined at the Bar of Christianity," (Philadelphia: Dickins, 1800), pp. 49–50.

181 "He is so true": *The Mercury and New-England Palladium*, Jan. 16, 1801, p. 1.

181 "Mr. Jefferson's conduct": Oliver Wolcott to Fisher Ames, *Gibbs Memoirs*, 2:401.

182 "His fantastic tricks": Charles Carroll of Carrollton to Alexander Hamilton, Apr. 18, 1800, *PAH*, 24:412.

182   "Against the dangerous": North Carolina Planter, "Address to the Citizens of North Carolina of the Subject of the Approaching Elections" (Raleigh: Hodge and Boylan, 1800), p. 12.

182   "The philosopher is nothing" and following: *American Mercury*, July 31, 1800, p. 1. For an example of Federalist references to Jefferson as a "mad specula[to]rist and the fanatical reformer," see *Connecticut Courant*, May 26, 1800, p. 1.

184   "is intriguing with all his might": Alexander Hamilton to James A. Bayard, Aug. 6, 1800, *PAH*, 25:58.

185   "It is admitted": *Maryland Herald*, Sept. 25, 1800, p. 1.

185   "These are always": Thomas Boylston Adams to William Shaw, Aug. 8, 1800, ed. Charles Grenfill Washburn, "Letters of Thomas Boylston Adams to William Smith Shaw, 1799–1823," *American Antiquarian Society Proceedings*, n.s. 27 (1917), p. 121.

186   "The candidates on both sides": Oliver Wolcott to Fisher Ames, Aug. 10, 1800, *Gibbs Memoirs*, 2:404.

186   "Here the candidates": Adams to Shaw, p. 121.

186   "The measures of": *Federal Gazette*, July 28, 1800, p. 3.

186   "a tried, firm": *Maryland Herald*, Sept. 25, 1800, p. 1.

186   "You may be certain": *Federal Gazette*, Aug. 14, 1800, p. 2.

187   "If ever an occasion": *Maryland Herald*, Oct. 30, 1800, p. 2.

187   "The right of election": *Federal Gazette*, Aug. 21, 1800, p. 2.

187   "I am aware": Alexander Hamilton to Charles Carroll of Carrollton, Aug. 7, 1800, *PAH*, 25:60.

188   "counteract the policy": *Maryland Herald*, Sept. 25, 1800, p. 1.

188   "Equity among the citizens": *Federal Gazette*, Aug. 11, 1800, p. 2.

188   "From present appearances": James McHenry to Philemon Dickinson, Sept. 3, 1800, *PAH*, 25:115.

188   "it more than probable": James Madison to Thomas Jefferson, Aug. 12, 1800, *PJM*, 17:401.

188   "Republican issue": James Madison to Thomas Jefferson, Oct. 1, 1800, *PJM*, 17:418.

188   "It may be truly said" and following: *Federal Gazette*, Oct. 1, 1800, p. 2 (address dated Sept. 16, 1800).

CHAPTER EIGHT: INSURRECTION
PAGE

190   "A fellow of courage": *American Citizen*, Sept. 25, 1800, p. 2.

191   "Death or Liberty" and following: "The Trial of Gabriel," *Journal of the Senate of Virginia* (Richmond: Nelson, 1800), p. 32.

191 "It is unquestionably": James Monroe to Thomas Jefferson, Sept. 15, 1800, *WJM*, 3:208.

192 "Upon that very evening" and following: James Thomson Callender to Thomas Jefferson, Sept. 13, 1800, *PTJ*, 32:136.

192 "was preparing": *Gazette of the United States*, Apr. 3, 1799, p. 3.

193 "The scenes which": James Monroe to General Mathews, Mar. 17, 1802, quoted in Douglas R. Egerton, *Gabriel's Rebellion: The Virginia Slave Conspiracies of 1800 and 1802* (Chapel Hill: University of North Carolina Press, 1993), p. 47.

193 "There has been great": James Monroe to Thomas Jefferson, Sept. 9, 1800, *WJM*, 3:205.

194 "The whole state": Thomas Jefferson, *Writings* (New York: Library of America, 1984), p. 289 (*Notes on the State of Virginia*, Query 28).

194 "While it was possible": James Monroe to Thomas Jefferson, Sept. 15, 1800, *PTJ*, 32:144–45.

195 "The sound of French": *New Hampshire Gazette*, Sept. 30, 1800, p. 3.

195 "Behold America": *Philadelphia Gazette*, Oct. 24, 1800, p. 3.

195 "The slave holders": *Gazette of the United States*, Oct. 1, 1800, p. 3.

195 "Truly Mr. J.": *Gazette of the United States*, Sept. 18, 1800, p. 3.

195 "to tread down": *The Courier*, Oct. 15, 1800, p. 2.

195 "The late revolt": William Cobbett, *Porcupine's Works*, 12 (London: Cobbett & Morgan, 1801), p. 141.

195 "He who effects": *Connecticut Gazette*, Oct. 8, 1800, p. 1.

195 "shallow": *Windham Herald*, Oct. 2, 1800, p. 2 (reprint from *Virginia Gazette*, Sept. 12, 1800).

196 "the boisterous sea": e.g., *Commercial Advertiser*, Oct. 1, 1800, p. 3 (quote from Thomas Jefferson to Philip Mazzei, Apr. 24, 1796, reprinted in Jefferson, *Writings*, p. 1037).

196 "If anything will": *Boston Gazette*, Oct. 9, 1800, p. 3.

196 "wholly false": *Herald of Liberty*, Oct. 27, 1800, p. 3 (reprint from *Aurora*, Oct. 7, 1800).

196 "While our administration": *The Times and District of Columbia Daily Advertiser*, Oct. 14, 1800, p. 2 (reprint from *Aurora*).

196 "There was not": E.g., *American Mercury*, Oct. 16, 1800, p. 3 (reprint from *Aurora*).

197 "According to our present": James Monroe to John Drayton, Oct. 21, 1800, *WJM*, 3:217.

197 "I doubt not": William Vans Murray to John Quincy Adams, Dec. 9, 1800, ed. Worthington Ford, "Letters of William Vans Murray to John Quincy Adams, 1797–1803," *Annual Report of the American Historical Association* (1912), p. 663.

197 "In Virginia": Robert Troup to Rufus King, Oct. 1, 1800, *LCRK*, 3:316.

197 "under the auspices": Jefferson, *Writings*, p. 289 (*Notes on the State of Virginia*, Query 28).

198 "Where to stay the hand": Thomas Jefferson to James Monroe, Sept. 20, 1800, *PTJ*, 32:160.

198 "reprieved for transportation": term from the time for the export of a convicted slave quoted in Egerton, *Gabriel's Rebellion*, p. 112.

199 "an evil of colossal": John Adams to William Turner, Nov. 20, 1819, *AFP*, reel 124.

199 "should fail to insure": Charles Cotesworth Pinckney, in ed. Edward J. Larson and Michael Winship, *The Constitutional History: A Narrative History from the Notes of James Madison* (New York: Modern Library, 2005), p. 106.

199 "Slavery is inconsistent": Albert Gallatin, Mar. 22, 1793, excerpt in *LAG*, p. 86.

200 "The spirit of the master": Jefferson, *Writings*, p. 289 (*Notes on the State of Virginia*, Query 28).

200 "worth diamonds": John Adams to Thomas Jefferson, May 22, 1785, *PTJ*, 8:160.

200 "take lessons upon": "A Candid Address to the Freemen of the State of Rhode Island on the Subject of the Approaching Election," rpt. in ed. Arthur M. Schlesinger Jr., *History of the American Presidential Elections, 1789–1968*, 1 (New York: Chelsea, 1971), p. 140.

200 "The insurrection": *Gazette of the United States*, Sept. 23, 1800, p. 3.

200 "We augur better": *Aurora*, Sept. 24, 1800, p. 2.

202 "His refusal": John F. Mercer to Thomas Jefferson, Nov. 10, 1800, *PTJ*, 32:436.

202 "It was the popular": *Federal Gazette*, Oct. 25, 1800, p. 2.

203 "The right of suffrage" and following: Oliver Wolcott to Fisher Ames, Aug. 10, 1800, *Gibbs Memoirs*, 2:404.

203 "I congratulate": Thomas Jefferson to Samuel Smith, Oct. 17, 1800, *PTJ*, 32:227.

204 "I see no other": *Federal Gazette*, Oct. 25, 1800, p. 2.

204 "I have now": Charles Peale Polk to James Madison, Oct. 10, 1800, *PJM*, 17:423.

204 "five, perhaps six": Gabriel Duvall to James Madison, Oct. 17, 1800, *PJM*, 17:424.

205 "The plan": *Centinel of Freedom*, Apr. 1, 1800, p. 3.

205 "at the total destruction": "At a Meeting of the Inhabitants of the Township of Gloucester," Aug. 4, 1800, p. 3, in *EAI*, Evans no. 37525.

205 "A considerable diversion": Alexander Hamilton to Charles Carroll of Carrollton, July 1, 1800, *PAH*, 25:69.

205 "Delaware is safe" and following: James A. Bayard to Alexander Hamilton, Aug. 18, 1800, *PAH*, 25:69.

205 "No doubt is": *Gazette of the United States*, Oct. 18, 1800, p. 3.

206 "Altho' our horizon": Caesar A. Rodney to Thomas Jefferson, Oct. 13, 1800, *PTJ*, 32:218 (Rodney writes the maxim in the original Latin, "Magna est veritas & prevalebit").

206 "The engine is": Thomas Jefferson to James Madison, Feb. 5, 1800, *PJM*, 17:227.

207 "On every important": *Connecticut Courant*, Aug. 18, 1800, p. 1.

207 "the unceasing use": Fisher Ames to Theodore Dwight, Mar. 19, 1801, *WFA*, 2:1411.

207 "arrest[ing] the rapid": Thomas Jefferson to James Monroe, Oct. 19, 1823, *WTJ* (Ford), 12:316.

208 "Our annual election": *Aurora*, Sept. 25, 1800, p. 2.

208 "It is intended": *Gazette of the United States*, Oct. 14, 1800, p. 2.

208 "CITIZENS OF PHILADELPHIA": *Aurora*, Oct. 14, 1800, p. 2.

208 "FEDERALISTS TO YOUR POSTS": *Gazette of the United States*, Oct. 14, 1800, p. 3.

208 "In a few days": *Gazette of the United States*, Oct. 11, 1800, p. 2.

209 "Men know his contempt": Ibid.

209 "The friends of *peace*": *Aurora*, Oct. 4, 1800, p. 2.

209 "If this be true": John Adams to William Tudor, Dec. 13, 1800, quoted in Page Smith, *John Adams*, 2 (Garden City, New York: Doubleday, 1962), p. 1034.

209 "Republicans will carry": *Herald of Liberty*, Oct. 20, 1800, p. 3.

209 "The elections in that state": Thomas Jefferson to Charles Pinckney, Nov. 4, 1800, *PTJ*, 32:242.

211 "We are so beset": *Carolina Gazette*, Oct. 9, 1800, p. 1.

211 "The citizens of Charleston": *City Gazette*, Oct. 8, 1800, p. 2.

211 "Mr. C. P.'s Ticket": *South Carolina State Gazette*, Oct. 11, 1800, quoted in Noble E. Cunningham Jr., *The Jeffersonian Republicans: The Formation of Party Organization, 1789–1801* (Chapel Hill: University of North Carolina Press, 1957), p. 189.

211 "You know we can form": Thomas Pinckney to John Rutledge Jr., Sept. 23, 1800, in Marvin R. Zahniser, *Charles Cotesworth Pinckney: Founding Father* (Chapel Hill: University of North Carolina Press, 1967), p. 222.

212 "I have taken post": Charles Pinckney to Thomas Jefferson, Nov. 22, 1800, *PTJ*, 32:256–57.

CHAPTER NINE: THUNDERSTRUCK

PAGE

213 "The rage of the Hamilton": John Adams to James Lloyd, Feb. 17, 1815, *WJA*, 10:126.

214 "for his part": Abigail Adams to Thomas Boylston Adams, July 12, 1800, *PAH*, 24:576 (quoting statement attributed to Hamilton).

214 "statement" and following: Alexander Hamilton to Oliver Wolcott, July 1, 1800, *PAH*, 25:4.

214 "base, wicked, and cruel calumny": Alexander Hamilton to John Adams, Oct. 1, 1800, *PAH*, 25:125.

215 "will be converted": George Cabot to Alexander Hamilton, Aug. 21, 1800, *PAH*, 25:75.

215 "*You* ought not": Fisher Ames to Alexander Hamilton, Aug. 16, 1800, *PAH*, 25:87–88.

215 "Whatever *you* may say": Oliver Wolcott to Alexander Hamilton, Sept. 3, 1800, *PAH*, 25:105.

215 "come too late": James McHenry to Alexander Hamilton, Sept. 4, 1800, *PAH*, 25:111.

215 "You see I am": Alexander Hamilton to Oliver Wolcott, Aug. 3, 1800, *PAH*, 25:54.

215 "It is plain": Alexander Hamilton to Oliver Wolcott, Aug. 3, 1800, *PAH*, 25:54.

215 "factious" and following: Alexander Hamilton to Oliver Wolcott, Sept. 26, 1800, *PAH*, 25:122.

216 "In writing an intemperate indictment": Ron Chernow, *Alexander Hamilton* (New York: Penguin Press, 2004), p. 619.

216 "letter" and following: Alexander Hamilton to Oliver Wolcott, Aug. 3, 1800, *PAH*, 25:54.

216 "Not denying to Mr. Adams" and following: Alexander Hamilton, *Letter Concerning the Public Conduct and Character of John Adams* (New York: Lang, 1800), pp. 4, 9, 12, 14, 20, 26, 29, 39, 47, and 52.

218 "The final section": Chernow, *Alexander Hamilton*, p. 623.

219 "Alexander Hamilton has been": *Aurora*, Oct. 21, 1800, p. 3.

219 "better that [the letter] should appear": *Salem Impartial Register*, Dec. 4, 1800, p. 3.

219 "The subject which now occupies" and following: Robert Troup to Rufus King, Nov. 9, 1800, *LCRK*, 3:330–31.

219 "I cannot describe to you": Robert Troup to Rufus King, Oct. 1, 1800, *LCRK*, 3:315.

219 "The press teems": Alexander Hamilton to James McHenry, Nov. 13, 1800, *PAH*, 25:236.

219 "Those amongst the Federalists": James McHenry to Alexander Hamilton, Nov. 19, 1800, *PAH*, 25:242.

220 "I regret": John Adams to Uzal Ogden, Dec. 3, 1800, *WJA*, 9:576.

220 "Among the very few truths": John Adams to John Jay, Nov. 24, 1800, *WJA*, 9:91.

220 "I shall not say anything": Abigail Adams to Mary Smith Cranch, Nov. 10, 1800, *NLAA*, p. 255.

221 "gross lies": Abigail Adams to Mary Smith Cranch, Nov. 21, 1800, *NLAA*, p. 258.

221 "Admitting all your charges": *American Mercury*, Nov. 6, 1800, p. 2.

221 "I am *bound*": George Cabot to Alexander Hamilton, Nov. 29, 1800, *PAH*, 25:249.

222 "We are all thunderstruck": Bushrod Washington to Oliver Wolcott, Nov. 1, 1800, *PAH*, 25:249.

222 "This letter": Robert Troup to Rufus King, Dec. 4, 1800, *LCRK*, 3:340.

222 "Our enemies": Robert Troup to Rufus King, Nov. 9, 1800, *LCRK*, 3:331.

222 "Hamilton's attack upon Mr. Adams": [Bishop] James Madison to Thomas Jefferson, Nov. 1, 1800, *PTJ*, 32:239.

222 "would have subjected": *Centinel of Freedom*, Oct. 28, 1800, p. 3.

222 "From what I have heard": James Monroe to James Madison, Nov. 7, 1800, *WJM*, 3:220.

223 "An eventful period": *Courier of New Hampshire*, Nov. 1, 1800, p. 1.

224 "The elections have" and following: James Madison to James Monroe, Nov. 10, 1800, *PJM*, 17:434.

226 "If war in any degree": John Adams to John Marshall, Sept. 4, 1800, *PJMar*, 4:257.

227 "'Tis said": Abigail Adams to Abigail Adams Smith, Nov. 21, 1800, *LMA*, 2:242.

227 "with the respect due": John Adams, Nov. 22, 1800, *Annals of Congress*, 10:724.

227 "unfitness" and following: Charles Carroll of Carrollton to James McHenry, Nov. 4, 1800, *LCJM*, pp. 473 and 476.

228 "Tomorrow, the electors": James McHenry to Oliver Wolcott, Nov. 9, 1800, *Gibbs Memoirs*, 2:445.

228 "Setting aside Pennsylvania": Thomas Jefferson to Thomas Mann Randolph, Nov. 30, 1800, *PTJ*, 32:263.

229 "the efforts of both parties": *Centinel of Freedom*, Nov. 25, 1800, p. 3.

229 "How disgraceful": *Newport Mercury*, Nov. 15, 1800, p. S-2.

230 "Putting Pennsylvania": Thomas Jefferson to Thomas Mann Randolph, Dec. 5, 1800, *PTJ*, 32:271.

231 "This I think": Charles Pinckney to Thomas Jefferson, Nov. 22, 1800, *PTJ*, 32:256.

231 "The situation of our country": Thomas McKean, Address, Nov. 8, 1800, in *Philadelphia Gazette*, Nov. 9, 1800, p. S-1.

232 "Could the monarchists": *Aurora*, Nov. 6, 1800, p. 2.

232 "A gracious Providence": *Philadelphia Gazette*, Nov. 11, 1800, p. 3.

232 "Their doctrine": *Gazette of the United States*, Nov. 5, 1800, p. 2.

233 "*Francis Gurney's*": *Aurora*, Nov. 17, 1800, p. 2.

234   "The leading Jacobins": *Gazette of the United States*, Dec. 13, 1800, p. 3.

234   "will have eight votes": *Aurora*, Dec. 3, 1800, p. 2.

235   "At the time": Theodore Sedgwick to Rufus King, Sept. 26, 1800, *LCRK*, 3:309.

236   "my situation": Charles Pinckney to Thomas Jefferson, Nov. 22, 1800, *PTJ*, 32:256.

237   "In this dilemma": Henry William De Saussure to friend, Dec. 4, 1800, in *Newport Mercury*, Dec. 30, 1800, p. 2.

237   "Contrary to my former advices": Charles Cotesworth Pinckney to John Marshall, Nov. 29, 1800, *PJM*, 6:508.

238   "Gen. Pinckney is well known": *Carolina Gazette*, Nov. 20, 1800, p. 2.

238   "The constitution and laws": *Carolina Gazette*, Dec. 11, 1800, p. 3.

239   "I believe we may consider": Thomas Jefferson to Thomas Mann Randolph, Dec. 12, 1800, *PTJ*, 32:300.

CHAPTER TEN: THE TIE

PAGE

241   "Splendid Intelligence": *The National Intelligencer*, Dec. 12, 1800, p. 2.

243   "It was badly managed": Thomas Jefferson to Aaron Burr, Dec. 15, 1800, *PTJ*, 32:306–07.

243   "There will be": Thomas Jefferson to James Madison, Dec. 19, 1800, *PTJ*, 32:322.

244   "The Feds in the legislature": Thomas Jefferson to James Monroe, Dec. 20, 1800, *PTJ*, 32:330.

246   "will be revived": *The National Intelligencer*, Jan. 23, 1801, p. 4.

246   "Some, tho' Federalists": Thomas Jefferson to Martha Jefferson Randolph, Jan. 16, 1801, *PTJ*, 32:475.

246   "My personal friends": Aaron Burr to Thomas Jefferson, Dec. 23, 1800, *PCAB*, 1:473–74.

247   "Keep the game": Robert Goodloe Harper, Dec. 24, 1800, *PCAB*, 1:474.

247   "A drowning man": *Herald of Liberty*, Jan. 5, 1801, p. 2.

247   "Mr. Burr would": *The National Intelligencer*, Jan. 12, 1801, p. 2.

247   "The considerations": Theodore Sedgwick to Theodore Sedgwick Jr., Jan. 11, 1801, *PCAB*, 1:482.

248   "There are many reasons": *Albany Centinel*, Jan. 6, 1801, p. 2.

248   "A profligate": Theodore Sedgwick to Alexander Hamilton, Jan. 10, 1801, *PAH*, 25:312.

248   "By persons friendly": James A. Bayard to Alexander Hamilton, Jan. 7, 1801, *PAH*, 25:300.

248   "He must lean": Henry Lee to Alexander Hamilton, Feb. 6, 1801, *PAH*, 25:331.

248 "I believe" and "He is a soldier": William Hindman to James McHenry, Jan. 17, 1801, *LCJM*, p. 490.

248 "To courage": Gouverneur Morris to Alexander Hamilton, Jan. 25, 1801, *PAH*, 25:329 (commenting on Federalist views of Burr).

248 "If Mr. Burr succeeds": James McHenry to Rufus King, *LCRK*, 3:362.

248 "Either will be bad": Uriah Tracy to James McHenry, Jan. 15, 1801, *LCJM*, p. 489.

249 "His very selfishness": Theodore Sedgwick to Alexander Hamilton, Jan. 10, 1801, *PAH*, 25:311.

249 "It is fashionable": Joseph Hale to Rufus King, Dec. 29, 1800, *LCRK*, 3:357.

249 "The Federalists": William Hindman to James McHenry, Jan. 17, 1801, *LCJM*, p. 489.

249 "If Mr. Burr should": *Philadelphia Gazette*, Jan. 5, 1801, p. 3.

249 "My little bark": John Adams to Thomas Boylston Adams, Dec. 17, 1800, *AFP*, reel 399.

250 "sending the last mission": James McHenry to Rufus King, Jan. 2, 1801, *LCRK*, 3:346.

250 "The President, I am told": Thomas Pickering to Rufus King, Jan. 5, 1801, *LCRK*, 3:366.

250 "I shall be in Quincy": John Adams to Cotton Tufts, Dec. 28, 1801, *AFP*, reel 120.

251 "How mighty a power": John Adams to Elbridge Gerry, Dec. 30, 1800, *WJA*, 9:577–78.

251 "turned and turned": Abigail Adams to Mary Smith Cranch, Feb. 7, 1801, *NLAA*, pp. 265–66.

252 "There is no circumstance": Alexander Hamilton to Oliver Wolcott, Dec. 1800, *PAH*, 25:286.

252 "has pretensions" and following: Alexander Hamilton to Oliver Wolcott, Dec. 16, 1800, *PAH*, 25:257.

252 "well" and "If there be": Alexander Hamilton to Gouverneur Morris, Dec. 26, 1800, *PAH*, 25:275.

253 "Burr loves nothing but himself": Alexander Hamilton to Harrison Gray Otis, Dec. 23, 1800, *PAH*, 25:271.

253 "No mortal can tell": Alexander Hamilton to John Rutledge, Jan. 4, 1801, *PAH*, 25:297 (enclosure in letter).

253 "I beg you": Alexander Hamilton to Theodore Sedgwick, Jan. 21, 1801, *PAH*, 25:328.

253 "Mr. Burr [is] the most unfit": Alexander Hamilton to James A. Bayard, Dec. 27, 1800, *PAH*, 25:277.

253 "I ought certainly": Alexander Hamilton to James A. Bayard, Jan. 7, 1801, *PAH*, 25:300.

254   "While making it": Alexander Hamilton to James A. Bayard, Dec. 27, 1800, *PAH*, 25:277.

254   "throw out a lure": Alexander Hamilton to Oliver Wolcott, Dec. 16, 1800, *PAH*, 25:258.

255   "They are about": Gouverneur Morris to Robert Livingston, Feb. 20, 1801, *DLGM*, 2:405.

255   "we shall profit": John Rutledge to Alexander Hamilton, Jan. 10, 1801, *PAH*, 25:309.

255   "giving additional fiber": Gouverneur Morris to Robert Livingston, Feb. 20, 1801, *DLGM*, 2:404.

256   "I dread this": Thomas Jefferson to Aaron Burr, Dec. 15, 1800, *PTJ*, 32:306–07.

256   "the richest provision": Thomas Jefferson to Caesar A. Rodney, Dec. 21, 1800, *PTJ*, 32:337.

256   "the mines of Peru": Thomas Jefferson to James Madison, Dec. 19, 1800, *PTJ*, 32:323.

256   "saw nothing in the law": Jonas Platt, Jan. 21, 1801, *Annals of the Congress*, 10:918.

256   "the most striking": Samuel Eliot Morison, in *LLHGO*, 1:200.

256   "He is extremely irritated": James A. Bayard to Andrew Bayard, Jan. 26, 1801, "Correspondence of J.A. Bayard," in Elizabeth Donnan, ed., "Papers of James A. Bayard, 1796–1815," *Annual Report of the American Historical Association for 1913*, (Washington, Government Printing Office, 1915), 2:121.

256   "the most splendid diamond": John Adams to John Lloyd, Feb. 6, 1815, *WJA*, 10:115.

257   "A few, indeed": Albert Gallatin to Hannah Gallatin, Jan. 22, 1801, *LAG*, p. 255.

257   "I arrived here": James A. Bayard to Richard Bassett, Jan. 3, 1801, "Correspondence of Bayard," p. 117.

257   "a refectory of monks" and following: Albert Gallatin to Hannah Gallatin, Jan. 15, 1801, *LAG*, p. 253.

257   "You may suppose": Albert Gallatin to Hannah Gallatin, Jan. 22, 1801, *LAG*, p. 255.

258   "There is a great want": James A. Bayard to Andrew Bayard, Jan. 8, 1801, "Correspondence of Bayard," p. 119.

258   "There is nobody": James A. Bayard to Caesar A. Rodney, Jan. 8, 1801, "Correspondence of Bayard," p. 120.

258   "I have concluded": Harrison Gray Otis to Sally Foster Otis, Feb. 1, 1801, *LLHGO*, 1:148.

258   "Not one room": Abigail Adams to Mary Smith Cranch, Nov. 21, 1800, *NLAA*, pp. 257–58.

258 "Party will believe it": Albert Gallatin to Hannah Gallatin, Jan. 29, 1801, *LAG*, p. 258.

258 "The Federal City": Albert Gallatin to Hannah Gallatin, Jan. 15, 1801, *LAG*, p. 254.

259 "Is it possible": James Madison to Thomas Jefferson, Jan. 10, 1801, *PJM*, 17:453.

259 "substantial violations": ibid.

259 "Whether the assumption" and following: Albert Gallatin, "Plan at the Time of Balloting," [1801], *WAG*, 1:19.

260 "In case of usurpation": Aaron Burr to Albert Gallatin, Feb. 12, 1801, *LAG*, p. 246.

260 "It was threatened": Albert Gallatin to Henry A. Muhlenberg, May 8, 1848, *LAG*, p. 249.

260 "resistance by force": Thomas Jefferson, *The Anas*, Apr. 15, 1806, *WTJ* (Lipscomb and Bergh), 1:452.

260 "We thought it best": Thomas Jefferson to James Monroe, Feb. 15, 1801, *PTJ*, 32:594.

260 "but in the event": Thomas Jefferson to Thomas McKean, Mar. 9, 1801, *WTJ* (Ford), 9:206.

260 "Let the two candidates": Thomas McKean to Thomas Jefferson, Jan. 10, 1801, *PTJ*, 332:433.

261 "The prerogative": James Madison to Thomas Jefferson, Jan. 10, 1801, *PJM*, 17:454.

261 "Let them order": Albert Gallatin, "Plan at the Time of Balloting," [1801], *WAG*, 1:23.

261 "shall immediately": U.S. Constitution, Art. 2, Sec. 1.

261 "the House shall": "Rules for the Election of President," Feb. 9, 1801, *Annals of the Congress*, 10:1010.

262 "We are to be shut up": Harrison Gray Otis to Sally Foster Otis, Feb. 9, 1801, *LLHGO*, 1:207.

262 "I hear both parties": Gouverneur Morris to Robert Troup, Feb. 1, 1801, *LGM*, 3:151.

263 "It is a chance": Harrison Gray Otis to Sally Foster Otis, Feb. 11, 1801, *LLHGO*, 1:208.

263 "The votes having been": *The National Intelligencer*, Feb. 13, 1801, p. 3.

264 "On the day": Albert Gallatin to Henry A. Muhlenberg, May 8, 1848, *LAG*, p. 249.

264 "I was informed": Benjamin Hichborn to Thomas Jefferson, Jan. 5, 1801, *PTJ*, 32:399.

264 "Mr. C's lady": Samuel Tyler to James Monroe, Feb. 9, 1801, "Original Letters," *William and Mary College Quarterly*, 1 (1892), p. 104.

264 "I am far from confiding": Thomas Jefferson to Thomas Mann Randolph, Jan. 9, 1801, *PTJ*, 32:418.

264 "By the arrangements": James A. Bayard to Samuel Bayard, Feb. 22, 1801, "Correspondence of Bayard," p. 131.

264 "phalanx": George W. Erving to James Monroe, Jan. 25, 1801, quoted in Morton Borden, *The Federalism of James A. Bayard* (New York: Columbia University Press, 1955), p. 87. Jefferson later used this term in this context. Thomas Jefferson to James Madison, Feb. 18, 1801, *PJM*, 17:467.

265 "A second ballot": Robert Troup to Rufus King, Feb. 12, 1801, *LCRK*, 3:391. In a similar observation by a Federalist member of Congress, Leven Powell wrote to his brother on Feb. 12, "Mr. Jefferson's friends believed that he would carry on the first ballot, and Mr. Burr's [friends were] still more certain that if [Jefferson] failed in the first that [Burr] would ultimately succeed." Leven Powell to Burr Powell, Feb. 16, 1801, "Correspondence of Col. Leven Powell," *John P. Branch Historical Papers of Randolph Macon College*, 1 (1903), p. 250.

265 "The business": George Jackson to James Madison, Feb. 5, 1801, *PJM*, 17:461.

265 "We are in conclave": Harrison Gray Otis to Sally Foster Otis, Feb. 11, 1801, *LLHGO*, 1:207.

265 "What the Feds": John Dawson to James Madison, Feb. 12, 1801, *PJM*, 17:464–65.

265 "*Unworthy* will he be": *Washington Federalist*, Feb. 12, 1801, p. 2.

266 "All stand firm": William Cooper to Thomas Morris, Feb. 13, 1801, *MAB*, 2:113.

266 "We request information": James Monroe to Stephens Thomson Mason and William Cary Nicholas, Feb. 18, 1801, *WJM*, 3:260.

266 "cabal, intrigue, and hatred": Thomas Jefferson to Maria Jefferson Eppes, Feb. 15, 1801, *PTJ*, 32:593.

266 "Representing the smallest state": James A. Bayard to John Adams, Feb. 19, 1801, "Correspondence of Bayard," pp. 129–30.

267 "In determining to recede" and following: James A. Bayard, "Deposition," Apr. 3, 1806, *Documents Relating to the Presidential Election in the Year 1801* (Philadelphia: Mifflin and Parry, 1831), p. 11.

267 "I have declared": Thomas Jefferson to James Monroe, Feb. 15, 1801, *PTJ*, 32:594.

267 "I have taken": James A. Bayard to Allen McLane, Feb. 17, 1801, "Correspondence of Bayard," p. 129.

267 "The clamor was prodigious": James A. Bayard to Samuel Bayard, Feb. 22, 1801, "Correspondence of Bayard," p. 132.

268 "explicitly resigns" and following: Theodore Sedgwick to Theodore Sedgwick Jr., Feb. 16, 1801, *PCAB*, 1:486.

268 "Burr has acted" and following: James A. Bayard to Richard Bassett, Feb. 16, 1801, "Correspondence of Bayard," pp. 126–27.

268 "Thus has ended": Albert Gallatin to Hannah Gallatin, Feb. 17, 1801, *LAG*, p. 262.

268 "They had but one": Albert Gallatin to Hannah Gallatin, Feb. 19, 1801, *LAG*, p. 263.

268 "Thus ended the electoral drama": John Cotton Smith, *Correspondence and Miscellanies of the Hon. John Cotton Smith* (New York: Harper, 1847), p. 220.

268 "This farce of life": Gouverneur Morris to Robert Livingston, Feb. 20, 1801, *DLGM*, 2:404.

269 "Yes my beloved angel": Harrison Gray Otis to Sally Foster Otis, Feb. 15, 1801, *LLHGO*, 1:208.

269 "I have heard": Abigail Adams to John Adams, Feb. 21, 1801, *AFP*, reel 400.

269 "The question": *Gazette of the United States*, Feb. 20, 1801, p. 2 (reprint of February 18 article from Baltimore).

269 "I was willing to take Burr": James A. Bayard to Alexander Hamilton, Mar. 8, 1801, *PAH*, 25:344.

269 "We consider this": Thomas Jefferson to James Madison, Feb. 18, 1801, *PJM*, 17:467.

EPILOGUE: INAUGURATION DAY, MARCH 4, 1801

PAGE
271 "May none but": John Adams to Abigail Adams, Nov. 2, 1800, *AFP*, reel 399.

272 "During the contest" and following: Thomas Jefferson, Mar. 4, 1801, *Annals of the Congress*, 10:763–64 (capitalization in original).

273 "I am in hopes": Thomas Jefferson to James Monroe, Mar. 7, 1801, *WTJ* (Ford), 9:203.

273 "The consolidation": Thomas Jefferson to Levi Lincoln, July 11, 1801, *WTJ* (Ford), 9:268.

273 "I know indeed": Thomas Jefferson to Henry Knox, Mar. 27, 1801, *WTJ* (Ford), 9:236.

273 "I consider the pure": Thomas Jefferson to John Dickinson, July 23, 1801, *WTJ* (Ford), 9:281–82.

273 "The frenzy": Thomas Jefferson to Thomas Paine, Mar. 18, 1801, *WTJ* (Ford), 9:213.

273 "What an effort": Thomas Jefferson to Joseph Priestley, Mar. 21, 1801, *WTJ* (Ford), 9:217.

274 "We may now say": Thomas Jefferson to Elbridge Gerry, Mar. 29, 1801, *WTJ* (Ford), 9:241.

274 "The storm is over": Thomas Jefferson to Samuel Adams, Mar. 29, 1801, *WTJ* (Ford), 9:239.

274 "a revolution in": Thomas Jefferson to Spencer Roane, Sept. 6, 1819, *WTJ* (Ford), 12:136.

274 "Party is an association": Fisher Ames to Theodore Dwight, Mar. 19, 1801, *WFA*, 2:1409–11.

274 "Today the new" and following: John Marshall to Charles Cotesworth Pinckney, Mar. 4, 1801, *PJMar*, 6:89.

275 "The Federalists": John Adams to William Cunningham, Sept. 27, 1808, *Correspondence Between Hon. John Adams and the Late William Cunningham, Esq.* (Boston: True and Greene, 1823), pp. 29–30.

276 "You and I": John Adams to Thomas Jefferson, July 15, 1813, *AJL*, 2:358.

276 "It is a great day" and following: Susan Boylston Adams Clark to Abigail Louisa Smith Adams Johnson, July 9, 1826, Adams-A.B. Johnson Manuscripts, Massachusetts Historical Society.

INDEX

monarchism of, 72, 157, 178
in New York, 87, 92, 95, 96, 102, 109
peace treaty with France opposed
by, 256
in Pennsylvania gubernatorial election, 58–61
pro-British sympathies of, 29, 145
Republican satirical creed for,
178–79
Sedition Act supported by, 35, 58,
61, 73, 76
and slavery, 199
on suffrage rights, 203
Thomas Pinckney supported by,
40, 120
Washington urged to run for third
term by, 39, 43
Hindman, William, 248
History of the United States for 1796
(Callender), 133
Holt, Charles, 76, 77
House of Representatives, U.S., 19,
22, 60, 78, 115, 121, 138, 255–58
direct election of members of, 84
portrait of Louis XVI in, 68
presidential election in, 83, 118,
240, 243–48, 253, 259–68, 274
Ross Bill in, 80
slavery and apportionment of seats
in, 250

Illuminati, Society of, 168–70
Immigrants, 103, 104
German, 60, 88, 103
Irish, 59, 60, 81, 88
Impressment, 30
India, British, 81

Jackson, George, 265
Jacobins, 27, 94, 148, 162, 215

fear of invasion by, 34
Federalist equation of Republicans
with, 45, 50, 51, 59, 61, 69–70, 84,
146, 177, 187, 189, 208, 234, 274
Jefferson denounced as, 96, 131, 247
secularism and, 28, 29, 94, 166,
167, 169, 173
slave revolts and, 195, 196
tax resisters characterized as, 128
Jay, John, 105, 152, 188, 245, 252, 263
as negotiator of American independence, 7, 216, 220
as New York governor, 42, 50, 86,
87, 107–9, 151, 220
in peace negotiations with Britain,
30, 46 (*see also* Jay's Treaty)
Jay, Peter, 105
Jay's Treaty, 30, 32, 46, 56, 102, 177,
211
Jefferson, Maria (christened as Mary),
266
Jefferson, Martha, 12, 158, 246
Jefferson, Thomas
Alien and Sedition Acts denounced
by, 35, 73, 78, 156, 225
anti-intellectual attacks on, 180–82
assessment of political landscape
by, 85–86, 154–55
and Burr's vice presidential candidacy, 117–19, 159, 184
Burr in tie for electoral votes with,
241–44, 251
Callender and, 133–34, 136, 162,
192
campaigning by, 155–59, 188
constitutional views of, 16–17
in Continental Congress, 14–15
death of, 276
and Declaration of Independence,
1–3, 5, 14–15
and Delaware elections, 206
early life of, 10–12

ILLUSTRATION CREDITS

Letters identify illustrations in the insert. The illustrations appear courtesy of the following sources:

A. Continental Congress Group: Library of Congress (LC-USZ62–14414)
B. John Jay: Library of Congress (LC-USZ62–50375)
C. Benjamin Franklin: Library of Congress (LC-USZ62–45167)
D. John Adams: Library of Congress (LC-USZ62–3992)
E. Abigail Adams: Library of Congress (LC-USZ62–10016)
F. Death of Washington: Library of Congress (LC-USZ62–3917)
G. James Madison: Library of Congress (LC-USZ62–3462)
H. James Monroe: Library of Congress (LC-USZ62–104958)
I. Anti-Federalist Cartoon: The Library Company of Philadelphia (1w/5760.F.6)
J. Thomas McKean: American Philosophical Society (M42.30.6)
K. Pennsylvania Election Broadside: Courtesy of The University of Georgia Libraries (*Aurora General Advertiser*)
L. George Clinton: Library of Congress (LC-USZ62–110647)
M. Alexander Hamilton: Library of Congress (LC-USZ62–48272)
N. Aaron Burr, 1792: Library of Congress (LC-USZ62–102555)
O. Charles Cotesworth Pinckney: Emmet Collection, Miriam and Ira D. Wallach Division of Art, Prints and Photographs, The New York Public Library, Astor, Lenox and Tilden Foundations (EM 15385)
P. Thomas Pinckney: American Philosophical Society (M42.31.34)
Q. Napoleon Bonaparte: American Philosophical Society (M42.16.18)
R. Timothy Pickering: Library of Congress (LC-USZ62–47649)
S. Washington in 1801: Library of Congress (LC-USZ62–4702)
T. Advertisement for Hamilton's Letter: Courtesy of The University of Georgia Libraries (*Aurora General Advertiser*)
U. Federalist Election Projection: © American Antiquarian Society (*Gazette of the United States*)
V. Republican Election Projection: From the collections of the Charleston Library Society (*City Gazette and Daily Advertiser*)
W. Jefferson Election Article: © American Antiquarian Society (*The National Intelligencer*)
X. United States Capitol in 1801: Library of Congress (LC-USZC4–247)
Y. Thomas Jefferson: Library of Congress (LC-USZ62–75384)

ABOUT THE AUTHOR

EDWARD J. LARSON is the author of seven books and the recipient of the 1998 Pulitzer Prize in History for his book *Summer for the Gods: The Scopes Trial and America's Continuing Debate over Science and Religion*. His other books include *Evolution: The Remarkable History of a Scientific Theory; Evolution's Workshop: God and Science on the Galapagos Islands*; and *Trial and Error: The American Controversy Over Creation and Evolution*. He has also written over one hundred articles, most of which address topics of law, science, or politics from an historical perspective, which have appeared in such varied journals as *The Atlantic Monthly, Nature, Scientific American, The Nation, The Wilson Quarterly*, and *Virginia Law Review*. Larson is a professor of history and law at Pepperdine University and lives in Georgia and California.